MY SPORTS HERO

MY SPORTS HERO

Famous New Zealanders talk about people who inspired them

By Wynne Gray

TRIO
BOOKS

FRONT COVER:

Centre photo – Colin Meads *(Peter Bush)*. Other photos, clockwise from top left – Sam Neill *(Dominion Post)*, Peter Snell, Tame Iti *(Dominion Post)*, Valerie Vili, Sir John Walker and Allison Roe *(Dominion Post)*, Richie McCaw *(Dominion Post)*, Rachel Hunter *(Dominion Post)*, Sir Edmund Hillary and Tenzing Norgay *(Alexander Turnbull Library)*.

PHOTO CREDITS:

Dominion Post: 10, 13, 15, 21, 29, 48, 50, 58, 60, 67, 82, 105, 107, 125, 127, 130, 132, 134, 141, 153, 160, 165, 169, 180, 183, 198, 202, 213, 216, 223, 230, 234, 249, 257, 263, 271, 273, 276
Don Neely: 11, 97, 99, 104, 116, 195, 220, 254, 282
Newstalk ZB: 79, 85, 124, 192, 237
Peter Bush: 17, 23, 37, 187
The Wellingtonian: 45, 144, 164, 221
Ivan Mauger: 177, 277
Photosport: 43
Bernie Wood: 113
Keith Quinn: 211
Woolf Photography: 228

Thanks to all those who supplied photos of themselves.

National Library of New Zealand Cataloguing-in-Publication Data

Gray, Wynne.
My sports hero : famous New Zealanders talk about people
who inspired them / by Wynne Gray.
ISBN 978-0-9582839-9-1
1. Athletes. 2. Heroes. 3. Athletes—New Zealand. 4. Heroes—New Zealand.
I. Title.
796.0922—dc 22

Published in 2009 by Trio Books Ltd, PO Box 17021, Wellington.

Design: Sally McIntosh.
Printed by Astra Print, Wellington.

CONTENTS

ACKNOWLEDGEMENTS

This book's incubation took some time. There was widespread support for the idea, and a raft of publishers liked the concept, but none nailed their support to the financial mast until Joseph Romanos at Trio Books took up the challenge.

With that necessary encouragement, the task started. It was over to me, but there were many helpers on the journey. They weighed in with their ideas, tracked down some of the subjects, helped ghost-write contributions and offered advice on likely story-tellers. I am indebted to all those in the book who gave their time and thoughts for interviews and those who were just as comfortable providing their own copy. You are all champions.

There were special moments tracking down people I had never met before, many circuitous inquiries, others where the responses were almost immediate. There were warm reunions with people who too infrequently passed across my radar, and there was always the support of my wife and three children as I went about this project.

I must also thank Sally McIntosh, who designed the cover of this book, and then set to work carefully planning and laying out each page.

INTRODUCTION

When Sir Edmund Hillary died, the national outpouring of emotion snapped me into action.

For some time I had been tinkering with the concept of compiling a book in which a range of prominent New Zealanders were quizzed about their sports inspirations. When they were growing up in this great little country and starting to inquire more about life's prospects, who were the sportsmen and women whose deeds encouraged them, made them proud, made them envious or offered them signposts for the future?

Did that concept really exist? Was it just a romantic notion or a saccharine schoolboy idea revisited?

As you will read, the answers were varied. Many of those I asked found it hard to pinpoint one special person. Some could not go past family, while others were guarded about worshipping others because it would have impinged on their ambitions.

The origins of this book can be traced back more than a decade, to when the *Sydney Morning Herald* ran a series of articles by its staff, each with the "hero" theme. Then the newspaper's rugby writer, Greg Growden, reworked the idea into a book. I liked the concept; it struck a chord. But it had only simmered until Sir Ed's death.

The chance of quizzing the mountaineer about his early inspiration was gone, never to be regained. I kicked myself for not having inquired about his sports hero. But at least Sir Ed had a full life and the experience of seeing his children grow through their teens into adulthood. He watched them have their heroes, he walked with them and talked to them on their journeys in life.

For several others during the course of this book's development, that delight ended way too prematurely. All Black prop John Drake will not be at courtside to see his daughters' progress. My neighbour, Scott Looney, lost his battle to share in his young children's joy on the sports field because of an accursed cancer. They were both heroes to their families.

Thinking about these people I have known, gone too soon, and talking to so many people during the compilation of *My Sports Hero,* I reflected on my own life. Not surprisingly, I thought first of my parents, whose encouraging role and selflessness in supporting my sports passions were an under-appreciated part of my teenage years.

There were others who flitted through my sports consciousness, people like Don Clarke and Bert Sutcliffe, who had books written about them. As a youngster, I was enthralled watching Sir Garfield Sobers' shotmaking, Peter Snell's power, Des Connor's dive-pass, Bishan Bedi's twirling deliveries and Tim Woon smashing the dimpled skin off a golf ball.

Subsequently, my working life has allowed me access to many of the great sports citadels of the world and to an array of sports luminaries. I've been able to see, close up, their range of talents and their temperaments.

Many sports stars who now dazzle our senses will I am sure remain heroes for today's schoolkids. Many of our impressions about sport these days are gleaned through the all-seeing lens of television, and much of our watching is done from the comfort of our couches, because we get far closer to the action than we can with the naked eye or even with binoculars at the park. Before the arrival of television, we had to make do with books, newspapers, movie newsreels and radio to feed our interest.

When a touring rugby or cricket side arrived in town, we did our best to get to the game or watch them practise somewhere. When the 1965 Springboks played in New Zealand and an immense forward scratched two lines across my autograph book rather than attempting to write his name, that act reinforced family tales about never trusting the All Blacks' greatest foe.

For a country with a small population, New Zealand has made enormous statements on the world sports stage. Swags of those names do not appear in the context of this book, but they are not forgotten. Men like George Nepia, Jack Lovelock and Ian Ferguson, women like Oliver Hollis, Erin Baker and Rebecca Perrott. When you scour one of the legendary TP McLean's books on New Zealand sport, you realise the extent of the sports threads in this country.

When teenagers in this millennium are asked in future about their sports beacons, they may wheel out names like Daniel Vettori, Ryan Nelsen or Irene van Dyk. It will be fascinating to see how that plays out and whether the broadening sports landscape in this country is reflected in those choices.

My thanks go to everyone in this book who agreed to contribute so generously of their time and their recollections.

When the book was just an idea and I needed some independent advice about the concept, I turned to Andy Haden, who was a fine All Black lock and these days is an agent and confidante of many famous New Zealanders.

My mission was two-fold. I wanted to gauge his thoughts on the project and then, armed with that affirmation, pressed him for help in contacting several of the stars in his stable. Andy was generous with his ideas and assistance, supermodel Rachel Hunter was willing to help, and after a little while I had my first chapter.

Rachel told of her schoolgirl efforts to emulate the athletics prowess of another North Shore girl, Allison Roe, and explained, in a delightful tale, how that panned out.

Chapter one was in the can and, armed with that valuable contribution, I was able to persuade others to join the project. John Clarke, holed up these days in Australia but known throughout this nation as Fred Dagg, came on board early. Dame Susan Devoy, Sir Bob Jones and Midge Marsden joined in and I was on my way, launching into a fascinating journey among not only New Zealand's media and sports stars, but also talking to achievers from the diverse worlds of music, film, business, politics and other spheres.

Some of the people in this book, I already knew quite well; others were contacted through a friend of a friend. Some I simply ran into at sports events or at airports. Some took months to track down, others did not quite pan out.

Along the way it was a delight to talk with many of this country's famous faces, like Fred "the Needle" Allen, who I had not seen for a while. I spent an afternoon in the Whangaparaoa sun with him while he recounted the deeds of his boyhood hero.

Other memories were my fascinating first-time encounters with Sam Neill, Valerie

Vili and Scott Dixon, reunions with old cronies like Oscar Kightley, global detective work to nail down AJ Hackett, copy written on the Cook Strait ferry by the irrepressible Gary McCormick and an immediate "let's do it" response from John Hawkesby. The copy flow from all my media colleagues was hugely appreciated.

I wanted to include Helen Clark, but it seemed as though I would miss her. She was flat out before the last election, then, after allowing her a suitable holiday break, the news broke of her impending job at United Nations. Suddenly she had launched into a hail of farewell interviews and speeches and I began to doubt I'd get her. Then a new Labour MP, Grant Robertson, offered to help, and so he did. The result arrived almost as Helen Clark boarded her plane to New York.

The result of months of badgering and begging is *My Sports Hero,* in which gifted people from so many walks of life share the memories and dreams that, in many cases, they've had for decades.

For some of those I asked, it was easy – they flowed into the task. For others, it was a struggle as they agonised over their choices and their words. Some needed cajoling, many needed reminding and a firm word, but no matter the method, they are all my heroes for taking part.

Wynne Gray **JUNE 2009**

Fred Allen

BERT COOKE

Fred Allen captained the All Blacks after World War II
and from 1967-69 was the most successful All Black coach
in New Zealand history.

It was a oncer, but it was worth it. I guess I am part of a dwindling group who was
fortunate enough to see Albert Edward Cooke, or Bert Cooke as he was known, lace on
his boots for the All Blacks.

Later on I saw Cooke play provincial rugby in New Zealand, but the only test I
saw him play was at Lancaster Park in 1930 against Great Britain in his last season of
international rugby. For a 10-year-old who fancied himself as a midfield back, this was
some treat. Our expectation about Cooke was matched by reality that day at Lancaster
Park when we saw him play a starring role in a narrow 13-10 win over the tourists.

The All Blacks had lost the first test at Carisbrook narrowly, and there had been
plenty of criticism of the team before the test because of the inclusion of a number of
veteran players. The tourists snatched a late 6-3 victory with a long-range try as their
wing narrowly outpaced the chasing Cooke. There were a number of changes for the
next test, at Lancaster Park, but Cooke was an automatic All Black choice as a record
crowd of 32,000 filled the ground on a brilliantly fine afternoon.

It was strange to watch the All Blacks turn out in white jerseys to avoid any confusion
with Great Britain, who wore dark blue throughout the series.

I was mesmerised by the way Cooke played. He was so light on his feet and his
anticipation and speed off the mark were very sharp. He was a predator, an assassin
and an artist all tied up in one magnetic bundle. For me, he was the man to watch,
though the great George Nepia was also in fine form. Nepia pulled off another of his
superb defensive saves when he shepherded the great British centre, Carl Aarvold, so
cleverly that Aarvold tried to score himself, though he had a team-mate in support
outside him. Nepia pounced and flattened him and stopped the move. It was a superb

piece of defensive work from a great fullback. But even so, to my 10-year-old eyes, there was none to match Cooke.

He was the Bradman of the rugby field, far superior to any other player I had seen in midfield. Cooke was a very light man, although he had a heavyweight defence and great instincts about every part of his play. He had tremendous speed and was very elusive, and for a young lad like myself, he played with all the panache, accuracy and skill that I wanted to emulate.

Cooke was a bit like another marvellous All Black midfielder, Johnny Smith, who seemed to be able to evade any defender when he put his mind to it. They could not only beat strong tacklers, they both had a number of methods for dodging defenders.

By all accounts Cooke had a tough upbringing and had some unsettled moments in his adult years. He moved from one province to another, but once he was on the rugby field he never had any difficulties. His balance while running at full speed was breath-taking, his timing was exquisite and, like all great players, he knew when to run, when to kick and when to pass. His instincts were simply brilliant.

In many ways, the great Lions and Irish centre of latter years, Mike Gibson, reminded me of the way Cooke played. Another player I never grew tired of watching was Bob Scott, a remarkable fullback and just the best sort of team player. He achieved some remarkable levels of skill during the 1949 tour to South Africa and but for some troubled goal-kicking, would have been remembered forever as a genius from that expedition.

But Cooke had just that little bit extra, certainly to these eyes when I was growing up as a mad-keen rugby youngster. He was an extraordinary talent and while we did not get to speak much, I did have the great pleasure of meeting him at several functions.

Like Richie McCaw and Daniel Carter, Bert Cooke would be an automatic selection in my best All Black side.

Chris Amon

JUAN FANGIO AND OTHER MOTOR-RACING CHAMPIONS

Chris Amon was, along with Denny Hulme and Bruce McLaren, one of the three famous New Zealand Formula One motor-racing stars of the 1960s.

When my sporting genes were starting to boil towards the tail-end of the 1950s, New Zealand had been through momentous rugby series against the Springboks in 1956 and the Lions in 1959.

Some years before, New Zealand had marvelled when Edmund Hillary had climbed to the top of the world.

Such events were celebrated deeply, and captured the public imagination far more than they would these days, when there is a surfeit of sport and widespread television coverage.

My interest in motor-racing was serious by then. I had always been interested in engines and learned to drive around the paddock in an old ute when I was about six or seven. I never imagined it would lead to my eventual involvement in Formula One events.

It was an odd trail. My initial ambition was to do a few hill-climbs. Having completed those, I thought it might be nice to do a couple of races near home. Then I pushed on to try a couple of other circuits, the summer series and a few races in Australia, before heading off to Europe to try my luck. I ended up doing that for 14 years before I gave it away.

I was extremely lucky to be asked to race in Formula One without having tested myself anywhere beyond Australasia.

Initially it was the machinery, the smell of the workshop and the technology that appealed to me. In those days the Germans, with Mercedes, were dominating.

I marvelled at the best drivers of the time, people at the top of their craft, like

The incomparable **JUAN FANGIO.**

Juan Fangio and Stirling Moss, and others like Mike Hawthorn and Tony Brooks. The wonderful thing was that as time progressed and they became my heroes, I got to know them very well.

The first time I met Fangio, I was still in awe of him. It was about 1967, and I was driving for Ferrari. On the morning of the Grand Prix at Nurburgring it was pouring with rain and there was thick fog. You could not see across the track.

The hotel we were staying in was actually at the back of the grandstand, and on the morning of the race I walked down the hotel corridor to find Fangio sitting in the foyer. I introduced myself and in his funny, squeaky voice, he said he was pleased I was driving that day and not him. He was a lovely person – you never heard anyone say anything unkind about him.

Stirling was much more gregarious, much more outgoing, a brilliant driver and thinker, too. I really only raced him twice out here when I was 17. It was his last season, because he was seriously hurt not long afterwards and went through a few bad times because of his head injuries. Fortunately he recovered and regained his outgoing nature.

Motor-racing was in my blood. My father helped me initially and we scrimped and saved enough to buy a car, but we never had the money to progress any further.

However, I was fortunate, and I suppose talented enough, to get noticed. We had a unique situation in New Zealand then, because about half a dozen Formula One drivers used to visit each year and race in what was an escape from the northern hemisphere winters. The beauty of this was that their team managers travelled as well, and my fortune was that I was spotted by Reg Parnell, who was running the Lola team.

He saw me driving in 1962 then again the next year, and approached me – I think it was at Warwick Farm in Australia – and asked me whether I would be interested in getting a Formula One drive if he could get it together.

It took me about a tenth of a second to answer. Parnell put the offer in such a way that it was not guaranteed, but he thought he could make it happen.

This was about February and I was a very anxious 19-year-old for about four or five weeks before the deal was confirmed. By then Jack Brabham had won a world championship and Bruce McLaren was emerging, and suddenly I had a few more people to look up to.

When I began, I was younger than anyone who had driven in Formula One. I think there is still only one driver who was younger than me on debut and that was Mike Thackwell, another Kiwi, who started the Detroit Grand Prix in 1981 when he was a few days younger than I'd been.

A few of the current drivers are pretty young as well and it is a very different sport these days, thank goodness, than it was in my day. Officials have managed to remove a lot of the danger, of which we were almost oblivious. In hindsight, it was a bit like going off to war for a few years.

They were fascinating times, and from a New Zealand perspective I remember the odd occasion in Formula One races when Denny Hulme, Bruce McLaren and I had the first three podium places, which was a bit special. You would have to put a lot of it down to Bruce, but we all had high standards at that time.

Jim Anderton

GARY BARTLETT

Jim Anderton has been a Member of Parliament since 1984, representing first Sydenham, and then Wigram.

The word "hero" suggests someone you admire from afar. A person you have heard or read about but never met, one whose feats you admire and would like to emulate.

This is not, however, the relationship I had with Gary Bartlett, fast bowler supreme for the Marlborough Hawke Cup team, Canterbury and New Zealand.

I first met him at the other end of the 22-yard cricket pitch in a Hawke Cup challenge match between Wanganui and Marlborough in Blenheim on February 24-25, 1961.

We had heard ugly rumours about the lightning speed of Bartlett and these had created apprehension in Wanganui's top batting order.

Michael Bell was our opening batsman and his high backlift was his trademark. I watched with interested anticipation for his first ball. He never got his bat anywhere near the ground or the ball. His middle stump was blasted out of the ground and cartwheeled end-over-end to reach the wicketkeeper, who was standing, I can assure you, a long way behind the batting crease.

As I passed Michael heading towards the pavilion after being dismissed from the first ball of the innings, I was struck by how happy he was – something I had never observed in any other batsman dismissed in similar circumstances.

Facing my first ball from Gary Bartlett – the second of the innings – I remember thinking, "He's only got a run of 10 or 12 yards, so he can't be all that fast." Big mistake!

He seemed to shuffle to the wicket and his bowling arm came from a long way behind his back. And then... nothing. I didn't see any ball bowled. I thought he still held it in his hand until I saw it in the wicketkeeper's gloves.

I think this was the first time in my life I had felt real fear, because I had no idea the ball had been bowled – I had not seen a thing.

For the next six overs I was unable to get away from the strike. I managed to snick one ball to the boundary through the slips, which was the safest place to put it because the speed of the ball off the bat made it virtually uncatchable.

Naturally I tried valiantly to push the odd ball for a single, but my batting partner, equally naturally, was resolutely not interested in running singles.

These were the days of no thigh pads, chest pads or helmets, and I was hit in just about every part of my body (except the head) and was literally black and blue for weeks after.

In the years to come, I realised just how lucky I had been. Bartlett subsequently played for Central Districts against the English MCC team at Cooks Gardens, Wanganui. His first ball to opening batsmen Roger Prideaux went for six byes. Yes – six byes! The English opener gratefully spooned the next to short leg and happily retired from the front-line.

The South Africans were the next to suffer when John Reid's famous 1961-62 side won two test matches on South African soil – the first time a New Zealand team had won a test match away from home. Bartlett helped gain revenge for the 1953-54 carnage that Neil Adcock had wreaked on Geoff Rabone's heroic but luckless Kiwis.

There were no radar guns in Bartlett's day, but I saw Tyson, Statham, Hall and Holding et al. In my view Bartlett was, and is still, the fastest bowler I have ever seen and he deserves an honoured place as a heroic and iconic figure in New Zealand's proud cricket history.

Kylie Bax

LORETTA JANE AND OTHER HORSES

Once a teenage beauty queen, Kylie Bax has become
a model and actress of international acclaim.

I really wasn't too thrilled about being a teenager. It was an awkward time for me. My mum decided I should chop off my long, golden locks which left me as a tall, lean, gangly, short-haired kid, and everyone thought I was a boy. Not my idea of fun at all!

I went to boarding school in my teenage years. And worse than that, it was an all-girls boarding school. So again not fun!

Okay, okay, I was meant to be doing all this in the interests of a good education, but that didn't stop me from hating it. I had dreams. They were dreams of not only escaping from the boarding school, but also of escaping into another world, away from New Zealand.

Growing up, my father was my special mentor. But if I had to nominate somebody outside my family, then there were a few who didn't know they had a hand in shaping different parts of my life at that time.

I'm a sports nut. I loved swimming and netball, and I loved my horses. I watched rugby (and I'm still an All Blacks fan). I was into beauty and so was my mum. I was very proud of Lorraine Downes and I loved watching Grant Fox kick goals.

However, my most enjoyable and memorable times were listening to and watching horse races, and spending time with my thoroughbred foals. We bred many foals and it was a quiet time, a thinking time, a relaxing and enjoyable time.

My first horse wasn't a superstar, but she was a great inspiration for life. How? You may ask. Easy! Her name was Loretta Jane. I have no idea where I came up with that name, but she was tough and feisty and demanded respect.

When I was nine, my father gave me the lead rope to walk her from one side of the paddock to the other. The first time I tried, we got half-way, before she pulled away and out of my hands. My dad caught her, brought her back to me and said: "Now this time don't let go! When she pulls to get away, don't let go, pull hard down and scold her with your voice."

My heart was racing because I knew she would try that same stunt again. We started off again, got half-way across the paddock and sure enough, she tried it on again. This time, remembering what my father had said, I yanked down on the lead rope and we walked peacefully on. Simple. That was one big lesson in my teenage years: demand respect and you will get it. If you don't, others will walk all over you.

It may be a surprise to many, given my love of horses, to find out that I don't ride. I am much more into the bloodlines and gauging who will be the best broodmares.

But I love going to the races. There was nothing quite like going to the Thames race carnival with dad and soaking up the buzz of the entire day. It was our home track and from the bird's-eye view at my parents' house up on the hills, we would watch the horses going through their trackwork every morning, then dad and I would team up to pick out the winners for the day, get to the course, eat the picnic fare and stand in our favourite "lucky" spot, just past the members' stand, to get the best view of the finish line.

The race meeting was always held at the beginning of January, round my birthday, and it was always beautiful weather, and you could guarantee that trainer Dave O'Sullivan with his jockey son Lance would combine to bring home at least three winners on the day. Great fun!

Andrew Becroft

CLIVE CURRIE

Andrew Becroft is the Principal Youth Court Judge
for New Zealand.

Boys always want heroes. When I entered the third form at Rongotai College, Wellington, in 1971, I was no different. The sixth and seventh-formers seemed to us as men, far removed and usually commanding instant respect. We quickly identified our own heroes among them. Mine was Clive Currie. He was two years ahead of me. Clive was immediately likeable and very popular. He was multi-talented, always calm under pressure, and someone of great integrity. Clive won the award for the best all-round sixth former. A year later he was head prefect, captain of the First XI cricket team and of the First XV.

Cricket was already my obsession. As a gangly fourth former, I struggled to flight my ungainly leg-spinners into the Wellington northerly. Leg-spinning, in those pre-Shane Warne days, was something of an oddity. Before my mid-teen growth spurt I could really turn the ball. I remember endless evenings at the Kilbirnie Park nets, supervised by Don Neely and Trevor Rigby.

Once, I bowled five of my best leg-spinners in a row to Clive. A left-hander, he carefully patted them on to the on-side. As he came down the wicket to hit the sixth, my embryonic "wrong-un" bit and turned the other way, leaving Clive stranded yards down the wicket. He gave the slightest nod of acknowledgement. Nobody else saw it. But I felt real pride. Mind you, I wasn't always so lucky. Bruce Edgar, also a fellow pupil at Rongotai College and a year ahead of me, told me in a similar situation that if I continued to bowl at him on leg stump he would hit me out of the ground. To my next delivery he did exactly that. Not only did it leave the park, but it also crossed Kilbirnie Crescent and landed on the second storey verandah of an apartment block on the corner of Wellington Road.

Even today, when I drive home from Wellington airport, I look at that verandah, and remember the bemused look of the elderly woman when she opened the door of her apartment and I asked if I could retrieve my cricket ball.

On another occasion, in a First XI trial match, I dropped a straightforward "skier" at mid-on. The worst fieldsmen are hidden there – it's a position Monty Panesar has

The end of a promising All Black career. **CLIVE CURRIE,** suffering from concussion, is assisted from the field during the test match against Wales in 1978.

recently made his own for England. Most of the team collapsed with laughter. There was nowhere to hide. Clive was bowling. He simply nodded in my direction, said it could have happened to anyone and returned to the start of his run-up.

In 1973, Clive was selected for the New Zealand Secondary Schools' cricket team. The next year, Bruce Edgar and Ian Smith (who had attended Rongotai College in his third and fourth form years) were also selected, followed by my friend Peter Rowe in 1976.

The just over 1000 Rongotai College pupils all came from fiercely working and middle-class families. Parents made huge sacrifices for their sons. We were encouraged academically and in sport. I often ponder why so many nationally prominent sportsmen (including the Rufer brothers) were produced from such a small part of Wellington's eastern suburbs.

Clive continued to excel at cricket. We always thought he would soon become what is now called a "Black Cap". And while he did represent Wellington at an early age (21), he only played three first-class matches, all in 1977, with an inconspicuous average of 14.75.

I admit it – I am a sick man: cricket statistics have always fascinated me. It is worth noting that Clive's highest score, 36 not out, was made on debut against Canterbury in January 1977 at Lancaster Park, against an attack comprising no less than Richard Hadlee, his brother Dayle, Alan Hounsell, Stephen Boock and Bevan Congdon. Wellington won. And by that time Bruce Edgar was already playing for Wellington.

Contrary to all our predictions, it was in rugby that Clive made his real mark. He quickly shone as a fullback for Oriental-Rongotai in Wellington club rugby. He played several games for Wellington in 1976 and 1977. However, when studying in Christchurch in 1978, he could not make the Canterbury team. The 1976 All Black, Richard Wilson, kept him out. The AllBlacks.com website records that Clive "... appeared for the South Island in the 1978 inter-island match, giving him the distinction of representing each island, and that was enough for him to make the tour of Britain as the first-choice fullback".

Clive made his All Black debut in October 1978 against Cardiff, aged 22. All of us who knew him were immensely proud. There was the realisation that All Black status was suddenly not that distant and unattainable. Clive played against London Counties and then made his first international appearance, against Ireland.

A week later, just 21 days after his All Black debut, his rugby career ended at Cardiff Arms Park. Eight minutes into that famous Welsh test, Clive, always beautifully balanced and safe under the high ball, fielded an up-and-under in his own twenty-five. As he caught the ball, aggressive Welsh second-five Steve Fenwick flew across the TV screen, viciously tackling him head-high, ball and all. It was a tackle that would have put Fenwick on report even if he had been playing rugby league. And it certainly would not have withstood the modern-day citings procedure. A concussed Clive was led shakily from the field, his jaw broken. He was invalided out of the All Black tour.

I don't think he ever played serious rugby again. Clive was replaced by Brian McKechnie, who kicked a last-minute penalty, securing a thrilling 13-12 All Black win. Had it not been for Steve Fenwick's reckless tackle, it might have been Clive Currie who became immortalised in rugby history. Oh, the fickleness of sporting success and the randomness of career-ending injuries!

What happened to Clive Currie? I don't know. I lost track of him. That is not the point of this story. For me, and for scores of my mates, Clive fulfilled our collective dream. He proved that it was possible for "one of us" to become representative cricketers and All Blacks.

Decades later, as I sit as the Principal Youth Court Judge, some things haven't changed. Boys still seek out role models like heat-seeking missiles. The only issue is who will that role model be? A gang leader? A repeat burglar who heads "missions" with kids in his orbit? That role model could, on the other hand, be an older pupil at school. Someone who has a sound values system that is a model for boys who come after him. This is part of how boys become responsible adult males, something, it seems to me, that most serious young offenders in the Youth Court have never experienced.

Equally, what stands out is the lack of "community connectedness". There is a sign outside Blenheim airport: "A kid in sport stays out of court". Trite? Simplistic? Not from my vantage point. Very few serious young offenders are involved in organised sport. Or indeed any form of organised community activity or club. Such involvement provides, as it did for me, much-needed team discipline, the pursuit of common goals, good role models and mentors, and connectedness with the community.

For me, there have been other heroes since then, of course. As a committed Christian myself, I was always hugely encouraged by the faithful Christian witness of test cricketers such as Bruce (Bags) Murray, Victor Pollard and Brian Yuile in the 1970s. And then there was the peerless Michael Jones in the 1980s and 90s. All enjoyed significant national and international success, although they never played on a Sunday. If only the young boys I see in the Youth Court had similar heroes and opportunities for involvement in sport.

More recently, my real hero has been my younger brother David. A former captain of the New Zealand volleyball team, he was involved in a very serious car accident in his early 30s, leaving him severely paralysed on the right side of his body – the result of a life-threatening head injury. He is the most competitive and determined person I have ever known.

With that same attitude he has fought over the years to cope with his disability with astonishing courage and grace. I respect him as much as any man in the world.

But it was Clive Currie who was my first sports hero. As I put the full stop to this article, I decided to search the Web. I found that Clive Currie won the men's doubles championship at the Ngataringa Tennis Club, at Stanley Point in Auckland, with an old South Auckland lawyer friend of mine, Ian Tucker. I suspect Clive could have excelled at many sports. I also noted a recent media release from Westpac Bank, announcing the bank's partnership with All Black captain Richie McCaw. Towards the end of the release, almost as an afterthought, a former All Black/now Westpac private banker, one Clive Currie, is quoted as explaining that among other things "...we all know that rugby can be tough on the body..." I suppose few All Blacks would know that better than Clive.

Sir Ron Brierley

JOHN REID AND RON JARDEN

Sir Ron Brierley has been the chairman and
a director of a number of large companies in
Australia, New Zealand and Britain.

As a Wellington schoolboy growing up in the early 1950s, I had two wonderful sports
heroes – John Reid and Ron Jarden who, coincidentally, had been schoolmates at
Hutt Valley High School.

By happy circumstance, my schoolboy hero quota was full all year round, because
during the summers John Reid mesmerised us at the Basin Reserve, performing
prodigious feats with bat, ball, and in the field. Came the winter, and Ron Jarden was
the idol of Athletic Park, speeding down the left wing to score vast numbers of tries
for University and Wellington.

John Reid and Ron Jarden weren't merely top-class sportsmen. They were exciting,
dominating, thrilling players and I was among thousands of the young and not-so-
young who followed them avidly.

Before the 1952 cricket season, I had some wonderful news. Bernie Paetz, the
master in charge of cricket at Wellington College, asked me and another boy to
become scoreboard attendants at the Basin for senior and first-class cricket. This
was a very important moment of my life. It gave me an official pass to the Basin, a
treasured item, and on top of that I was paid 10 shillings a match. My appointment
coincided with the upgrading and repainting of the scoreboard. That first season was
extraordinary – there was a succession of wet Saturdays, so there was virtually no club
cricket before Christmas.

We scoreboard attendants took our lives in our hands. The large metal plates that used
to spell names and signal numbers would go flying on windy days and were a constant
threat to all within close range, especially the scoreboard boys. It was dangerous work.
The ladder went directly up, at no angle. When the winds got up, it became difficult

to lean across to change numbers and neither of us boys would go to the top on windy days.

I saw some great cricket while sitting on the scoreboard, but nothing has stayed in my memory like John Reid's 283 for Wellington against Otago in January 1952. He smashed 41 boundaries and a six that day. At 150 he hit a ball straight up in the air and was dropped. So, in a way he played two innings. John Reid always kept us busy. We used to do the score in 10s or at the end of each over.

After that 283 Reid was confirmed as my cricket hero. Over the years there were disappointing days when he got out cheaply, but there were also occasions when he batted with such power and aggression, or bowled so purposefully that he couldn't help but excite.

Ron Jarden was Reid's rugby equivalent. It helped that he was in the attractive University club side, which always seemed to be scoring tries. For Wellington, Jarden was amazing. As I think back now as an adult, it is incredible to consider that Ron averaged more than one try a match in an era when kicking into touch was so prevalent.

I grew up in South Wellington, attending Island Bay Primary School and Wellington South Intermediate before heading to Wellington College, so Athletic Park fitted right into my zone.

I lost count of the number of tries I saw Ron score. He had an ability to beat his man by sprinting towards him, then swerving past, and his speed off the mark was amazing.

Strangely, I never saw Ron's most famous try, or non-try as it became. He was playing for New Zealand Universities against the Springboks in 1956 and got the ball well in his own half, then set off on the most breathtaking run, beating a succession of tacklers to score an impossible try. It was only then that everyone's attention was drawn way back downfield, where the linesman, Eric Tindill (a New Zealand test cricket and rugby representative) was holding out his flag – Ron had brushed the touchline at the start of his run.

I wasn't at Athletic Park that day and ever since have cursed that I missed my rugby hero's most brilliant moment.

My affection for Ron grew over the years because of our mutual involvement in the stock market. He was a most astute and hard-working businessman and like all his friends, I was shocked by the news of his early death in 1977, following a heart attack.

Peter Bush

GRAHAM MOURIE

Peter Bush is one of New Zealand's most acclaimed newspaper photographers.

Graham Mourie was lying on a small table still clad in his muddied All Black strip. The doctor bending over him was about to begin stitching his torn eyebrow, and barely gave me a glance as he attended to his needlework. But Mourie, with a slight smile of recognition, gave me a wink.

No, we were not in a front-line trench, but deep in a Murrayfield medical room, which was now doubling as a temporary operating theatre.

The test, won 20-6 by the All Blacks, had finished an hour before, and I was in the medical room under false colours after I had managed to persuade the security men guarding the room that I was a member of the All Black management, and that because of strict New Zealand insurance conditions, we were obliged to record photographically all player injuries while on tour.

A member of the media? "Never."

With great haste I took a couple of shots, thanked everyone profusely for their co-operation and vanished down one of the gloomy corridors before my subterfuge was discovered.

The year was 1979 and the ABs were on a 10-match tour of Scotland and England, with one match against Italy on the way home. From 1978 the All Blacks, with myself in tow, returned each year to Britain for long or medium tours of the four Home unions.

Graham Mourie was 26 when he captained the 1978 All Blacks on their 18-match Grand Slam tour. That '78 tour still remains the happiest, if not the best, tour I have been on.

Much of the success and enjoyment of that tour can be attributed to the selection of the manager, Russ Thomas, the coach, Jack Gleeson, and, most of all, to the captaincy of the Taranaki flanker and farmer, Graham Mourie.

While I had photographed Mourie in a number of games – provincial and test matches – I doubt whether I had spoken more than a few words to him before the tour.

What a change the '78 tour was. Not only was I invited on a number of occasions to ride on the team bus, but I found myself sitting next to, and chatting with, Mourie, who always expressed genuine interest in what touring as a rugby photographer entailed.

On the field, Mourie best exemplified that intriguing and mysterious "X factor" that individuals, in sport and in other walks of life, are born with or develop at an early age.

Examples abound of troops following their leaders against overwhelming odds and to hell with the risk.

In Mourie's case, some of these qualities came to the fore when, usually with 10 or 15 minutes to go and the game delicately balanced, he would drop to one knee, call his men around him and without raising his voice ask them to hang in there, dig deep and go for victory.

Games where his captaincy was shown at its best were the 1978 Wales and Scotland tests, and the ill-tempered midweek game against Bridgend, where he held the team together in a brawl that threatened to wreck the Grand Slam tour.

After the Scottish test, I rushed to develop and print some pictures for wiring to New Zealand, and then went back to the team hotel, where the All Blacks were to join the Scottish team at a formal dinner.

For this dinner Mourie was going to wear a Maclean tartan kilt and velvet jacket, all lent to him by the Scottish coach, Nairn MacEwan. It would make a good picture and Mourie told me he would wait for me at the dining room entrance.

Despite my best efforts, I arrived 10 minutes after the start of the dinner. But Mourie had patiently waited outside the dining room with a couple of agitated officials urging him to please be seated. I was grateful for his patience – he made a good picture in his Scottish regalia.

At the end of the tour, he invited me to join the team at their farewell party at the team's London hotel, in the upmarket Park Lane area.

The dress code for attending the day-long party was as informal or fancy as you felt. I came in "drag", dressed by a woman journalist friend. I did make the mistake of travelling via the underground, and attracted some knowing stares and salty remarks.

The party was a fitting end to a memorable tour, and it made for some equally memorable pictures.

Back in the United Kingdom again in 1980 for the Welsh Rugby Union centenary, New Zealand played five games, four against Welsh club sides that had previously beaten All Black teams over the long years.

The second game was against Llanelli, as it was for the 1972-73 team that lost an ill-tempered match 9-3. As Mourie later said in his brilliant autobiography, it was the match he feared the most. On the day of the 1980 game at Strady Park, up at the north end of the ground, stood a stark reminder of the 1972 defeat – Llanelli 9 V Seland Newydd 3. Some locals said it was the original scoreboard, unchanged from 1972.

The All Black victory apart, the game is probably best remembered for the ordering off of lock Graeme Higginson by Scottish referee Alan Hosie. I was lucky to be close enough to capture the incident as Hosie directed Higginson to take an early shower. In the same frame can be seen an exasperated Mourie and anxious Llanelli players Phil Bennett (the captain) and Ray Gravell.

Referee Hosie had wrongly assumed that Higginson had kicked someone on the ground. The three players managed to get this viewpoint across, and Hosie reversed the order and signalled the end of the game. Mourie and Bennett could justifiably feel proud of their diplomatic gesture. The ordering-off would have sunk the Welsh Union celebrations in mid-stream.

As a captain, Mourie was definitely a man for all seasons.

On the train back to London after the game, I sat with John Reason, the seasoned rugby writer for the *Daily Telegraph*. Reason was not one of the All Blacks' greatest fans and he spared little time in giving me his venomous account of the game and the Higginson incident.

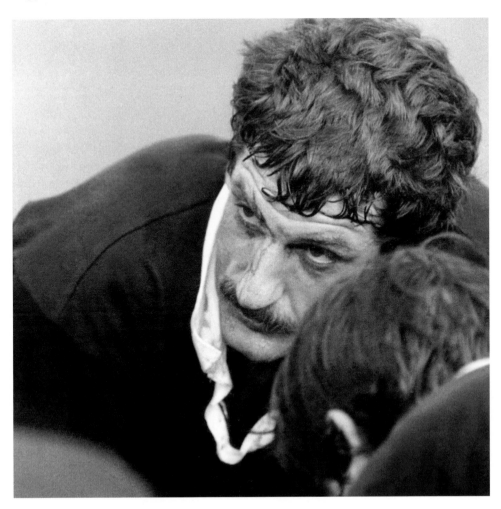

He was angry, he said, and felt betrayed that Hosie had reversed his decision to send the All Black off. With a note of grim satisfaction he told me that he would make sure that Llanelli would be the last top-level game Hosie would control. It made for a long, hard ride back to London.

In 1981, there was the end-of-year tour to Romania and France.

Romania, still behind the Iron Curtain, was full of surprises and secret police. With mighty relief, we moved on to La Belle France.

No New Zealand player in my time has ever been as popular with the French, venerated even, as Graham Mourie. Long before New Zealand rugby players made France their preferred home-away-from-home, Mourie was a feature of French rugby.

He had played for PUC, the famous Paris University Club, spoke French better than most Francophiles and was now captain of their most feared and respected foe, the All Blacks.

In 1983, at the invitation of publisher John Blackwell, I teamed with Graham Dingle and Graham Mourie and illustrated a series of adventures they were undertaking for a book project.

It was a complete break from the rugby world, and we set off in high summer for the Bay of Islands, then took a boat from Russell to Piercy Island and the famed Hole in The Rock that runs under it.

We landed on the island, climbed to the top of the historic rock, and then both Grahams prepared to abseil down the sheer south face of the island.

To capture the abseil I went back on the boat and focused my camera as the two figures set off on their perilous descent. Dingle, one of New Zealand's top mountaineers, completed the descent in a couple of minutes. Mourie, following him, was about halfway down when the figure of eight plate he was using to feed the rope through slipped. Mourie, a fair bit heavier than Dingle, came whizzing down the rope trying with his bare hands to slow the fall.

When he touched the boat deck, his hands were smoking – the rope had burned through the skin of some of the fingers, leaving deep bloody gouges. I thought it was bone sticking through.

While shocked crew members rushed to help, I recorded the scene and thought that would spell the end of our big adventure trip.

But Mourie then showed the gutsy grit that had made him such a sterling All Black skipper. With his hands dressed and taped, he was ready for the next jaunt.

Our odyssey continued with diving at the Poor Knights Islands, exploring deep caves in the Waikato, a swift climb of Mt Egmont, and some mustering at Mesopotamia Station at the head of the Rangitata River. Our odyssey finished with a gruelling trip to Hollyford Valley.

It was a magnificent journey. I felt privileged to have been invited, and that journey confirmed to me that Graham Mourie was a man for all seasons. He was thoughtful and quiet at times, but when he spoke he was always worth listening to.

He demonstrated what a wise move it was by Jack Gleeson to appoint him All Black captain back in 1978.

Jan Cameron

DAWN FRASER

Jan Cameron, an Australian who has settled in New Zealand, has been head coach of our recent Olympic and Commonwealth Games swimming teams.

It was a heady time for someone as fascinated as I was with swimming to watch Dawn Fraser show her formidable class in 1960 at the Rome Olympics.

Several things helped. Our families lived not far from each other in neighbouring Sydney suburbs and the newspapers then were full of her exploits. They had been four years earlier in Melbourne as well, but I was not quite so tuned into swimming then and to Fraser's outstanding exploits.

I could not get enough of the coverage in Rome, where Fraser was up to the job once more, and it further encouraged me to shoot for the big-time, to train harder and aim to make a games team myself, which I was fortunate enough to achieve four years later in Tokyo.

Dawn trained in the Drummoyne pool in our suburb for a while and there were many other great names in Australian swimming there, like Jon Henricks and John Konrads, whose deeds encouraged us all to aim high. About that time, our coach, Forbes Carlisle, asked me to start in his squad. I was very young and very raw, but when I saw Dawn Fraser's exploits and what she could do, it spurred me to have dreams and aspirations as well. She was a global superstar and you can just imagine what it was like if she was in the area and came down to the pool for a training swim.

Fraser was big-time in a sport that was booming in Australia. She would be alongside Herb Elliot, Shane Warne and Ian Thorpe of athletes in modern times in Australia, up with the best of the best. It was such a privilege, eventually, to swim with the woman who had been my guide, my inspiration, my hero, and a yardstick for swimming feats.

I was a decade younger than Dawn and initially chosen as the reserve fifth swimmer for the 4 x 100m relay at the 1964 Tokyo Olympics, but my times kept coming down and I managed to push my way into the starting line-up. It was great being around Dawn, who was selfless about sharing her tips, experience and knowledge with the rest of the team. Her charisma and leadership drew the team even tighter and while we came second in the final, we also broke the world record. It was magic and much of it was down to Dawn's inspiration.

I remember swimming against Dawn in a time trial before those games and beating her. I was young and had no fear. I was at an age when I had little trepidation and felt invincible. It is only later in your career when you realise how big the stage is and what the ramifications are that you feel more vulnerable.

When the chips were down, though, Dawn showed her class. She was a brutally tough swimmer, someone whose mental strength was as powerful as her stroke, very charismatic, a winner.

She came from a difficult background, a loving but tough childhood, where she had to fight and scrap her way to the top. We were never friends because of the age difference, just team-mates, but her example has stayed with me and I have tried to instil her instincts and drive in my pupils during my coaching career in New Zealand.

Dawn Fraser was the Michael Phelps or Ian Thorpe of her time, a superb swimmer, an inspiration, just one of the best.

Olympic silver medallists – the 1964 Australian freestyle relay team.
From left: Robyn Thorne, **DAWN FRASER,** Jan Murphy (Cameron) and Lyn Bell.

John Campbell

PETER MCGREGOR

Working for TV3, John Campbell has become a noted
television current affairs interviewer.

In 1973, when I was nine, the Plunket Shield cricket final was between Auckland and
Wellington, at the Basin Reserve.

My dad and I went. A father and son outing of sandwiches, cordial from plastic
bottles, third-degree sunburn and the northerly sweeping along that fat, straight
stretch of road from Courtenay Place.

Three and a half decades on, I recall both teams contained names that can still
provoke a schoolboy's smiling awe: Bruce Taylor, Richard Collinge, Ewen Chatfield,
Bob Cunis, Terry Jarvis, Mark Burgess and Geoff Howarth.

Great players, all of them. But the greatest player that day, and in the Campbell
household for many years afterwards, was a man named Peter McGregor.

Before I go on with this story, I need to put things in context.

I grew up in Wellington. This is more important than mere biography, because
unlike patrician Aucklanders and bolshy Cantabrians, Wellingtonians don't expect
to win. We hope we'll win, with an almost quixotic longing, but that's quite different
from expecting to. Throughout my life as a Wellington supporter, I have understood
that victory isn't rightly ours.

Which is just as well. In the 45 years of my existence, Wellington has held rugby's
Ranfurly Shield, for example, on just three occasions, defending it for a grand total of
just six games, an average of one successful defence every seven-and-a-half years of my
life. Facts like these shape you. Rational expectations simply can't survive in that kind
of environment. Success becomes incongruous.

I was at Eden Park at the end of 2008, when Wellington won the Ranfurly Shield
for just the third time in my life. It felt strangely awkward – like borrowing an older

person's suit.

So when, on December 16, 1973, Auckland batted first, made 209, and Wellington slumped to be 179-8 in response, my father and I understood we had done what we were destined to do. We had made it to the final, we had restricted Auckland to a gettable total, and then, because this is always the script, we had conspired to lose.

Richard Collinge came and went for a duck. Wellington were 186-9, with 24 runs needed and Ewen Chatfield and Peter McGregor at the crease.

There is no sentence in the entire history of cricket less likely to inspire confidence than that last sentence – 24 runs required – and Ewen Chatfield and Peter McGregor the men to get them. We were doomed, and my father and I joined the sad but not entirely surprised or surprising exodus of fans streaming along the embankment to the gate.

I have no idea why we stopped. Maybe it was about getting full value for money – we are of Scottish descent, after all. But stop we did. We stood at the northern exit of the Basin waiting for that final wicket to fall. And waiting. And waiting. And waiting.

And it didn't.

For Wellington to win, Chatfield had to survive a relative eternity and McGregor had to score. As I have already suggested, both outcomes seemed unlikely. Chatfield is a fine man, and he was a brilliantly tenacious and accurate bowler, but his test batting average was 8.57 and even that lowly figure implies a prowess not readily apparent in his technique. He prodded. Sometimes the ball hit the prod. Sometimes the ball missed. Either way, the prod itself had little to do with determining the outcome.

But ball by ball, Chatfield did survive and Peter McGregor did score. The afternoon traffic roared around the Basin Reserve, but inside you could have heard a pin drop. McGregor scores a single. Chatfield prods. Chatfield prods again.

They passed 200.

And my father and I, and a growing huddle of people who had also stopped at the exit, and others who had hurried to the ground after hearing this unlikely progress on their car radios, stood in silent prayer.

And then it happened. Peter McGregor hit a four. Wellington had won. *Chatfield not out 6, McGregor not out 26.* The Basin erupted. My father, who was not given to such outbursts, did a little dance. Men in walk-shorts and knee-length socks shook hands with the strangers beside them.

Happiness spread out from the Basin over the entire city. Wellington had beaten Auckland, to win.

We went home, euphoric. What a wonderful day. The following week my young sister was given a kitten. Despite the fact that Sally had no interest in cricket, and the kitten was female, we named it McGregor.

Michael Campbell

THE ALL BLACKS AND GOLF

Michael Campbell was for a decade New Zealand's No 1
golfer and in 2005 won the United States Open.

Many things were important to me as I grew up in Wellington in the 1970s. My family
and my mates were a huge part of my life, but like many Kiwi kids I had a fascination
with sport, particularly rugby, and like most, my heroes were the All Blacks.

The men in black were all my idols, though I had a special fondness for Ebony
and Ivory – Bernie Fraser and Stu Wilson – who would scorch along the wing for
Wellington, doing their best to warm us up while we froze our backsides off watching
from up in the Millard Stand. Colour-wise, I used to relate a bit more to Bernie Fraser,
as he raced in for his tries in that corner of the ground he used to call his own. Stu
Wilson may have had a bit more to his elegant game, but he was tall, skinny and white,
so we used to yell just that bit harder when Bernie scored.

I used to go with my dad and watch many games from up in that creaky old structure,
while the wind usually howled through from Cook Strait and made conditions very
tough to play rugby in. It was extra special when the All Blacks came to town. This was
our national team, the best rugby side in the world, and there was always a magnetic
pull about the occasion, because they were so much a part of our culture.

And when they travelled overseas there was something extra special about being
woken by my dad in the early hours of the morning to watch our All Blacks take on
teams in Europe.

When I played, I was a hooker for a start, then a halfback, so my special interest
was watching how Sid Going then Dave Loveridge controlled a game and how they
operated. It was just amazing how Super Sid was able to wriggle through the smallest
of gaps when he was running with the ball, while Trapper had to be one of the sweetest
passers of the ball ever.

Whenever I played, I imagined that I was able to combine their fantastic talents, while I also tried to deliver the sort of leadership authority that Graham Mourie imparted every time he took his team on to the field.

About that time I was also starting to get interested in golf, because we had moved from Cannons Creek to Titahi Bay, and the course was only a few minutes from our place. Television had also moved on and I was captivated by the coverage they used to have of the Masters, usually the last nine holes of the fourth round.

Very soon my list of sports heroes swelled as Jack Nicklaus, Arnold Palmer, Greg Norman and Seve Ballesteros came into my world.

I remember it was a very fine balancing act on the last day of the Masters. I'd watch as late as I could before I had to get my skates on and make it to school before the first class. Even then I was trying to take parts out of all those champions' games and include them in the way I tried to play.

Seve just had the most magic short game. He was a genius for imagining shots and then making them happen. Norman struck the ball so beautifully and consistently that you yearned to repeat his shot-making. Nicklaus was just so mentally tough, so hard to beat, so determined, that you wanted to emulate that when you went out on to the course with your mates.

There was also a part of me that said I wanted to show the world that Maori could also play golf. As a race we had proved to be magic rugby players in the All Blacks, but as I was growing up the best New Zealand golfers were all European – Bob Charles, Greg Turner, Frank Nobilo, Simon Owen. I wanted to crack that mould and show that a little Maori kid from Titahi Bay could foot it with the best.

I guess I knew from a very young age that I was not going to be an All Black, but I wanted to prove to people that I could play top-level sport, that I could match our best crop of golfers and could succeed and be an example for other Maori.

Daniel Carter

JOHN KIRWAN

Daniel Carter is regarded as the best rugby first five-eighth in the world.

Ever since I could walk, it seemed that rugby was a huge part of my life. I grew up loving the All Blacks, wanting to be one and following everything about them.

I was only four, but can still recall watching the first World Cup and being pulled along by all the hype of the occasion as the All Blacks secured the greatest prize in their rich rugby history. Along with the rest of the nation, I was dragged in by the whole tournament, and top of my favourites list was John Kirwan.

That try he scored in the opening game against Italy was breathtaking and it just seemed right he should score another in the final to kill off the French. There was no argument. JK was my special hero – I wanted to play like him and score tries like he did. I followed his career through to its conclusion with the All Blacks. Whenever I played, I tried to impersonate JK. He just stood out.

Later on I marvelled at the exploits of others like Andrew Mehrtens and Graeme Bachop, but even when JK switched his allegiance to rugby league late in his career, I continued to follow his progress.

I was lucky enough to meet him in the early stages of my All Black career. We became good friends and I have stayed with him and his delightful family in Italy. It was reassuring to discover that my hero on the field was equally special off the field. Too often people find out their idols are very different in real life, but JK was very down-to-earth, a very genuine, caring sort of bloke. He makes time for people and he was very helpful to me, talking about his experiences and discussing how to handle being in the limelight.

The first time I met him, he had come down to my shop in Christchurch to do an interview for television. We did the job and he stayed around afterwards to chat, and

we found we were on a similar wavelength. He gave me his details and suggested we get together again in future.

JK was the marquee player of his era. He revolutionised wing play with his power and speed. His deeds were just magnetic at that first World Cup and beyond. I did not necessarily want to play on the wing, but I did want to play like him. He wanted the ball, he was always about scoring tries with his mix of strength, sidesteps, fends and pace.

During his career, JK also managed to indulge his love of surfing and has even managed to persuade me of the benefits. I started to learn and was looking forward to getting away to some spots like Biarritz a few times during my time in Europe, until I got injured.

While JK was a marvellous All Black, he has also shown me how to keep a good balance in my life, the importance of keeping my mind occupied with a variety of things away from rugby. He is a busy coach, but he values his family networks in Italy and New Zealand. He also eases the clutter when he goes surfing.

I train and play as hard as I can. When my time is needed in rugby, then I'm full on. But away from that I enjoy many other business opportunities and relaxation. It is very important to have that balance, and for that sort of guidance, I am indebted to JK.

I would suffocate if I was breathing rugby 24/7. You have to keep things fresh to deliver your best work.

Sir Bob Charles

A WEALTH OF EARLY INFLUENCES

Sir Bob Charles is the best golfer produced by New Zealand.
He won the British Open in 1963.

It will come as no great surprise to those who know me when I say it is difficult to pinpoint one individual who was a sporting beacon in my life. There were many people who helped and instilled values in me which have been at the core of my life, but to boil an inquiry such as this down to one person is too narrow.

If others judge me they would probably suggest my nature leans towards the introverted side of life and if I was summing up my nature I would say I am very much my own man and always have been. Even as a teenager, I did not have many heroes or people I looked up to, although I was influenced a little later by people like Kel Nagle and Peter Thomson.

When I won the New Zealand Open as a country-raised teenager, I had never competed against either. Bruce Crampton was second in that tournament, Thomson came third and was already the British Open champion, and it was from that encounter really that I started making some connections with people who were to be lifelong friends and confidantes and offer help in my sport and life.

The following year – 1955 – when I was the defending champion at Middlemore, was the first time Kel Nagle came over to compete. I later became very close to him and travelled a great deal with Kel, his wife, Jean, and my wife, Verity.

My upbringing was fairly standard, though as an only child and one who was quite reserved, I tended to latch on to the circle of friends of my parents, Ivor (it was actually dad's middle name because he was christened Albert Ivor Charles) and Phyllis. My parents were typical of their generation – not demonstrative, and very private, and I think I have followed them in that regard.

I was a typical kid of that generation growing up in the 1940s in New Zealand. You had respect for your elders – most people did. You stood up if a lady entered the room, you doffed your hat and you opened doors for others, and all those sorts of things that counted for manners.

My parents both played golf and as someone with sporting instincts I was also keen to play, but had to wait until my 15th birthday before I was permitted to join the Masterton Golf Club. Much of my parents' spare time was spent at the golf course, so it was natural that I gravitated in that direction as well. We lived about 15 minutes' walk from the course and once I started getting involved and understanding some of the game's intrigues, I soon had the bug for the sport.

Golf was then a winter sport in New Zealand, which was a nice counterpoint for me because I was heavily involved in cricket in summer when I was at Wairarapa College.

My parents immersed themselves as committee members at the local golf club. They always supported my interest and gave me a set of Norman von Nida clubs as a present for my 18th birthday, just before I won the New Zealand Open. Much of their spare time was spent on the golf course.

Dad was a schoolteacher and also a very strict disciplinarian. He and my mother believed in the dictum of the day, which was "spare the rod and spoil the child". Not that I was beaten much at all, but there were definite rules that had to be adhered to.

I would bike to school, to the YMCA and to the golf course – life was pretty easy, pretty good in those days. I was a country kid who was fortunate enough to discover I had an aptitude and a love for the game of golf and I took to it quickly.

About that time I took out a *Golf World* magazine subscription that I still have running and I am proud to say that every tournament I have won has received coverage in that magazine, and that my picture has been on the cover on more than one occasion. My other golfing Bible was a book called *Power Golf* by Ben Hogan. It contained all sorts of advice and some fantastic photos of him in action at Augusta.

My mother and I won the mixed foursomes at the Masterton Golf Club when I was 17 and the prize was a book by Henry Cotton. It gives me enormous pride to know that he and I remain the only two golfers to have been knighted. I read the story of his life over and over again and imagined myself in his spikes in the photos throughout the book. Most of the coverage was about the game in Europe, and I recall being fascinated by his account of a tournament he was involved in at Crans-sur-Sierre in Switzerland. It was a magnetic travelogue and that also influenced me.

They were all collecting forces that pushed me into a life of golf.

I was an avid reader and can recall Sam Snead's book on golf, which was inspiring for a young fellow like myself. I thought there could be nothing better than to turn pro and travel the world. I was sure it would be marvellous and it has turned out to be a very privileged life.

My life evolved, it gathered pace. There were no sudden decisions, which I guess was reflective of my nature and the times.

I moved to Christchurch in 1956 and was accepted as a member at Shirley, where I met two other people who influenced me greatly.

Arthur Dennis was the general manager of Winstone Building in those days, an Englishman, a very well-educated man who caddied for me in my amateur days throughout New Zealand. He could spare time only at the weekends, but he always came out and supported me.

Another great friend, Ian Cromb, later travelled the world with me. I was 20 then, by nature a shy, retiring, private individual, but also someone who was indebted to a core group of quality individuals whose manners, advice and guidance have been the backbone of my very fortunate life.

Julie Christie

SIR COLIN MEADS

Julie Christie, a pioneer in New Zealand television, was the founder of Touchdown Productions.

It was 1989. I'd been working in television for all of a year as a junior production assistant and researcher when the "job of a lifetime" landed on my desk. It wasn't a lucky break. I don't believe in luck, preferring to put such things down to good timing and/or good management. My "good timing and good management" was that I was the only one of the 50 employees at the television production company who knew anything about sport. I'd spent most of my newspaper journalism career as a sports sub-editor. This job of a lifetime was producing a new TVNZ series, *Mud and Glory: Great Rugby Stories.*

I was 27, and statistically 27 is your most entrepreneurial age – the age you are most likely to make your first million – if you're going to make it at all! Perhaps the fact that I was 27 was a sign because before that, I'd had little of the driving ambition that has plagued me for the 20 years since.

The truth was, I did know a bit about sport, but I fibbed when I said I knew much about rugby. I just didn't care that much for the sport, preferring rugby league – what do you expect when you come from the West Coast of the South Island! Fortunately, there was no-one around with the knowledge to catch me out, so suddenly I was the producer of a television rugby show. But I figured the series wasn't really about rugby; it was about heroes.

I began the job with two heroic ambitions – the first was to get Buck Shelford to perform a haka, bronzed, oiled and topless with full moko and feathers in his hair, for the opening title sequence. The second ambition was to find the long-lost anti-hero, Keith Murdoch. Both ambitions were achieved, but neither would leave the sort of lasting impression – and a lesson for life – that one episode of the series did. As part of

the job, I was to travel to the United Kingdom to film four episodes. We'd do part of the Keith Murdoch story at the Angel hotel in Cardiff, we'd film convert John Gallagher at his new Leeds league club, and in London we'd talk to brainy Black David Kirk.

But first there was the episode that would leave the biggest impression – I was to follow Colin Meads on his return trip to Wales.

Colin Earl Meads had given up international rugby 18 years earlier, after 133 matches from 1957-1971. He'd toured Wales only twice, the second time 22 years earlier, and had been the target of every Welsh player. They believed that to fell Meads was to fell the All Blacks. But I was to see in every face we met that the fanatical Welsh revered him above all other players, past or present.

He'd played his rugby with the hard, uncompromising qualities of the Kiwi farmer – the same qualities they revered in their miners – so there was an unbreakable bond between the Welsh and Colin Meads. They were miners, he was a farmer. When the Welsh played the All Blacks, to them it was the miners versus the farmers. And in 1989, that hadn't changed like it has today.

Wherever we went, Colin proudly wore his maroon and gold King Country blazer, offering a taloned hand to every Welshmen we met, and there were thousands. His huge clawlike fingers are the result of rheumatic fever as a child, but also gave him a unique one-hand grip of a rugby ball as he ran towards the tryline.

What surprised me was that as a 27-year-old New Zealander I knew so much less about Colin Meads than any 10-year-old Welsh kid. He was literally mobbed by children as young as five. I could not work out how they would even know who he was, but they did. He was a god in that country and it was the first time I had seen true heroism, and hero worship, so close up.

These people had respect for the man like I had never seen before. Everyone wanted to talk about the 1963 All Blacks' loss to Newport... 1963! I was two years old then! How did these kids know so much about this man and this game? Obviously great moments in history include rugby matches in the Welsh schools, but not in ours!

He told me how he married Verna in 1957 – at a "very young age" – on the basis that marriage wouldn't interfere with rugby. I imagine such a proviso is not part of Marriage Guidance 101 these days, yet this couple provided a lesson in respect. Verna said she felt proud to be married to such a great talent.

His All Black captain, Wilson Whineray, said: "He would never be beaten. We might be, but he never was." Colin also spoke, with some sadness, about how he felt his success had put too much pressure on his children to do well in sport.

Colin's answer to the Welsh adoration on our tour was to say that on his All Black tours to Wales, he was more loathed than loved by the Welsh and it wasn't until he was famously sent off in Scotland in 1967 and banned for two matches that the Welsh suddenly went wild about him and the cry came out: if you can't play for the All Blacks, come and play for us!

Twenty-two years later, the great Welsh halfback – and now fabulously wealthy – Gareth Edwards landed on Cardiff Arms Park in his private helicopter to be interviewed about Meads. He called him a gentle man and the greatest forward ever. Legendary flyhalf Barry John talked of touring New Zealand in 1971 with the British Lions, who all looked up to Meads and revered that famous No 5 jersey.

Meads' answer to the gushing accolades? "I was never that great, just a member of a good team!"

Yes, Colin remained humble. You couldn't help but be struck by his shyness, yet this was the man whose backchatting of referees was legendary. His explanation? "I never struck a referee who didn't need some help."

Only in countless tiny bars in the back of countless public houses in countless Welsh villages – bars that felt to me as if a woman had never previously ventured there – was the shyness drowned in countless pints of beer. But never once did even gallon after gallon of the local brew have any effect on this giant of a man, other than to make him join in the endless singing of Welsh rugby anthems.

Am I eulogising or idolising a saint? Well, I don't mean too. He didn't ever pretend to be one. He even talked about using Keith Murdoch as an enforcer to sort out an opposition player. Murdoch apparently couldn't wait for Meads to give him the signal – he was into the bloke at the first scrum and was soon sent off.

Meads taught me a lot about what it means to be a New Zealander. His 15-season test career embodied New Zealand's heartland – you would never see a New Zealand man as "New Zealand" as this one. He said it himself in his famous tanalised fenceposts TV commercials – "tough, rugged, durable". He could have been talking about himself.

The visit to Wales came just three years after the rebel Cavaliers tour to South Africa and, as a result, the Welsh were convinced that every New Zealand player of the amateur game was actually getting paid. They continuously asked Colin what he was getting paid to appear in the show. The answer was nothing, of course. He'd even folded that hulking body and those long legs into an economy class seat to travel over there. One night, after at least 10 pints in yet another pub, he cheekily pulled one of my pigtails (they were the answer to a bad hair day!) and said again:

"They want to know what you're paying me."

"Tell them the truth," I said.

"She says I'm not allowed to tell you," he bellowed with laughter.

When I again watched the Meads programme of *Mud and Glory: Great Rugby Stories* nearly 20 years after I produced, wrote and directed it – my first TV programme – it was still a moving story, a great story. It had not aged. I would make it no differently today. It's not that I've learned nothing in the past 20 years in television, but that the story was so great then and it still is now.

It just took the Welsh to make me, and a lot of New Zealanders who watched it, understand. How disappointingly New Zealand of us!

I had been brought up in the West Coast coal-mining town of Greymouth and taught the meaning of old-fashioned values like respect, but, in Wales with Colin Meads, I saw what it really meant. And I learned how to tell a story about love, passion and guts. Over the next 20 years I would make countless television programmes about heroes, or starring heroes, but it was back in 1989 when I learned from a bunch of kids 12,000 miles away that I was walking beside one truly great hero.

Mike Chunn

THE FIRST XV

Mike Chunn was a member of the New Zealand band Split Enz and is the man behind Play it Strange, a charitable trust that develops secondary school students' musical and writing skills.

In August 1964, my form one class went on a trip to Wellington. Most of us were 12 years old, but we felt like explorers of experience and maturity seeking whatever lay lost out there at the end of New Zealand's vast roads. An overnight bus trip and a pie at 4am in Palmerston North set the scene for an adventure far from the rut of day-to-day life and the blight of arithmetic.

From the camping ground, that fine Saturday, we drove off in high anticipation to Athletic Park, where the All Blacks were to play Australia.

I'd never seen grown-ups play rugby. I had played for the Otahuhu 12th grade in my red and black jersey. But I knew the local All Blacks by name and had seen them in their civvies.

Pat Walsh turned up at our end-of-year 13th grade trophy presentations in the clubrooms at Sturges Park. He looked like a film star.

And there was Mac Herewini, who owned the dairy in the mall by the picture theatre in the main drag. I would ask him for a Snappy Bar at half-time and stare at him long and hard as he turned to the Empire confectionery boxes to get me one. They were tuppence.

Then there was Waka Nathan. I saw him in the street once. He walked past and I imagined tackling him. He seemed about twice my height. And we all knew him as "the Black Panther".

So there we were at Athletic Park, aghast at the spectacle. A huge crowd beyond anything I'd ever seen. Rows and rows of faces, pensive and expectant, in towering grandstands. And us down by the sideline in makeshift stands of our own. Hundreds of schoolboys. Waiting. So silent compared to our usual blabbering selves. And then out they came from the tunnel. The national anthems. The haka. Stunning. And the game began.

What do I remember most? Running on to the field after the game. Smelling the grass and walking close behind one of the forwards with his jersey off. Towering above me. It seemed so very clear to me. This sport, this ceremony, this perfect combination of quick thinking and physical prowess, was the perfect pursuit.

That night, still buzzing from the game, we all went to see a movie. It was *A Hard Day's Night*. Another spectacle, another team effort with quick thinking and musical prowess. A perfect pursuit. It was an epiphany and I wanted to be a pop star like the Beatles. How could you not?

The next year I was 13 and off to boarding school. The concept of being a pop star was alien to anyone there so it murmured away in my head for five years. But when it came to rugby, there was a perfect objective in the form of the First XV. For four years I was thrilled, inspired and motivated by that beautiful combination of 15 young men. Each time I watched them it took me back to that day at Athletic Park. Why?

I used to think of rugby as a microcosm of living life on our wacky planet. What else was there to hang on to? Life in the classroom, with its permutations and combinations and too much silence? The playground and the superficial societies within? The darkness of the dormitory?

Even though as a teenager at boarding school I had virtually no understanding of the world around me, I knew about the concept of allies and enemies. I knew about the love of your fellow man. I knew about humility and strength and stamina and teamsmanship. I knew about victory and loss.

And there they were in a concentrated, choreographed state of strategy and purpose in an 80-minute game of rugby. Each Saturday, I stood on the sidelines around Auckland watching my First XV and relished all that was to be had.

The individuals. The great players who weaved through the opposition. Youths who captained the boys as if they had captained armies. The ones who always moved forward, were never driven back. The lineout jumpers high above the rest. The great fullbacks who sent the ball soaring through posts. And like my Otahuhu All Blacks, real and present, so too these First XV players. Names that rolled off our tongues. No Smiths, Browns or Joneses in our lot. Names like Gilhooley, Cotterill, Coleman, Hoki, Rejthar, Faire and Miskell. They walked past you in the quadrangle and you imagined tackling them. They were real.

The whole team. The collective will and the unified spirit. Beautiful to watch and moving in its most successful moments when your heart beat faster and theirs did, too.

The philosophy of rugby in its practical execution is a model for life. And for me as a youth at school it bent and shaped me in real terms. My First XV team was the working engine. It was the practical embodiment of that belief system.

And at the end of each game I would walk on to the paddock and smell the grass. And walk behind them, jerseys draped over their shoulders.

It was revolution on the paddock.

The revolution in my head was amply supplied by the Beatles. So did I ever don those special First XV colours to enact all that I had gleaned from the years of watching and absorbing? Yes I did. After 60 minutes in my first game, I had both bones in my right leg broken in two. And that was the end of my rugby career.

So I became a pop star instead.

Helen Clark

STACEY JONES

Helen Clark was the New Zealand Prime Minister from 1999-2008. She is now head of the United Nations Development Programme.

The electorate of Mt Albert that I was privileged to represent for 27 years is in the heart of rugby league country, so I suppose it was only natural that I would follow the sport closely.

Over the years I've seen some great New Zealand rugby league teams and met some very admirable players, but for me one man has stood out – Stacey Jones, whose career I have followed since his early days.

He broke into the top level at a very opportune moment, just as the Warriors club was being formed in the mid-1990s.

From the minors' grade to now, from his earliest playing days with Ponsonby Ponies and the Mt Albert Rugby League Club, followed by his successful association with the Pt Chevalier Rugby League Club, Stacey showed natural ability verging on brilliance. He was always a player who could change a game with one special piece of football.

His ability from an early age to read the game helped him to stand out from his peers and it was obvious he had rare talent.

Stacey was always destined to be a rugby league star. He played representative league for Auckland right through the various age levels and this culminated in his being appointed captain of the Junior Kiwis in 1994.

Soon after, Stacey was spotted by the Warriors' Auckland-based National Rugby League franchise, at almost exactly the same time as he was selected for the Kiwis.

Stacey had an extremely long career with the Warriors and he was a great crowd-puller. He won many matches for his club with his ability to spot a gap, time a pass, or deliver a pinpoint kick just when it was needed. It was not surprising that he was voted the Warriors club's first life member.

He then made a decision to have a family OE, and played a couple of seasons for the Catalans club in France.

When Stacey returned home, it was not long before he had been re-signed with the Warriors, and he quickly made his presence felt again. Some worried that perhaps he wouldn't be the player of previous years, but in no time he was the Stacey of old, and his team-mates clearly responded.

Stacey, who fans call "The Little General", is a great family man. Although naturally shy, he has never let his fame change the person we know, love, and admire, and I find that his most endearing quality, ahead of any outstanding play on the field.

He will go down as one of the best players rugby league has ever seen, and not just in New Zealand. Watching Stacey over the years has given me many hours of pleasure, and that feeling is magnified because he is such a modest individual off the field. In short, a great New Zealander.

Jackie Clarke

MICHAEL JONES

Jackie Clarke is a singer and a television and stage actor.

I'll have to be careful here, otherwise people might get the mistaken impression that I'm a stalker! I first met him in about 1992 at one of those roof parties they held at TVNZ. His mother was there and I remember seeing him across the room and suddenly my heart rate went out of control.

For years I had been going on about how I loved Michael Jones and of course I still do, but this was like a moment from a movie. Our eyes met, and he came towards me, like in a Hollywood script. I melted – I couldn't say a bloody word!

I was pathetic. I was absolutely incapable of going up and introducing myself and saying I'd had an indecent obsession with him for years and I thought he was amazing.

It was deeply unusual for me. I was absolutely awestruck. There is something unusual about meeting those godlike creatures and you are so shocked when they descend to earth that, like me, you end up going: "Blah, blah, blah." Michael drove the conversation and then introduced me to his mum.

It was highly unusual. He was so smooth and just started off a conversation with: "Hi Jackie, oh you're Samoan and so am I." And then he continued talking about our mutual heritage and I was just going "blah, blah, blah" and probably had impure thoughts while there he was, such a paragon of purity.

That's why I dug him so much. The reason I love him, in a pure and impure way, is because of the Sunday thing. I love that. I think that's what really turned me on to him, because here was somebody who was the best in the world. In that first World Cup, in that All Black team, which was probably the first that I really identified with, there he was, kicking arse, and yet he was also saying he was not going to play on Sundays.

Now I'm not really religious at all, but I think I took a step back and thought: "Oh my God, somebody who everybody wants a piece of is being incredibly brave and mature to put his stake in the ground and not be swept along by the tide, especially when his decision involves the national religion of rugby."

That is why I have always thought: "What a man."

All the way through, no matter what was happening, no matter if the team really needed him, he had the courage of his convictions. How cool is that?

To be able to maintain personal integrity with all that going on around him was great. You see so many All Blacks who get swallowed up by the whole experience – it is so much bigger than *Ben Hur*. So I guess that was the first time that I have ever gone: "Wow, somebody has done something that is incredibly full of integrity and what a hero that makes him." To me anyway.

Of course, there is that No 7 thing, too. It is a magical number and for me he is the first of a whole series of gods who have played in that position. He was followed by Josh Kronfeld, who is also Samoan, and Richie McCaw, who is probably Samoan as well.

I once bumped into Michael having coffee and we had a chat. It was very casual. I kept my cool and I think I said more than three words to him that time. He was so sweet, such a soft voice and such a sweet man. I have never got his autograph, though I wish I had. I couldn't even begin to ask. How would you do that? "Blah, blah, blah," all over again. I just live for our next meeting, but I would love for our sons to meet him.

I'm obsessed with rugby. I love the drama, the ongoing complexity of the game, and that fact that, on paper, while we are the best team by miles, what happens on the day is what counts. I love the multi-layered nature of the game, and I get totally involved in its characters. I watch a lot of the sport. For me it is like really good theatre and I get incredibly emotional and vocal when I watch, because I get so tied up in it. I get drained by the way New Zealanders react to it sometimes. It is a game, a great game, and we should celebrate it.

The psychology of public opinion is such a huge factor in the way the game is played. It's a lot like music, and playing in a band is a lot like playing in a team. All that rehearsal that goes in, then when you get there on the day you have to kind of throw it all away and be in the moment, be free and uninhibited. Any kind of black shadow over the psyche is so damaging. It is a tough wait to play gigs at night, in much the same way as it is a long delay for the All Blacks before they run out at night.

With us musos, there is often a drive to the airport the same day, then setting up the gear, sound-checks, dress-rehearsal and then you are really buggered by the time you get on stage to play.

But you have to find a fifth gear, you have to tap into that mentally. I might get agitated, but when I get on stage I have to say: "Nothing matters now. Give it all, let it go." My brain has to be free, just like Michael and the All Blacks.

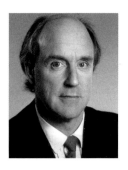

John Clarke

TERRY LINEEN

John Clarke, who invented the character Fred Dagg, is an acclaimed television actor and writer, with a particular talent for comedy.

In Palmerston North in the winter of 1959, I sat down and wrote to an All Black. I was 10 years old and the letter was in my best handwriting.

The letter was to Terry Lineen, the All Black second five-eighth, who could float through gaps which he identified using radar. He was elegant and gifted, and as someone once said of a pitcher in American baseball: "He could throw a lamb-chop past a wolf."

The next player who combined strength and subtlety in this same way was Bruce Robertson, who drifted upright past opponents who seemed to accompany him and offer whatever assistance they could. It was ridiculous and it looked easy, and no-one else could do it.

In those days there were four tests a year, rather than one a week, and they actually mattered. Nobody sang the national anthem and if a player scored a try he returned to his position in solitude and waited until the fuss had died down. Nobody got paid. The players all had other jobs. Like Ed Hillary, who climbed the highest mountain in the world, but was really a beekeeper. The only way to watch rugby at that time was to be at the game or hope that a few seconds of test match footage appeared in the local news section at the pictures.

For the kids of Palmerston North, however, there were the All Black trial matches between the Possibles and the Probables, imaginary sides made up of real players. Squadrons of us primary school kids would fill the Manawatu Showgrounds and watch our heroes before sprinting into no-man's land after the match and getting everyone's autographs.

The national selectors should have paid more attention to us at these fixtures. We were good. We went for balance in a side, but we rewarded flair and our selections stand up well to this day. Basil Bridge and I picked Kel Tremain a year before the selectors did. Kel ran flat; nothing deceptive, but he processed things fast and he was up on the opposition like a writ. The selectors ignored him until the Lions scored four great tries against us in the first test in Dunedin and the NZRFU referred to our notes and popped Kel on the side of the All Black scrum for the next 10 years. That first 1959 Lions test match was the Dunkirk of New Zealand rugby. On the one hand firepower, élan, tactics and quick thinking. On the other hand (ours) Don Clarke kicked six penalties. As Churchill said at the time: "We must be careful not to assign to this deliverance the attributes of a victory."

Observant kids on bikes, having been in attendance at the Manawatu Showgrounds, had sensed this would happen. We'd made a few changes, but they hadn't been introduced. We'd picked Red Conway, for example. How he'd missed selection for Dunedin we couldn't understand. He'd come down from Taranaki and he'd taken the trial match apart. He was all over the paddock and was one of the first forwards we'd ever seen turn up among the midfield backs looking for part-time work.

We'd also earmarked the big Waikato lock Pickering. I was so confident I got his autograph twice. He said: "You've already got mine," but I wasn't convinced and he gave it to me again. I may be the only 60-year-old in the world with E A R Pickering's name signed twice, one above the other because he was right and because he was genial. (I'll leave my autograph book to the state. It's an important record. It's not just mine. It belongs to the nation.)

A lot of people think selection is easy. It isn't. We had our difficulties. We were troubled by the Briscoe/Urbahn question at halfback and we didn't spot Ralph Caulton, the Wellington winger who looked as if he'd arrived to check the gas meter and then zipped over for two tries in a dream debut in the second test at Athletic Park. I was there that day and Keith Quinn was a ballboy. After the match, Keith got the ball from the final kick and returned it to the kicker, Donald Barry Clarke, the famously accurate porpoise from Morrinsville, whose brother, Ian, was still propping the New Zealand scrum at 112. Don thanked Quinny very much, and recognising a good keen man, gave him a pie.

Terry Lineen wrote back to me.

John Clarke,
18 Milverton Ave,
Palmerston North.

The letter thanked me, encouraged me and thought perhaps I might be interested in the signatures of the All Blacks who played in the third test against the Lions (which we won 22-6). These were all on a separate sheet. Each player was named and each had signed next to his name. I still feel good about this letter.

When Fred Dagg appeared on television in the 1970s, he got letters from kids all over New Zealand. Every kid who wrote to Fred Dagg received a reply. The reason Fred wrote back to all those kids is that Terry Lineen wrote back to me.

Lana Coc-Kroft

LESSONS OF THE 1981 SPRINGBOK TOUR

Lana Coc-Kroft, Miss Universe New Zealand in 1988,
is a television and radio personality.

My background is a sporty one, but to be fair, I am much more of a participant than an armchair viewer, probably because I was the last of four children. I was required to be quick off the mark to get enough dinner, to use the bathroom or to escape my older brothers' super-length backhands.

Home life was very typical of middle New Zealand. Weekends were all about us playing sport. My sister and I played netball and hockey and it was rugby for the boys.

However, there were always two events that drove us, as a family, on to the couch. The Olympic Games and rugby tests were family events to be marked on the calendar. Chips, dips, pickled onion and cheese toasties, friends rallying round, and beer consumed. As a teenager, I wasn't inspired so much by individuals, as I was by these historical and memorable events.

I was about 13 when the Moscow Olympics took place, a very impressionable age. I wanted to climb into the television and become a super-athlete, bask in the limelight after a record-breaking performance, shed tears on a podium and sing my national anthem with unabashed pride.

I had the urge to push myself to physical limits and train to represent my country at any high-profile events. At school I ran a little harder, swam a little faster and trained a lot more – but sporting glory was never for me, a jack of all and a master of none.

I mention the Olympics because they inspired me and I was spellbound by them. However, it was not this event or any of those individual athletes that left the most lasting impression on my teenage years. That came a year later, when the Springboks toured New Zealand.

It was the first time I was truly initiated into the world of sport and politics.

JOHN MINTO leads a protest against the 1981 Springbok tour.

The Springboks didn't just come to New Zealand, they came to my house. My parents were both avid rugby fans. I have a warm, fuzzy, long-standing memory of dad or mum slipping into my bedroom in the middle of the night and the excitement of being allowed downstairs, snuggled up, to watch the All Blacks take on the world. They are some of the fondest memories I have of my childhood.

In 1981, when the Springboks came, the warm fuzzies shot out the door and my understanding of the power of sport changed for me and gave me a greater understanding instead of the power of conflict.

My father believed rugby was the greatest game, our national sport and should be played without political interference. Basically he believed sport should reign supreme over every outside issue and should not be influenced by political conflict. My mother, on the other hand, loved rugby through and through, but intellectualised that as much as this sport could send a positive message, it could not be seen to condone atrocities that were publicly accepted in a world forum.

Apartheid needed to be addressed and abolished. By making a stand here in New Zealand that under no circumstances would we support any travelling team or export from South Africa, the world could make a formidable stand against the South African government and its unwillingness to change its apartheid policy.

That battle was fought not only outside Eden Park and on the streets of New Zealand, but in our very own lounge. I was witness to some spectacular arguments that were won time and again by my mother, much to my father's frustration – he being a man of strength and history, she being a woman of incredible intelligence, political awareness of current events and compassion.

Our house became divided, as did many households in New Zealand. A truce was eventually called and my parents would agree to disagree.

I have memories of my rugby heroes, with fatigued faces, being interviewed and expressing their frustration at not being able to play the sport they loved without interference. I saw the passion of the protesters making enormous personal sacrifices to get their message across. I also recall the horror of seeing our police force resorting to shields and helmets and state-of-the-art batons, and lining the streets to keep the peace.

But most of all I remember thinking that even though I passionately loved playing sport and always played to win, nothing was more important than the safety, peace and unity of mankind, and that in the end we need to remember it's just a game.

Julie Coney

MARTINA NAVRATILOVA

Julie Coney is a former New Zealand netball captain and is now one of the two directors of Auckland firm coneystanleyEvents, a specialty hospitality service provider.

I was fortunate when I was attending Dunstan High School in Alexandra to run into two women who shaped my feelings for sport and, especially as far as netball is concerned, gave me the drive to go as far as I could.

One was Elaine Kaye, who helped to coach netball at the school and the other was Jude Henderson – Miss Henderson – a teacher.

They both had a lot of belief in me and that gave me the confidence that I needed to make progress in netball during school and after I'd left.

It was not an easy thing coming from a wee place like Alexandra in Central Otago to believe you could match some of the big names from major centres around New Zealand, but Elaine Kaye and Jude Henderson offered me a vast amount of encouragement and sound advice.

While I was at Dunstan, we entered a team in the South Island secondary school netball championships, a very exciting development for us. The first year, we went to Invercargill and the next year Christchurch. It was quite a thing for a small school like Dunstan High to be matching it with some of the big high schools of the South Island, schools like Villa Maria and Sacred Heart. We had a talented little team, tried our hardest and went very well. We learnt a lot about ourselves at those tournaments, what we were capable of.

At the same time, I made the Otago Country team and played at national tournaments in Invercargill and Hamilton. I made a point of watching as many games as I could on the No 1 court, where the top teams played.

The player I really focused on was Yvonne Willering, the Auckland goal defence. She played in the same position as me and she was a real star. I really loved the way Yvonne played, her reading of the game and the way she could make amazing intercepts. I tried to emulate those aspects of her play.

I was proud later in my netball career to play alongside Yvonne and then to be coached by her.

But extending my sights further than just netball, I'd say my sports hero, if that's the right word, was Martina Navratilova, the tennis player.

It's a funny thing. I suppose lots of teenaged girls would have had Chris Evert, Martina's great rival, as their hero, but Martina was always the one for me.

I felt she was the most incredible athlete. She had an amazing career – she was nearly 50 when she finally retired from the pro tour.

She started winning Wimbledon titles in the late 1970s, and after that she became ever more dominant, at the Australian, the US Open, the French, and in singles and doubles. I used to play a lot of tennis, and began by watching her on television and followed her career from there.

I admired her work ethic, the way she was so committed to her sport and how she maintained her fitness.

Even now I visit her website because she has written training programmes for summer, autumn, winter and spring. Martina has surely been one of the most inspirational figures in the history of sport.

I was delighted to finally meet her a few years ago when she came out to play an exhibition series against Monica Seles. Our company sold the hospitality at the Auckland event and afterwards I was introduced to her. I told her that I thought she had had an incredible career and was a marvellous athlete, and she was very gracious, but I don't think she had much idea what netball was!

Belinda Cordwell

EVONNE CAWLEY

Belinda Cordwell is the best women's tennis player produced by
New Zealand. She reached a career-high world ranking of 18th.

When I was young I was mad about sport and tried as many as I could. But tennis was
always a favourite, and one of the stars when I was growing up was Evonne Cawley of
Australia.

She was just the sort of combination a young girl looks up to – she was a wonderful
player, who won the Wimbledon singles title twice, she was a bit exotic, with her
Aborigine looks, and she was very laid-back and friendly.

Our whole family used to get up in the middle of the night to watch the Wimbledon
finals when they were televised live. I remember those times well – pitch black, the
excitement of a Wimbledon final, and hot chicken noodle soup and toast to keep us
going in the middle of the night.

In the 1980 final, Evonne Cawley, who was by then a mother, played Chris Evert (or
Lloyd as she was at the time), in the final.

I remember when Evonne came on to the court, she had matching white Fila gear.
Fila was famous at the time as the sponsor of Bjorn Borg, who had been winning the
French Open and Wimbledon for years. When Evonne walked out looking so good in
her Fila gear, we all remarked about what it would be like to be sponsored by Fila. I
had a poster on my bedroom wall of Evonne looking superb in green Fila gear.

That match really put Evonne on the top of my personal hit-list. She upset Chris
Evert to win her second Wimbledon title nine years after her first. She played gracefully
and had a very appealing all-court game.

A year or two later my father was travelling back to New Zealand from a business
meeting overseas when he noticed Evonne on the same flight. Being rather formal
about these things, dad wrote her a note, telling her his daughter was a fan of hers and

that she would love to get the chance one day to challenge her.

He asked the air hostess to pass it to Evonne and waited to see what would happen. Well, Evonne wrote a very nice message, telling me she hoped I would continue to make progress as a tennis player and to make sure I enjoyed the game.

When dad got home he gave me the note and it became one of my most cherished mementos.

By the time I got on the professional tour in the mid-1980s, Evonne had retired as a player. I saw her on the odd occasion at big events, but never really had the chance to say anything more than a quick hello. I've never had the opportunity to sit down and tell her what her act of kindness meant to an 11-year-old girl in Wellington.

There was one nice touch (for me) though, at the Australian Open in 1988, when I reached the fourth round. On the way I played Nicole Provis. Because Melbourne was her home town, there was a lot of interest in the match, and Evonne was brought in to commentate on it for television.

I got a special thrill when I learned later that Evonne had been a commentator, and I was very glad that evening to play one of my good matches.

Martin Crowe

SIR JOHN WALKER

Martin Crowe is regarded by many as the finest batsman
produced by New Zealand.

New Zealand has had many sporting greats, many heroes for people to latch on to.
Choosing one might be difficult for many people, but for me it's a straightforward task.
If you ask me to identify a person, a hero from the sports world, someone I saw when I
was growing up and thought I'd like to mirror some of his or her achievements, then
John Walker, the Olympic champion and world record-holder, has to be my choice.

It goes like this. The first cricket test I ever went to was at Eden Park when I was
six years old and Garfield Sobers was picked to play for the West Indies. I was super-
excited about going to see this supremely gifted man, but he scarcely did much in
that international and didn't tour New Zealand again, so that chance of some hero-
worship diminished.

Then I was involved in completing school projects on that remarkable English
cricketer Colin Cowdrey, based on his book, but I never saw him play, so that choice
went out the window. I decided to turn to a local talent – Mark Burgess. I thought that
would be much easier, and Burge was a bit of a hero in Auckland when Grafton played
Cornwall, but he did not quite sustain his form at international level.

What I do remember well is the 1974 Christchurch Commonwealth Games. I was
in Eastbourne and had been stung by a jellyfish at Days Bay the day the games began,
and Dick Tayler won the opening long-distance race, the 10,000m.

John Walker was absolutely outstanding during those games. The blonde hair, the shell necklace, the black singlet and the silver fern – it all added up to a pretty powerful message.

Then Walker broke the world record and won gold in '76 in Montreal. Those performances made an enormous impression on me, because I was into my teenage years, starting to mix a lot more with adults and starting to think about wearing the silver fern.

It was not the running, but the sporting inspiration. It was what Walker achieved, an Auckland lad on top of the world.

I met Walker very fleetingly during his career, then got to spend a couple of days with him when we put together a television documentary on his life after he had retired and was starting to feel the effects of Parkinson's Disease. We went out and interviewed him at his saddlery in Manurewa.

He was late because he had been unable to press the numbers to open the gate at his house, and was extremely apologetic. We had waited a while to schedule the chat because he had not been in great shape, but on that day he was in outstanding form.

I could not believe how sharp his mind was. Obviously his body was frail and had betrayed him, and he was apologetic and very humble. Yet the way he reflected on his career was just like it was yesterday and he did not say it with any arrogance. He just explained things matter-of-factly.

He could remember it all, which is probably why he had a long life as a runner – it meant so much to him. He had a gift, and he made the most of it so that he really went well beyond his use-by years to be still running competitively when he approached his 40th birthday.

I think the Olympics were much a more a special event then than they are now. There is a tainted weariness about the Olympics now, and because we have so much great international sport all the time, they have become just another event.

But in those days the Olympics were on much more of a pedestal. As a keen, young sportsman I was taking plenty of interest. Walker was in one of the glamour events, the 1500m. That got me thinking about history, legacy and great traditions of New Zealand sportsmen. You begin to appreciate all the things like pride, the silver fern, the national anthem and all those sorts of things, and that all came together in 1976.

As I sat next to Grant Fox in my form class at Auckland Grammar, I started to dream about what I was going to be and I was thinking about being a test cricketer scoring a century at Lord's. Foxy and I had a conversation then, a bet in our first year at Grammar, about who was going to play the most tests for New Zealand.

John Walker had the look of someone who might have been brought up at Piha Beach running into the wind, doing all his training out there on the west coast. He had that ruggedness about him, the look of a tough and determined man.

I loved the individual nature of his sport and the tactics that were so crucial. Walker was responsible for everything once he got out on the track. I could relate to that because while I played cricket in what was perceived to be a team sport, there was also a huge amount of individual responsibility.

Grant Dalton

SIR JOHN WALKER

Grant Dalton is a sailor whose projects have included
the Round the World race and the America's Cup.

Many households still had black and white television, but this performance was all colour. It was John Walker at his best, his long hair flowing, the beads, the black singlet, his hands outstretched to salute his triumph in Montreal in 1976, when he won gold in the 1500m.

Walker was the favourite, a remarkable middle-distance athlete who had broken the "impossible" 3min 50s barrier the year before and was expected to hit paydirt at the Olympics.

Many favourites in previous Olympics had failed to live up to the hype or meet expectations, but Walker did not fit that category as he psyched out his rivals to claim gold.

I expected him to win. I believed he would. However, I became alarmed and got a little twitchy as I watched the race unfold. The first 1000m seemed way too slow as the rest of the field deliberately took the pace out of the race in the only tactic they had to try to counter Walker's excellence. They figured someone might be able to outsprint the Kiwi champion in the race for the line, but Arch Jelley had trained Walker well. He had him in superb condition and I was exhilarated when he took off on the final lap, showing all that power, balance and control as he accelerated and left his rivals behind.

Any doubts I felt earlier were washed away as Walker belted his way to the tape and the victory podium. He answered all the sceptics, and all his rivals and showed just why he was the world's top middle-distance runner.

At Gothenburg on August 12 the year before, Walker had become the first person to crack the magic 3min 50s for the mile as he held his form for what seemed an eternity down the final straight before the official stopwatches clicked off at 3min

49.4s. It was one of those moments, like his Olympic gold, which just stick with you. The coverage in the papers, on radio and television went on for ages as we all revelled in our champion's deeds.

At one stage I remember running up one of the steeper streets in Parnell in Auckland, trying to keep up a certain level of fitness. Then Walker and Dick Quax came past as though we were in quicksand. They were on a training run, but the speed and effortlessness of their running styles was awe-inspiring.

I have never been involved in athletics or been connected to any people in that sport, but Walker's star qualities were a magnetic mix for teenage Kiwis in the 1970s. He was one of us, he was our man on the world stage, he showed there were no barriers if you worked hard, he made you proud, and he was a New Zealander at the pinnacle of his global field.

I got a real buzz from meeting John at one of the recent Halberg Awards ceremonies. I am not a massive sports nut or anything like that, but it was a special moment to meet someone who was such a classy example for someone like myself.

JOHN WALKER bursts through the tape to win the 1976 Olympic 1500m gold medal at Montreal. Behind him are Ivo van Damme (103), Paul-Heinz Wellman (446), Eamonn Coghlan (514) and Frank Clement.

Jane Dent

COUSIN NIKI

Jane Dent was a television broadcaster who later moved into the world of public relations.

Heroes were different back in my formative years – the 1960s and early 70s. You really didn't get to see them close up. TV was black and white and grainy till 1974, so sports stars like Peter Snell seemed out of reach and unreal.

But somehow someone in my family got his autograph for me after the '64 Olympics and I knew it was special.

Sport was a big feature of country life near Raglan in those days. At community sports days, we couldn't wait to watch the wood-chopping, cross-country, three-legged races and the "toss the rolling pin" competition, which on one occasion I paid for my cousin to enter because I knew she'd win.

Actually, she was my first real hero – three years older, a champion discus thrower, school rep hockey player, and an accomplished swimmer who had once saved me from drowning.

Niki was as tough as any boy, and played rugby long before it was deemed suitable for girls. Her favourite line to me was: "Jane, don't be such a girl."

People said I should be a great runner, given my height and long legs. I wasn't.

Cousin Niki demanded that I excel at something. I took to high jumping with a vengeance; endless hours of backyard practice, scissor-jumping over a bamboo rod balanced between two stakes. I made the Waikato inter-secondary school championships!

But tennis was my passion. Niki's family and mine played at the local tennis club every summer weekend and when I went to boarding school it was the only thing I remember with any fondness. This was it. I was going to be a professional tennis player, like Billie Jean King or Evonne Goolagong.

The only things missing were talent, application and killer instinct.

Never mind, if you can't do something yourself you can always follow around after others who can, and still have a good time. After all, I'd done that with cousin Niki.

Clearly, a career in sports journalism beckoned. I joined what was then the NZBC (TV and radio) in 1973. There was an obligatory side-track into general news reporting because women simply didn't do sports reporting back then.

"OE" in London provided the glorious opportunity to tag along as "assistant" with a photographer friend to Wimbledon, to watch the greats, Martina Navratilova, Chris Evert and Bjorn Borg. I saw some heroes close up and in colour at last.

After my return to Auckland in the early 80s, some enlightened male colleagues at TVNZ encouraged me to specialise in sports news reporting and eventually to become the first woman to present the sports news.

Coverage of women's sport was a different matter. I can remember almighty rows in the newsroom with me insisting that a Susan Devoy story was much more "bloody interesting" than yet another rugby, league or soccer preview.

I also felt passionate about increasing coverage for lower-profile sports like yachting. My lucky break was covering the America's Cup in Fremantle in 1986. It was New Zealand's first entry into sport's oldest competition, and with all the drama of protests and personalities, I was hooked.

Being a yachting reporter took me all over the world, including covering an obscure event in 1987 run out of the Aga Khan's yacht club in Sardinia, where I met my wonderful future husband, Peter, another Kiwi journalist.

We were still covering yachting, both working for TVNZ, eight years later when New Zealand finally won the America's Cup off San Diego. It was the undoubted highlight of my 23-year broadcasting career and it was then time to do something different.

My timing, early in 1996, was very fortunate. John Hart had just been appointed the first All Blacks coach of the professional era and he offered me the chance to become the first woman media liaison officer for the team.

It was a rare privilege to be part of the All Blacks management group, travelling everywhere with the team. Balancing the needs of media with those of the players and management was always hard, but the job was hugely stimulating and gave me a fresh perspective on my former journalist colleagues.

Four years and 52 tests later, I hung up my filofax full of rugby media contacts and moved into another demanding but highly satisfying role, overseeing international public relations for Tourism New Zealand.

It's all about promoting New Zealand as a fabulous holiday experience for international visitors, and it's not surprising that sport plays a big part in helping inspire people to visit our country.

Over the past few years, we have taken a giant inflatable rugby ball to Paris and London, and a waka to Valencia for the America's Cup.

When I joined Tourism New Zealand after working in male-oriented domains, the mainly female environment created new challenges for me – nothing major, but I hadn't anticipated the difference working in a room full of women.

It's definitely not okay these days to tell anyone "don't be such a girl", but I still hear Niki saying that to me.

Thanks cuzzie. You helped me get a long way and it's high time I told you.

Dame Susan Devoy

BRYCE TAYLOR

Dame Susan Devoy won the world title four times and is widely considered the finest women's squash player of all-time.

Squash was a booming sport in the '80s and Bruce Brownlee was the New Zealander touted as the great hope to dethrone Jahangir Khan on the world stage. He travelled the globe in that quest and reached about sixth in the world before a hip disease stopped his progress.

His coach was Bryce Taylor, a Kiwi who was competent enough as a representative player in New Zealand, but had far greater success as a coach. He just had a knack for it, and he and his partner, Marie, went to the United Kingdom with Bruce to help him in his quest for world supremacy.

They were based in Beaconsfield in London, and I ran into them in 1982 as an 18-year-old fresh out of Rotorua. I had gone to Britain to do my thing on the world circuit and while I was there had run into another Kiwi, Stu Davenport, who told me about this coach who lived down in London.

I didn't think too much more about it. But apparently, when I was playing in my first British Open, Marie was watching and she encouraged Bryce to come and have a look at how I was playing.

Anyway, we got talking and they made me an offer to live and work with them in Beaconsfield. It was tempting, but I returned to New Zealand to win my first national title before retracing my steps to Europe. I again fell into the familiar frustrating pattern of living and training hard and getting beaten in the first rounds of tournaments.

However, I found some comfort linking with the other Kiwis on tour and, as usual, timing was everything. It was important to have a base and having a full-time coach was also critical. I'm sure I would have made it by myself, but it would have taken an awful lot longer. Bryce gave me the technical advice I needed.

I was always fit, and if anything I over-trained, but Bryce gave me the specialist advice and I have not seen many squash coaches since with that expertise and ability.

He had the knack of coaching. His special skill was being able to break down the game. I know I can't do that as well as he can – it's a very special gift. I remember we spent an entire season changing my forehand. He had that skill to identify problems and the expertise to fix them.

Bryce was technically top-notch, and he lived and breathed the game. He was totally immersed in it. He had a full-time job running the Oasis club in Marlow, near Henley, but still found time to teach me.

It was the start of a nine-year pupil-teacher partnership – totally professional – and

A happy moment for coach **BRYCE TAYLOR** and Susan Devoy.

a very interesting partnership, because he was most definitely the boss. Several times I remember trying to challenge him, but I soon learned to listen and take it all in. It was very much a tutor-pupil relationship and he never charged me one cent during our time together.

It was amazing. Marie was equally adept because she did all the mothering. She was also a talent scout who tended to all our emotional needs and also cleaned, washed, cooked and kept everything going. The pair of them were immersed in the deal.

It wasn't always rosy. Like the time I travelled to the British Open, in the north of England, in 1983, after having a spat with Bryce. He told me to go on my own, saying he'd had enough of my histrionics. I beat my first two opponents, but I remember looking through the glass and up in the stands during those games to see where Bryce was. There was no sign. When I reached the quarters, I was sure he would make an appearance. During the match there was a fair amount of lip, bad behaviour, lots of mouthing off from me and at one stage I was two sets down. Then Bryce turned up.

He just materialised, sat down and looked straight at me. "If you say another word I will rip your tongue out," he warned me. I won the match and got to the semis.

We were not the greatest mates, but he was a fantastic coach. Ironically, our friendship got stronger once my husband, John Oakley, came on the scene because Bryce and John got on really well and are still good buddies.

John was someone who could take the training issues away. It was also a time when I grew up a great deal, when I did not spend every waking minute on squash. I guess I got some more balance in my life.

Bryce was great – he was an expert motivator, and used to leave notes in my training bag all the time, sort of pep talk notes. We cleaned out a cupboard the other day and I found one of the notes he left me from the world championships in 1991. He was very astute in motivating me, he trained me really hard and, technically, he was extremely sharp.

He was a cool critter, and never changed his persona. He was very matter-of-fact. He would say one thing – he could boil his team-talk down to one issue.

He was very professional, very well-groomed and taught me a huge amount about life, sport and growing up.

When I went back to Britain a few years ago and saw him, it was the first time in a long while that I had seen him relaxed, and it almost completed the circle. He became paranoid about the Lady Di thing [when Bryce Taylor organised for secret photos to be taken of Diana working out in a gym, and got heavily criticised for doing so]. In fact, I think he became depressed.

We had a nice light-and-dark relationship. We attracted a cool group around us. He had a great sense of humour and always loved entertainment.

The sad thing was that when he returned to New Zealand for a while after the Lady Di incident, squash officials lost a great opportunity to employ him. If someone had had the gumption then, that would have given Bryce a renewed focus, but sadly New Zealand lost the chance of having a great coach.

Scott Dixon

KENNY SMITH AND AYRTON SENNA

Motor-racing driver Scott Dixon has twice won the
Indy Racing League championship and in 2008 won
the famous Indianapolis 500.

Growing up in Auckland with petrol running through my veins, it was easy to fall for
the motor-racing guidance of Kenny Smith.

I was very fortunate to live close enough and to be able to tap into his knowledge
bank, because Kenny was someone who was generous with his time, information and
advice. If you wanted to learn, Kenny was all too happy to help. He was someone who
had been there and done that. He was a very talented all-rounder.

Like most New Zealanders, he was hands-on and had learned to do everything
himself. Kenny worked hard at everything he did, from cleaning the car to fixing the
engine. He could be fiery, but he was always very determined and gave generously
whether it was his time, his knowledge or experience.

He was always around when I was starting to make my way through the ranks, learning
my craft in the go-karts before moving into Formula B when I hit my teenage years.

We were away racing at Manfeild about that time when my other hero, Ayrton
Senna, was killed. We had been up most of the night watching the television coverage
when we saw the crash and I remember going to bed, then waking up a few hours later
and being told that Senna had died.

It was a sad, difficult time for all those who admired his driving, but Senna's death
did not have as much impact on me then as it would these days. All I could think about
was that it was such a shame that we would not see Senna again on the motor-racing
circuit because he was a great talent, an aggressive racer who excited you every time
you watched him behind the wheel.

Senna gave his all. He could be a little bit untidy at times, but that was half the
fascination. You knew this guy was driving on the edge all the time. He rarely backed

off or resorted to a cautious, tactical approach.

He just went out there and drove as fast as he could all the time. For a young spectator who soaked up the atmosphere, that approach was compelling probably because it was the antithesis of how I approach my time behind the wheel.

It is not my style – it was all a bit frenetic and ragged, but that was half the appeal of Senna's approach.

Senna would often be up against Nigel Mansell, who had the advantage of a far superior car. But somehow Senna pulled the maximum out of his machine. No matter the conditions, he drove on the edge, left nothing behind. For us motor-mad teenagers, that was a compelling package. His talent was all natural, he had a flair about his driving, he was ultra-competitive, he had great instincts and the sheer will to win, which is crucial to be a top racer.

He wanted to dominate, there was no alternative. Michael Schumacher had the same concentrated focus. Michael Phelps was another who showed that determination in his swimming, while Lance Armstrong's cycling supremacy was just mind-boggling. I have read all Armstrong's books and have found great inspiration from his preparation, homework, skills and focus. If enough of those characteristics appear consistently in my work, I will be on the right track.

The brilliant **AYRTON SENNA**.

Christopher Doig

JOHN GRAHAM

Christopher Doig is an international opera singer and was chief executive of New Zealand Cricket for six years.

It is inevitable when one is a passionate sports follower or player that certain characters or personalities leave a lasting impression. For me, in my chosen sports of cricket and hockey, former internationals like Alan "Banjo" Patterson and Ernie Barnes in hockey and Walter Hadlee and John Sparling in cricket provided the inspiration for an impressionable young school-leaver, trying to find his feet in the ranks of senior grade sport.

However, on reflection, the sports personality who has had the greatest and most enduring influence over me comes from an entirely different sport. DJ Graham was one of three All Blacks on the staff of Christchurch Boys' High School when I attended that school. Pat Vincent and Tony Steel were the others, but there is no question that most of the boys of the school, including me, were influenced by the inspirational presence of John Graham, inside and outside the classroom.

It was, therefore, with some considerable sense of anticipation and delight that I learned DJ had been appointed as principal of Auckland Grammar School, where I had started my teaching career the year before.

DJ was typically outstanding in that role and gathered around him an exceptional group of individuals, who were encouraged to debate issues, educational and otherwise, and who understood, as a consequence of the environment that DJ engendered, that you had an indisputable responsibility to get the best out of not only yourself, but every pupil you came into contact with.

That small group of fledgling teachers included Graham Henry, Murray Deaker and Dave Sims, all of whom have done well in their respective lives and careers subsequently and each of whom will, I am sure, attribute much of that success to the special influence of John Graham.

John encouraged my singing career without really fully understanding it and certainly enabled me to pursue an international career through generously offering me two consecutive periods of leave of absence to allow me to test my abilities in the international arena in Vienna.

In the context of that background, it was little surprise then that many years later, after I had been appointed to the role as chief executive of New Zealand Cricket at a time when the sport was at its lowest ebb, with a team in disarray, desperately in need of strong inspirational leadership, I searched into my own experience and realised that if DJ Graham had been able to inspire such ambitious dedication and determination in our impressionable lives and had continued to do so for countless adolescents over the years, he might be able to weave some of that same magic with the New Zealand cricket team.

While the decision to offer a rugby player the important role of team manager raised several eyebrows – although fewer, it has to be agreed, than when it was announced that an opera singer was to become chief executive – John Graham's legacy to the players is assured.

Under his and Steve Rixon's leadership, New Zealand cricket enjoyed one of the most stable and productive periods in its history with the players relishing the clearly-defined structures and fair disciplines. John encouraged many of the players to read good literature, to educate themselves in advance about the various cultures of the places they were touring and generally provided the same tough, uncompromising, but supportive, environment he had given us many years before at Auckland Grammar.

Sandra Edge

ALICE CHESLEY

Sandra Edge represented New Zealand at netball from 1985–95 and is often judged to have been the world's finest centre.

My first sports hero, when I was a youngster growing up at Tokomaru Bay, north of Gisborne, was a local netballer named Alice Chesley, who these days is Arihia Matahiki.

She was beautiful and played very elegantly, and I used to love watching her. She was 10-year-old Sandra Edge's version of the ideal netballer.

A little later, as my sports horizons broadened, my hero was Bjorn Borg, who always seemed so calm and unfazed, even in the middle of a Wimbledon final. I played tennis pretty seriously until I was about 16, and he was the man, so cool and in control, so focused and emotionless. I wasn't like that at all, which might be why he impressed me so much.

Then I started to get a bit more serious about netball, and some of New Zealand's leading netballers began to catch my eye.

I remember watching Marghie Matenga, the Wellington goal shoot, on television and loving the way she played, her flair and movement. She was inspiring.

In 1979, when the New Zealand team was away at the world champs in Trinidad, I played in my first national tournament, in New Plymouth. I was 16, and represented Poverty Bay. National tournament was a huge event in those days and it gave players from the smaller associations the chance to watch the best players. I remember being very impressed with the Wellington defender, Liz Neilson, who was only in the early stages of her career, but already looked pretty good to me.

It's funny to think that in later years I played for Wellington and New Zealand with Marghie and Liz (who was Liz McJorrow by then).

Once I moved up the netball ranks, I didn't really have heroes as such, not in the sense that a youngster might. But I used to look at my team-mates and marvel at their ability. I'd admire Leigh Gibbs for her doggedness and determination, Margaret Forsyth for her grace, Rita Fatialofa for her all-round skills and toughness.

I suppose the player who attracted me most from overseas in those years was Anne Sargeant, the Australian shooter. She was very tall, but she moved very gracefully and was a wonderful player.

But by that stage of my career, I was past having heroes. By then it was more a case of admiring the skills of great players.

For a genuine sports hero, I suppose I would go back to Alice Chesley in those days long ago at Tokomaru Bay.

Marc Ellis

MUHAMMAD ALI AND VARIOUS WELLINGTON RUGBY PLAYERS

Marc Ellis played for New Zealand at rugby and rugby league and has become a noted television personality.

Sorry, you can't pin me down on one special sports person. There have been just too many.

My initial hero was Muhammad Ali. What an athlete, what a boxer, what a champion. One of my first vague sports memories was sitting in bed at home watching the Rumble in the Jungle while the old man shuffled and shadow-boxed round the room during the fight. Both were classic efforts.

I was lucky enough to meet the great man, not the old man, when I was on tour with the All Blacks in Scotland in 1993. He was involved in a book-signing deal and while he had never heard of the All Blacks, he liked the name so got his minders to let us skip the queue, which was about 2km long, and we ended up having our photos taken with Ali.

He did seem to be a little surprised when the All Blacks turned out to have a large number of white faces, but he was a gracious host and had a genuine aura about him.

As I worked my way into rugby, my heroes were the Wellington superstars from the Ranfurly Shield era of the 1980s. The team was full of them, blokes like Stu Wilson, Bernie Fraser and Murray Mexted, and it was always great after matches had finished to get out on to the paddock and be near our champions.

On one occasion, I am reminded by my father, I came sprinting back and told him quite proudly how I had touched Bernie Fraser on the back! I didn't want any signatures, I just wanted to stand beside my heroes. And they always seemed to oblige by staying out on Athletic Park for about an hour after every game.

That era coincided with the *Magnum PI* series on television and he was probably an equal hero of mine. He sported a great moustache, which is likely why I also admired Murray Mexted – because of the slight resemblance.

I recall kicking my rugby ball on Philip Myers Park in Wadestown one day (I used the lone tree as the goalposts and kicked over it) when a car pulled up and a booming voice called out: "Good kick, lad." I turned around and saw Murray Mexted looking at me. Suffice to say my feet scarcely seemed to touch the ground as I sprinted home to tell my folks.

The players through that great Wellington era always seemed very approachable and low-key. They achieved their triumphs with a certain style and made the city feel as though they were also part of that success.

Having met many of those players since, I can confirm they are really down-to-earth guys. When we went to watch them play, they impressed as people you aspired to be. They were not too aloof and you thought you could get there if you wanted it badly enough.

It is important for youngsters to be inspired like that. My belief is that it is your folks' role to ensure you get enough stimulus and if they can motivate you to enjoy certain things, then it is only natural that the closer you get to sport, music or art, you will be inspired by people at the top of those fields.

Here in New Zealand it seems sports heroes are a lot more accessible for youngsters than people from other walks of life. Sadly it's harder for kids to meet their favourite artists or musicians in person.

MUHAMMAD ALI (left), pictured with two other immortals of boxing, Sugar Ray Robinson (centre) and Joe Louis.

Sean Fitzpatrick

EDWIN MOSES

Sean Fitzpatrick, New Zealand's most capped rugby player, was All Black hooker from 1986-97, and the captain for six years.

When I think through all those rugby players who made an impression on me, I come up with names like Grant Batty and Gareth Edwards. Then there was the thrill of watching the Olympics in colour for the first time on television and seeing guys like Daley Thompson, who were just out of this world.

People like that stick in my mind, but it was the firepower of champion hurdler Edwin Moses that made an even greater impression on me. It was a great thrill later to get to know him and to be able to appreciate even more what he was like and how he was able to achieve those magnificent feats.

Over 10 years of running the 400m hurdles, and I looked it up again just to check, he won an incredible 122 races in a row, 106 in consecutive finals.

That sort of success is mind-boggling and trying to relate to that is very difficult. Reading about him, Ed was apparently not overly fast. But his mind had to be the sharpest of all athletes. He demonstrated that when he altered his style to use 13 steps between hurdles to compensate for his lack of high-end speed.

Incredible as it may seem, he was not the most devoted trainer, either. He would go out and do his stuff for an hour or so and then leave, while others used to spend much of the day on bits and pieces. Moses did not have the advantage of going to an elite school with a track programme, either. In fact, I don't think his college was into track and field much and didn't even have a proper athletics track.

His desire was extraordinary though, his will to win, the focus, concentration, unwavering belief. I guess they are all the sorts of things I admire in a sportsperson.

There he was aged about 48 and he was still having a crack at qualifying for the Athens Olympics.

The only reason he thought about making that squad was to show he could still do it. I think he still could have produced a respectable time, even though he had a bit of a knee problem. Eventually his doctor had to tell him that while he might be able to produce a qualifying time, he would go close to killing himself. Ed was not ready for that – he had too many other things he wanted to do.

I met him when he became chairman of Laureus. He had no hair and no beard. I found him a good person, a dedicated person, someone who enjoyed a drink and even the occasional cigarette and still looked pretty much in his physical prime at about 6ft 3in and 90kg.

He is a great person to be around. He has one of those deep, growly voices, he exudes confidence, and he makes things happen, which is so important for the charities he supports. We were all up at St Andrews a few years ago involved in some work and Zinzan Brooke was there, too. Zinny could not believe his eyes when Moses appeared. He was like a kid at the park getting his photo taken and asking for his autograph. I think those items still hold a prominent place in his house.

There is a swagger about Moses, the sort of confidence bred from being a champion. When he gives people his autograph he writes 47.02 – his world record time for the 400m hurdles. He is proud of what he has achieved, but he is also very generous with his time and in his efforts for others. He worked in the financial sector for a while after he finished sport, he helps kids and he spends a third of the year helping out our society.

Ed epitomises everything that a New Zealander would understand. He was not the fastest guy in the field, he was not the flashiest runner at school, but he was so incredibly determined and had such a remarkable will to win, all the qualities I admire so much.

I took him to watch a rugby test at Twickenham a few years ago, when England hosted Scotland. It was the first game of rugby he had seen. He really loved it and one day I hope to repeat that deal and take him to watch the All Blacks live.

Jeanette Fitzsimons

ROB HAMILL

Jeanette Fitzsimons became an MP in 1996 and was co-leader of the Green Party in Parliament from 1999-2009.

I recently had the privilege of meeting and getting to know Rob Hamill and his wife and three small boys. His legendary rowing across the Atlantic for 41 days in a small boat about a decade ago must be the best example of sheer determination I have heard of. He also won the race – the first of its kind – for New Zealand. And then he did it again!

His book describes the consequences of lack of sleep, physical pain, cramped conditions, alternating optimism and despair, and the challenge of seeing no-one for 41 days except his one rowing companion, who didn't talk much. I don't usually read this sort of book, but I found it gripping.

In person he is an unassuming Kiwi, still looking for ways to make a difference and committed to the environmental cause. If I ever think of giving up in the face of difficulties, I think of Rob and lift my game.

Bill Francis

RON JARDEN

Bill Francis has been involved in broadcasting for more than 40 years, as a reporter and then as the manager of Newstalk ZB and Radio Sport.

I was just eight years old when I met my hero. I was a bit of a runt (and still am). This had an influence on my naming at birth with, reputedly, my racing-loving father winning through, because he was enamoured with the ability of the most famous jockey of the day, Bill Broughton.

Even at eight, growing up in Masterton, I was seldom without a ball in my hands. I had older brothers steeped in sport and our 1950s family grouping, outside of politics, never strayed far from rugby around the dinner table. My first season of midget rugby was as a winger, before rather naturally progressing to halfback, who in those days wore the No 7 jersey. So sport was a dominant part of my life from very early.

I had two childhood sports heroes, cricketer John Reid and rugby player Ron Jarden, but it was an encounter with Jarden that clinched his status as my No 1 poster-player.

Jarden was big news in the mid-1950s, idolised by many more than just me. He was a world-class winger, powerfully built, just 5ft 8in, but about 13st. He had exceptional acceleration, was a try-scorer extraordinaire, possessed a devastating centring kick, and won matches with his goal-kicking. Jarden had me hooked.

Checking the rugby almanacks, I'm staggered to think I was only eight when I met with my hero. In those days Wairarapa-Bush used to play one or two games as combined unions (this was long before amalgamation), often in preparation for a match against a touring team.

So it was on a chilly August day in 1955 that my brother George and I, armed with autograph books, headed for Solway Showgrounds, venue for the Wairarapa-Bush match against Wellington. Our entry was gained via the backyard of an adjoining house. We would sprint down the driveway and leap the back fence before the white-coated brigade arrived. Paying at the gate was an option not even remotely contemplated.

That day Wairarapa-Bush, as was usually the case, struggled, holding Wellington to 29-9, but my attention was riveted on every movement by R A Jarden. Because Jarden was my focus, just for the day I was forced to heartlessly abandon my hometown heroes, "Kiwi" Blake and Johnny Lett. Jarden didn't disappoint. For 80 minutes he had me enthralled as he scored three tries, kicked two penalty goals and four conversions for a total of 23 points.

I can still picture him, prematurely balding, mummified right knee, strong and fast. Rather than age him, the receding hairline merely served to emphasise intelligence and command.

It was half-time, though, that's remained with me forever. I was small enough to sneak into a position on the steps leading down to the changing rooms, and as the players re-emerged for the second half I thrust my book in front of Jarden. He signed, smiled and then patted me on the head and said: "You're a small boy to be collecting autographs." More than half a century later, I can still savour the pleasantness and the kindness of how those words were spoken.

Despairingly, I can't find the autograph book, but I do have his book *Rugby on Attack*.

I still have, in a scrapbook, the cut-out of Jarden from the cover of a school pad.

A year later I gave a morning talk on the All Blacks to my class (it was 1956 – Springbok year) with Jarden as the theme, and I still have the glossy *Auckland Weekly News* team photos that I used to illustrate the talk.

The same year I made a plaster-of-Paris mould of Jarden and painted in the All Black jersey. I don't have that any longer. His nose got chipped off and he lost the arm carrying the ball, the remains disappearing into a hole down in the back garden.

Of course, I continued to follow his career and life, and was dismayed by his early retirement from rugby at age 26. He excelled in his yachting career with Barnacle Bill, his stock-broking career marked him down as a high-flying businessman, and at a time after I'd joined the NZBC, he was chairman of its board.

And then, tragically, aged only 47, a heart attack and death.

In a long broadcasting career, I've been fortunate to meet and get to know many of the outstanding sportspeople of my youth. I never did get to meet Jarden again after my fleeting 1955 encounter. I regret that.

Down the years I've admired Grant Batty, Bryan Williams, John Kirwan and other wingers, but none to my mind have supplanted the one and only Ronald Alexander Jarden.

Temepara George

SANDRA EDGE

Brilliant netball centre Temepara George first played for the
Silver Ferns in 2000. She won *Dancing with the Stars* in 2008.

Sandra Edge was the best centre in the world, so she was a perfect person to try to
emulate, certainly for a netball-crazy teenager growing up in New Zealand.

It wasn't just her surname that attracted me to watch her play, it was what she could
do on the court and how she held herself so well away from the game.

My family always made sure we watched international matches on television,
whether it was rugby or netball, and I saw Sandra play quite a few times on the small
screen before I was fortunate enough to spend a season soaking up all the lessons she
gave us when we played for the Collegiate club in Auckland.

When I first went on court, I was in awe of everything she did and I took as gospel
everything she said to us. She was on a pedestal for me.

I remember my coach saying to me after the first quarter in one game: "For
goodness sake, will you stop looking at Sandy and play your own game." I tried to snap
out of it, but it was hard because she had always been my role model and here I was
playing alongside her.

She was the captain of the Silver Ferns and her leadership showed in the way she
played. She was always involved in certain plays and when there was turnover ball she
always seemed to be in the thick of either trying to recover or make the opposition
pay if we had the intercept.

She had a great brain, superb anticipation and massive skills. She loved being
captain, she loved leading and encouraging us to go with her.

When I got to meet her, she was like I imagined the person on the TV to be.
Initially I was too scared to talk to her because I was frightened I would say the wrong
thing. You would kind of just walk past and say "Hi", and then think, "Oh my God, this

is too much".

Everything that she did, everything that she portrayed on court, transferred off it as well. She was a lovely person, but while on the court she was really determined and in the zone. You could see that off the court as well, because Sandra was so focused on what she needed to do. She always made time for everybody, she always wanted to help us improve when she took us for sessions.

I played alongside her and she was at all our trainings, so I was able to soak up much of her specialist advice. It was like having a personal assistant to coax and guide me through that season.

I could see what she did and why and also all those things she put into her training ethic, so she was ready every time she went on to the court. It was all those little details that you normally would not see, which made such an impression on me. She was selfless, but also passed on a lot of information just by being there.

She would be saying: "Come on Bubby, you've got it all in there, you've just got to play your own game. Concentrate on your own game, don't try to be like anyone else. Just play it, you've got it all there." I remember she did a drill and I would watch videos of her practising that, to try to emulate how she pinched intercepts.

Seeing how she communicated with others helped me because I was so young. She was a great inspiration but above all, she wanted us to play our natural games. She did not want to change us too much; she wanted us to develop our own styles and own games. She never took away our natural skills.

I had the fortune to play alongside Sandy for only one year, but it was probably worth about five times that amount of experience.

When I made the Silver Ferns I would telephone Sandy from time to time for advice on certain aspects of leadership and netball in general. She was always very approachable and willing to give as much help as she could.

Later in my career when I was dropped from the Silver Ferns, I also rang her and she told me not to worry about it, just to go and train harder and go stronger.

Early on, I had a meeting with my club coach, Jan Lundon, and she asked me what I wanted to do in netball. My reply was all about being like Sandra Edge, before my coach suggested I should be myself and someone for younger people to look up to. I nodded and mumbled some agreement, but as I walked away I remember saying to myself: "Nah, I still want to be like Sandra Edge."

My original sports passion was touch rugby, but training clashed with netball. I really wanted to play touch, but I'm glad that I decided in favour of netball. There was a lot more to it – it was a sport with more of an international future and it had that champion, Sandy Edge.

Phil Gifford

DON CLARKE

Phil Gifford has for more than 40 years been a leading media figure – print, radio and television – and a successful sports book author.

My nine-year-old grandson Joshua sums up his All Black heroes succinctly. "Dan Carter is a very good kicker, but I like Richie [McCaw] best because he's brave."

In 1956, when I was his age, there were many All Blacks I admired, but the chosen one by a long stretch was fullback Don Clarke, a man who could kick the ball so high, according to radio commentator Winston McCarthy, that it would "have snow on it".

With hindsight, what made him such a fascinating player to me?

In simple terms, he was god-like on a footy field. There was a majesty about him, a powerful charisma that even a kid could recognise.

Better still, at that time my parents had a dairy farm at Motumaoho, about six kilometres out of Morrinsville, and Clarke, or DB Clarke, as every newspaper of the time called him, played his club rugby for Kereone in Morrinsville.

So it was that in 1956 I found myself being introduced by my father to DB Clarke himself, on the sidelines at Campbell Park, at the end of a club game. The massive size of the hand he thrust out for me to shake is one memory, and grey mud caked on bandages around his knees another.

Already I had absorbed kitchen table gossip about his crook knees, which, although he was only 22 at the time, had already been operated on.

Not that his delicate knees stopped him from starring for Waikato in the first game of the '56 Springbok tour, when we heard McCarthy crackle through the Philco radio that Clarke had kicked a left-foot dropped goal from near halfway that "was still climbing when it went through the uprights". Waikato won 14-10.

A few weeks later, he was finally in the All Blacks, and a nine-year test career had started.

What were the components that made him special? For a start he was, even by today's standards for a fullback, a very big man, between 105kg-110kg, which in the '50s made him heavier than most test locks.

There was more. He had a habit, when the ball was dry, of catching a high kick with his hands above his head, not trying at all to cradle the ball with his arms.

That hand-eye co-ordination was reflected in his cricket career, where he was a medium-pace bowler who would also occasionally destroy an attack with the bat. He was good enough to play against an MCC side just after he'd turned 17.

But back to rugby. When he ran, he was dangerous, faster than his size made him look, with a devastating hip bump that could knock a would-be tackler on his butt.

Above all, of course, there was his kicking.

He played when the rugby balls were leather, and on a wet day they absorbed water until they felt solid right through.

He was so strong, and had such perfect technique and timing that when the flat, reinforced toe of his right boot hit one of these sodden lumps of leather the smack echoed, and the ball flew crazy distances.

I was lucky enough to see him play a lot. In my high school years we lived at Waihi, where he played several times for Morrinsville against the local side. I'd hitchhike to Hamilton to see him play for Waikato. I took buses to Auckland to watch five of his test matches.

The Waihi games are the most vivid.

For a terrible moment in Waihi in 1961, standing by the fence at Rugby Park with schoolmates, I thought we'd contributed to the death of a local player.

Fielding a kick, a Waihi back shaped to kick to touch, right next to where we stood. We all screamed "kick and chase, kick and chase", and he did.

Unfortunately it was Don Clarke who caught the ball. He ran forward, straight at the kicker, who then took the full force of a massive, steely hip with his head and shoulders.

With the possible exception of his parents in the stand, nobody was more pleased than we were when, after what felt like minutes, signs of life returned to the prone Waihi body.

A year later, on the sandier surface of the local recreation ground, big Don placed the ball for a penalty in the middle of his own 10-metre line.

There was little wind, but the ball was dry. It crossed so high above the bar I swear there was 10 metres to spare. I know that the best round-the-corner kickers are more accurate, but to see Don Clarke kick was to see staggering, almost supernatural, power.

FOOTNOTE: *If Clarke kicking at the Rec ground is a clear memory, so too is the visit one warm night in the 1962-63 summer of an Auckland sprint troupe including the Junoesque Doreen Porter, a Commonwealth Games silver medal winner in '62. Strikingly attractive, running in small stretch pants, she glazed the eyes – and for years would haunt the dreams – of every adolescent boy at the ground.*

Colin Giltrap

BRUCE MCLAREN

Colin Giltrap is the owner of New Zealand's biggest car dealership conglomerate.

For as long as I can remember, motor-racing has been my passion, and I have been fortunate enough to have welded that enthusiasm to my business interests. For such a small country, New Zealand has produced some incredible drivers on the world stage, from the smooth Denny Hulme to someone like Scott Dixon, who has shown what a premium talent he has become on the Indy Car circuit. Denny became Formula One champion in 1967, which was a marvellous feat. But for me, special inspiration came from Bruce McLaren, who was a massive influence on anyone in New Zealand who was interested in motor sport or the motor industry.

He did not quite become top of the Formula One heap, finishing runner-up in 1961, third the following year and again in 1969. It seemed only a matter of time before Bruce would repeat Hulme's feat, but he was killed the next year while he was test driving at the Goodwood circuit in England. He remains my hero. He was an inspiration for anyone in New Zealand who was interested in motor sport or the motor industry and I am thrilled his legacy remains through the car naming rights and the McLaren Trust.

His parents had a garage in Remuera Road in Auckland, and I would often see Bruce putting in some hours there when I dropped in to fill up the car or get some repairs done. From there, that contact escalated as I followed Bruce's successes at Pukekohe and Ardmore. Soon I was following him around a lot of the Formula One circuit. He made his name as both a technical expert and a driver. Bruce was a special engineer and that talent was recognised by General Motors when they contracted him to build Can-Am cars for the series in America. That was one of Bruce's greatest fortés. In the end they used to call it the Bruce and Denny Show because the Kiwis were so

dominant. I watched a number of those races and there is no question that the pair's regular successes put New Zealand up in lights on the world stage.

The current motor-racing guru in America is Roger Penske. I know he used to admire what Bruce did in the design-and-build world and was always trying to pick his brains to help him get ahead.

I was fortunate to know Bruce and his wife, Paddy, quite well. We used to socialise with them when we were in London and it was always great to hook up with them and catch up with the latest motor-racing ideas. Bruce was a really genuine, nice guy, an incredible person really, and it was easy to see that people all around the world used to respect him so much for his design, build and driving skills. He was an incredible package of talent, one of those fortunate people with that rare gift of being able to both design and drive cars. He was an engineer first, the brains behind the development, design and driving, and it was a shocking waste when he was killed test-driving one of his cars.

Bruce and Denny dominated the best in America in the Can-Am series. They were so far ahead of the others it made you proud to be a Kiwi. They hastened the global awareness of New Zealand, and they created enormous interest in this country because of their special talents.

The Tasman motor-racing series also helped, because many of the drivers from Europe used to travel down here to be involved in those races and to escape from the winters in the northern hemisphere. All those guys used to socialise together. They were mates and they would go to Lake Karapiro to water-ski and then head off to Lake Taupo for some fishing, or Paraparaumu, where the Amon family lived. It was quite a nice life, quite a decent lifestyle, although the risks were immense.

Anyone fortunate enough to meet Bruce or spend some time with him would have noticed how low-key he was, almost reserved. He did not need to be in the spotlight, and did not crave that sort of recognition. Bruce was very quiet, a real thinker, very genuine, a helluva nice guy.

I remember being in New Zealand when I heard the news that he had been killed. There is always that sort of danger in motor-racing and Bruce's death underlined the risks and the loss of a truly great man. His funeral at St Mary's Church at the top of Parnell was a massive event and in subsequent years his reputation has probably increased.

The McLaren name is synonymous with motor-racing and New Zealand throughout the world today. Every modern driver understands the connection – McLaren Mercedes is still emblazoned on the car and that says it all. Had Bruce not had such a reputation, then the name would have been well and truly scrubbed by now.

I remember buying his E-type Jaguar from him at one stage. It was one of the first in the world, painted in British racing green, and when he said he was going to sell it, I couldn't let the chance go by. Not long after, though, I took the 3.8 litre factory-built machine to Australia and ended up selling it. I didn't have enough money just to hang on to it. Now, of course, I wish I'd kept it, but circumstances were different then.

I guess Bruce was a flashing star on the world stage, but his name and reputation have stood the test of time. This is really saying something, because Ron Dennis [long-time McLaren Group chairman and CEO, now retired] or Mercedes could have changed the name. Instead they retained it to underline how much they respected Bruce and his work.

He was one of the few people who was an engineer and a driver. Most people do not build cars and drive them as well. There have been a few, like John Surtees and John Cooper, though Cooper did not drive his cars in Formula One. Bruce had a gift and that heritage is part of the reason why we are getting good recognition in the A1 series. That is his legacy.

Mark Graham

GOD, MY FATHER TOM AND THE YATES BROTHERS

Mark Graham played 29 tests for the Kiwis, and was captain in 18 of them. He later coached the Warriors.

The only real hero I have had throughout my life is God, and you can't go any further up the ladder than that. He is the ultimate, and there is no better person to worship, and to try to emulate his life and teachings. He was and is the super-hero.

Out on the sports field there have been a number of guys I have looked up to, who have taught me a lot about life, the game and how we should treat one another. From my very early days, that person was my father, Tom, who worked ultra-hard at everything he did.

He started off working on the roads and ended up managing a number of companies. He was tough and strong, worked tirelessly and showed me the benefits of hard graft. There was no easy method to reach your targets. It was all about hard work, sweat, being honest with yourself and putting in.

Down at the Otahuhu Rugby League Club, the men who taught me more than anything in my early days were the Yates brothers, Simon, Victor and John. They had legendary status at the club and were very tough men among a group of blokes who could all stand up for themselves.

These guys taught me how to look after myself and how prepared you had to be for anything that might be dished up to you in those early days of my rugby league career.

It was a very tough game then, more unruly than it is now because the rules were more lenient and the officials not so stringent. League was a test of fortitude from club level to test matches. The club stuff was as tough as all hell, while the provincial stuff could be pretty brutal. But there was something magnetic about it and we always made sure we wagged school midweek if there was a touring team in town and we could get along to a packed Carlaw Park, which would be just booming with attitude. It was a fabulous experience and even though there was a certain fear factor when you were involved, those big games were just hypnotic.

Sometimes I think officials might have come up with some interesting discoveries if they had used a metal detector test on players before internationals. Some of them were carrying all sorts of bits and pieces, and sometimes it seemed as if anything went except guns and knives. The environment was as tough as nails.

Rugby league is in a much better state now. It is still a remarkable test of courage, and internationals, especially, need to be like that, but officials have eliminated the out-and-out filth and skulduggery.

In my early days at Otahuhu, we had to deal with those situations and the Yates brothers were the best advisers. They were plain old tough, and totally unflinching, and I must say just great to have on your side. Once the game was finished they were real gentlemen, showing respect to their opponents off the field. Those are lessons that never left me during my career.

Warwick Gray

THE 1935-36 ALL BLACKS AND THE 1945-46 'KIWIS'

Warwick Gray, long-time sports follower, is the father
of Wynne Gray, author of this book.

I've been asked to write about a New Zealand person who thrilled me by his or her
sporting prowess. It seems to me that most of the other contributors to this book,
because of their age, will select a person from the 1950s or 60s onwards. Because of
this, and because I have lived somewhat longer than most of them, it behoves me to
concentrate more on the 1930s and 1940s.

I cast my mind back to the 1930s and immediately think of Jack Lovelock at Berlin
and that memorable phrase of radio commentator Harold Abrahams, "My God, he's
done it". Athletics, however, never made me quiver with excitement after the days
when compulsory school House runs had to be endured.

In the 1940s, we were necessarily starved of heroic sports achievements because
the efforts of young men and women then were set on achieving much more in the
service of their country.

So there it was, no-one from New Zealand came into my recollection as coming
within the brief that I had been given during those two decades. Yet I've always loved
sport and in the end have decided that during this 20-year period, it was a team rather
than a single person that excited me and waxed my ongoing interest in sports.

Accordingly I claim the privilege of age to depart slightly from "New Zealand
sporting person" to "New Zealand sporting persons". Seeing I have transgressed into
the plural form, I will risk editorial ire because I cannot separate the exhilaration that
I got from my selections in each of the decades that are under review.

The 1935-36 All Blacks thrilled me because it was the first time I was old enough
to enjoy, understand and follow the fortunes of our heroes of international sport,
especially when the team was going overseas to meet the foe.

My first recollection is the team photograph that appeared in the *Weekly News*,
and I can recall that photograph and name the team now, although it was more than
70 years ago. Jack Manchester was holding the ball with the "little ones" like Joey

In Memory of a Great Team
The KIWIS 1945-46

Sadler, Eric Tindill (soon to be a double All Black), Merv Corner, Rusty Page etc sitting cross-legged on the floor at his feet. And from that time until the final disaster at Twickenham [a loss in the test against England], I followed the fortunes of that team with the intensity of the young.

For the record, those All Blacks played 30 games and won 26, including tests against Scotland and Ireland, drew one early match with Ulster and lost (oh, what disasters they were) to Swansea, Wales (our traditional rivals), and, in the last match in the British Isles, to England, when we hoped they would redeem their loss to Wales, but were defeated by some 14 points – and that without the All Blacks scoring.

I concede that this team was not the best All Black team I have seen, but for me they were the first. They were young men who were gods and they thrilled me. There were some very good players like Caughey, Hart and Oliver in the backs and King and McLean (brother of the equally famous rugby writer) in the forwards. It was well nigh impossible to get direct reports of matches and summaries (sometimes marred by static from the BBC) were usually the first reports we could get, but I tried to never miss them and I'm sure many others were glued to their wirelesses as well.

Remember that these representatives of ours were away from home for more than six months – it took seven weeks to travel to the United Kingdom by ship – with little thought of personal or financial hardship. They were the All Blacks and that was enough for them, their families and for me.

They were proud and they made New Zealanders proud. And it was this sense of pride and patriotism that many of them carried through to the war that was to start four years later and in which three of that team were killed or died from their wounds.

From the 1940s, I have picked the 2nd New Zealand Expeditionary Force team of 1945-46. This team was always known, of course, as the Kiwis. Why did they thrill me as they did?

That's easy to answer – they were the revivalists of exciting rugby. They knew how to play 15-man rugby, not just the 10-man game that we had become so used to, from school rugby through to provincial sides. We, the spectators, came away from the first home match with eyes shining – rugby was an exciting game.

For me, before July 1946, all that mattered was that our rugby side won. Now it wasn't the be-all and end-all. It made us cheer; it made us excited. It was a skilful game played by everyone in the team from privates to those with field rank.

It didn't matter so much that the first game at home, against Auckland, ended in a 20-20 draw. The Kiwis deserved to win, or so we spectators thought. But so what? There was only one international – Charlie Saxton, the skipper – but there were others who would rise to greatness in rugby, and all 25 of them brought back to us who had grown used to stodgy, unimaginative rugby that the game was alive.

And so it proved, because that team deserves the credit for initiating the revival of an art that had been somnolent for too long.

And a post-script: That team introduced to us as its commentator Lieutenant Winston McCarthy, who in his own right contributed much to the enjoyment of our national sport by the public of New Zealand.

Wynne Gray

COLIN SNEDDEN

Wynne Gray, the author of this book, has been a journalist since 1975 and has been the *New Zealand Herald's* chief rugby writer since 1989.

My transistor radio was a hand-me-down present from my grandfather. I carted it everywhere. It had enough power to latch on to the short-wave test cricket commentaries from Australia and All Black tests round the globe, and a strong leather case that helped its long-term existence. The radio bounced a few times, it fought back against sand, wind and saltwater and best of all, it had an earplug that allowed me to listen long into the night, when I was supposed to be doing my homework.

It allowed me to embrace my sporting passion while also obeying my parents' wishes that I be outside and away from the television.

Summers were great, staying with my grandfather, whose bach became his permanent house not far from Takapuna Beach. Those times were a superb potpourri of swimming, catching shrimps in the rock pools, fishing from the local hotspots, scaling the cliffs, scouring the village shops and pick-up games of cricket with any other youngsters fortunate enough to be on that strip of sand.

Another attraction was that my grandfather owned a television, although there were restrictions on our viewing times. We all seemed to watch the news – which may have had something to with the fact that glamorous presenter Alma Johnson lived just down the road – the *Town and Around* programme that starred another local identity, Keith Bracey, with his jaunty hat and pipe, while I recall we had a dispensation to watch *Laramie*, a late-night western. Occasionally we managed to sneak in some footage of the Plunket Shield cricket when we went home to make lunch, while the transistor radio always allowed me to keep up with the scores.

My love for cricket was fired initially by my father's encouragement, underscored with works like *Bert Sutcliffe's Book for Boys*, while I gleaned further insights into that sporting world from commentator Colin Snedden, who lived close to my grandfather.

I was able to get the latest reports from Snedden and other domestic cricket commentators while I was down on the beach indulging in all the summer activities.

When tests were played in Australia, I could listen to those crackly shortwave broadcasts across the ditch with Alan McGilvray leading the charge.

My father, through his business dealings, knew Snedden, who had played one test against England in 1947, as a bowler and late-order batsman. To a small schoolboy, the snowy-haired, deeply-tanned Snedden looked intimidating. He stood well over six feet and it seemed incongruous that such a massive man would only bowl off-spin, and was here bowling to me on the beach.

My father had managed to acquire a composite cricket ball, which made the game far more realistic when the tide was out and the pitch was hard-baked, instead of trying to hit shots against a tennis ball which stalled and steepled in bounce from soft sand craters. Snedden appeared to be bowling from the clouds when he joined in several of our summer clashes, but he was generous enough to aim away from the sticks so we could later talk about the day we kept out the test bowler.

If matches were being played at Eden Park, it seemed just a little more personal listening to Snedden and his broadcasting colleagues. During the winter, Snedden also commentated on rugby, and I still have a letter excusing his inability, one year, to get more All Black and Wallaby autographs because he had been occupied with his work commitments for a Bledisloe Cup game on the other side of the ground.

Snedden's help made me feel even more connected to my club, provincial and national sides. He had been the tangible link between my love of sport and events out on the field. Cricket or rugby, as it was in those days, it did not matter. Through his work, Snedden, with broadcasting cronies like Alan Richards, Jim Read, Bob Irvine and newspaper scribes like TP McLean, Alex Veysey and Don Cameron, embellished my sporting fascination.

Jason Gunn

LANCE CAIRNS

Jason Gunn is a television personality, well-known to modern audiences as the host of *Dancing with the Stars*.

Cricket was, and still is, my passion. But I have given up wanting to be Lance Cairns.

I never quite achieved his stature, but on a good day if I really got in the groove and was seeing the ball well I could flick the odd ball from my brother or cousins over to the Donaldsons, several properties away, with the same one-handed Excalibur swish that captivated us all when the mighty Lance Cairns did the deed. We would wear the beige clothing, of course – it also doubled or, was that trebled, as daytime kit and evening wear – and everything was very cool.

A bit like Lance, I had an unorthodox bowling style, and I would get the old tennis ball and tape it heavily on one side to accentuate the swing I could get in the two arenas we played in, one in the backyard of our house and the other out on the tougher surface in Reading Street.

Even if I say so myself, I was an incredibly dangerous bowler out in the cul-de-sac because of my style and the cut and movement I could deliver with the ball. If the batsmen could have worn full body armour and helmets, they would have.

I had the in-swinger à la Lance sorted out to perfection, and also had a sneaky little delivery that held its line or even meandered away from the batsman a little. It was a beaut and in those games you had to back yourself. It was a bit tricky to start with and it's fair to say I'm glad I was not the wicketkeeper while I was going through my apprenticeship, learning where to target my mean in-swinger. I was hooping it around so much at one stage that there were far too many leg-side wides and byes, but once I got in the groove and sorted out the target area... lethal, man I was lethal!

Lance would have loved it and I'm sure he peeked out from behind the curtains of the neighbour's house just to get a few tips.

They were great summers in the cul-de-sac in Ilam. We had neighbours, friends, passers-by – they would all be involved in some of those games, either in the Gunn backyard or out on the street when the track might have had too much water in the backyard.

When we played on that alternate strip, there were usually all sorts of dramas. The geraniums were always in trouble. They really suffered when we went scurrying through them looking to cut down a run or two or to take a difficult catch.

It was marvellous having the choice of two tracks, for wet or dry weather, because it meant there was never a problem getting a game on.

Cars were banned if they ever looked like attempting to drive through one of our games. Motorists were advised to stop where they were, to park beyond the boundaries and then skirt us and walk to their destinations.

Nothing would get in the way of those matches. Little did we know that at one stage, while we were reliving another famous episode from New Zealand's rich cricket history in the '80s, one of the neighbours, Mr Sheldon, was doing some video work for Jeremy Coney.

We discovered that later and I also only learned that on that one day when I was not involved in one of the games, that one day when I had to go and visit nana, Coney, the man himself, came into the street and actually rolled his arm over as well. I was devastated when I found out what I had missed. I was not that old, but I would have backed myself to have rearranged Jerry's poles with one of the Lance specials if I'd ever got the chance.

Apparently he was not out in his brief stint at the wicket, but got tonked a bit when he bowled those dibbly-dobbler-type things.

I would have loved to have had a crack at him, too, with those menacing, swinging deliveries, but nana took precedence. My hillbilly harrow would have been a cracker against his bowling. I used to shave the shoulders of my bat, à la Lance, and dad had bought some orange and black tape, which we used to add to the bat.

Those were the days. In later years I met Lance and his son, Chris. I never quite got round to telling Lance how I imitated him, but I'm sure he would have been very proud.

A J Hackett

UNCLE JIM

Alan John (AJ) Hackett is an entrepreneur who popularised
the extreme sport of bungy-jumping.

There have been a number of people in my life who helped inspire me, and as a
result pushed me over the edge to take on life to the max on our gorgeous planet.
There were legends like that great athlete Peter Snell, then John Walker, who just kept
coming back and smashing the Kiwi Knocking Machine, but in many ways my life was
shaped by two of my uncles.

Don Bates was my mentor, someone who was a decade older than me and
something of a hero, but I would have to plump for another uncle, Jim Bates, who was
an inventor and an explorer. He managed to integrate his marvellous ideas with some
of his sporting expertise.

The most famous, or certainly the most public, of his achievements came in 1958
when his expertise with Massey Ferguson tractors meant he became involved in
Edmund Hillary's celebrated trip to the South Pole on those agricultural vehicles.

My uncle Jim had a passion for inventing and one project he became embroiled in
was when he was asked to design a special honey extraction machine for a beekeeper
named Hillary. From that first contact, their friendship grew and they ended up
working and exploring together.

Uncle Jim was involved in establishing an engineering company in the late 1940s,
which was a remarkable achievement, given his start in life.

When he was 10, he was still unable to read, and his exasperated mother took him
aside and managed to stimulate that skill by welding it to his interest in machinery
and engineering. He could relate to those ideas, understood he had to ramp up his
motor skills if he was going to work in those arenas, and so learned to read outside
the school system.

Uncle Jim was obviously a creative man, a passionate inventor, someone who was closely aligned to the dairy industry in New Zealand. He was also a yachting adventurer, and someone so trusted by Hillary that they went on a tractor expedition to the South Pole together.

He had five children and it was always a great thrill when we travelled north to stay with the clan on what was then a rural property at Whangarei Heads. It was a magnificent retreat. There was a foundry there, a massive workshop, a yacht moored out in the bay, and all sorts of mischief for us to get involved in as we mixed some part-time schoolwork with lots of play. It was a great part of New Zealand and those times hold special memories for me as I was growing up.

There were no real rules and my uncle Jim was very open to all of us staying there. He spent a great deal of time in his workshop building or tinkering with his creations. It was fascinating for me – I was in awe of his ideas and would spend as much time as I could watching what my uncle was making. He was not one of the world's great communicators. In fact, he could be quite blunt, but when he felt it was appropriate and the inquiry was not too off-beam, he would discuss his plans and ideas. It was best just to watch and digest what he was doing.

In later years, uncle Jim suffered from dementia, which is a cruel disease for anyone, let alone someone with such an inquiring temperament.

But his passion has stayed with me, the way he pushed the boundaries, moved barriers, was tuned into adventure in the mountains and on the oceans. It has trickled down through the family's bloodlines and I think much of his spirit has continued with some of my plans and adventures.

Sir Richard Hadlee

DICK MOTZ

Sir Richard Hadlee is the finest cricketer produced by
New Zealand. For a time he held the world record for
most test wickets.

I grew up in a household where there was a lot of talk about sport, and particularly
cricket, so not surprisingly the big sports personalities of my early years made a lasting
impression on me.

On the world scene, the man who towered over everyone was Muhammad Ali.
He always seemed to be having epic fights and was never far from the news. I was
a soccer player, so Pelé was also held in the highest regard. The big three of golf,
Jack Nicklaus, Gary Player and Arnold Palmer, set the standard and opened the door
for the professionals of today, and, a little later, tennis players Bjorn Borg and John
McEnroe were huge figures.

In New Zealand, Edmund Hillary was the biggest name. He climbed Mt Everest in
1953. I was born in 1951, so I don't remember the actual event. But moving through
our education system, you soon learned about his historic feat, and he remained a
much-admired figure for the next 50-odd years.

Our middle-distance athletes, specially Peter Snell and Murray Halberg, loomed
large, but it was cricket that always drew me.

The focus was on cricket and through the odd bits of black and white film, listening
on the radio and, especially, going to Lancaster Park to watch, I learned a lot about
New Zealand's leading players, the likes of John Reid and Bert Sutcliffe. Bert always
seemed to bat beautifully, and my first coaching book was *Bert Sutcliffe's Book for Boys*.

But to a lad growing up in Christchurch, Dick Motz was the special hero. I related to
him because he bowled fast and was a big hitter. He was the special hero of Lancaster
Park and that ground did become like a second home to me. Dick was the first New
Zealand bowler to take 100 test wickets, and that was a benchmark, something to aim
for and try to go beyond.

In my younger days I wasn't a big autograph-hunter, but I worked on the Lancaster
Park scoreboard for a while and sold programmes. I also collected bottles and returned

them to get a refund. If I got enough, I could make tuppence and buy an ice-cream. I must have been a nuisance, going up to people watching the cricket and asking: "Do you want your bottles?"

Dick Motz was Canterbury's leading pace bowler throughout the 1960s, when I was at my most impressionable. And there was always his batting. It was a bit hit-and-miss, and his innings were generally pretty quick, but he could whack 'em over the fence, and we schoolboys lived for those days.

I actually played against Dick once, just as I was starting out and he was ending his career. He opened the bowling for Riccarton at Hagley No 3. I was playing for Lancaster Park and was terrified. In fact, I was so nervous I don't even remember what happened, but I felt proud to have played against my schoolboy hero.

Roger Hall

JEFF WILSON

Roger Hall is an actor and playwright, known for his comedies, including *Glide Time,* which carry a serious vein of social criticism and feelings of pathos.

Near the end of my one-man play, *C'Mon Black,* when Dickie Hart is describing the tragedy of the World Cup final in Johannesburg in 1995, he says the following lines: "Kronfeld wasn't up with the pace. None of them, really, were on the pace the way they should be. Something was wrong. Wilson went off and vomited. I mean for Wilson to go off he must have felt like death, that kid's so keen. And you knew then the food poisoning story was true."

I was there on that fateful day, and once Wilson went off I quoted Private Frazer, the Scotsman from *Dad's Army:* "We're doomed." Indeed we were.

It was my son, Simon, who first heard of Jeff Wilson. He went from Dunedin to Invercargill playing basketball for his school, Logan Park. On his return he spoke in awe of this boy, "Jeff Wilson". As Wilson has often said, basketball was his first sporting love.

Later, during an exchange game, we billeted Jeff, this nice-mannered, fair young man. "We billeted Jeff Wilson": it's one of my claims to fame.

I can't remember which game I saw him play first. Otago presumably. But he had that electricity that when the ball got to him, you felt anything could happen. Fast, a sidestep... and rugby brains. Defence, too.

People forget his defence. He was outstanding, racing diagonally across the field to cut off the winger on the opposite side of the pitch, cutting him off and cutting him down.

Once, about 15 metres from his own line, Wilson made a great tackle and was instantly up on his feet to make a second tackle. He did the job of two men in a moment. The commentators never even mentioned it.

Then there was that sad moment against Australia, one of the first tests he played, when the game was his, a moment when New Zealand would have scored a last-minute win, and Gregan crashed across him, knocking the ball out of hands. Cruelly, this moment is shown again and again in previews for the Bledisloe Cup. (Why not show one of his great tries?)

I remember his regret, his self-blame, telling his father (something like) "I stuffed it up". Maybe, but the fact was that he was on the wrong end of one of the great defensive tackles of all time.

Not only was Wilson one of our greatest All Blacks, he was also one of the cleanest. I can't recall him ever being penalised for anything remotely dirty.

A lot of people forget his cricket. A career cut short, alas, by the introduction of Super 12 and the lamentable intrusion by rugby into our summer.

Memory is so fickle, but my memory tells me he was called into the one-day Black Caps side against Australia in the 1992-93 summer. I was organising the Dunedin Writers' Week and had to show an English writer the sights, so I took him out to the Otago Peninsula. I said: "I don't mind doing this, but if I miss seeing Wilson having a good knock, I'll never forgive you." We called into the Portobello pub and Wilson *had* indeed playing a quick match-winning innings and I *had* missed it.

In cricket, Wilson came back once too often for Otago and failed. Damn. He was human after all.

In 2005, Jeff and I both went on *Intrepid Journeys*, I to Uganda, he to Eastern Europe. Eastern Europe? Huh! God, they sent a 66-year-old man to Uganda and they sent a fit young buck to eastern Europe. But, hey, at last we had something in common.

And we would meet at the *Intrepid Journeys* party at the end of the year.

My chance to tell him how much I admired him.

Alas, I was the gushing fan. (I introduced myself as "Simon Hall's father".) On and on I went, saying much of the above. He bore the rantings of this boring old fart as long as could before finally saying: "Why don't you talk to Adine over there. She's the captain of the netball team."

I did, briefly, but in all honesty I wasn't equipped to talk about netball (she was as nice and as patient with me as Jeff had been).

After that, I slipped out into the night. There was no-one else there I wanted to talk to.

John Hart

CARDIGAN BAY

John Hart coached the All Blacks from 1996-99 and is now a director of the New Zealand Warriors.

My life has been bordered by rugby and it would be easy to select someone from that code, but at the same time, extremely difficult to isolate one person as my inspiration. Of course, I cannot ignore rugby because it has been such a huge part of my life, from the days when my brother used to mow Bob Scott's lawns and the massive impact that the 1956 Springboks tour had on New Zealand.

I was one of those kids who slept out at the ground before the fourth test to make sure I got tickets, queuing up with my brother until we got the valuable goods and then charging, with a whole lot of others, around Eden Park to get our preferred standing place, from where we watched the famous Peter Jones try.

Four years later I was back at the same venue for a midweek game, a sell-out. We biked to the ground to watch Auckland play Canterbury and this time managed to get into the West Stand, from where we saw Waka Nathan score that incredible match-winning try.

My life was starting to be shaped by rugby and I took great pride that same year when I entered a competition in *New Zealand Truth* and came third in a contest to pick the All Black squad to travel to South Africa. It was a bit embarrassing, however, because I had to confess to my parents about entering the competition in such a newspaper. I was able to appease them when my electric frying-pan prize arrived.

Subsequently I had great times as the Auckland and All Black coach, that magnificent era with the Blue and Whites in 1983-85 and then all the emotions of helping to make history at Pretoria in 1996 as coach of the first All Black side to win a series in South Africa. Fabulous times – so many great memories and so many great players that it would seem unfair to single out one moment or one champion.

Two stars meet – **CARDIGAN BAY** and Hollywood actress Jayne Mansfield.

So I have turned to my other great sports love, horse-racing. It was in my family's blood, with my grandfather spending time as a bookmaker and my father extremely interested in the sport of kings.

A number of close mates had horses and I have made great friends with people like Ray Cotter, who trains teams at Te Rapa. At one stage I wondered whether I might try my skills as a race commentator to try to emulate the styles of such great callers as Peter Kelly, Reg Clapp and Sid Tonks.

I remember my mother telling me how proud she was when she had listened through my bedroom door and thought I was repeating my homework when really I was practising my race calling.

My best mate from Mt Roskill Grammar, David Sixton, shared my sporting loves, so it was no surprise we should find ourselves at Alexandra Park in late December 1963 to watch Cardigan Bay go round off 78 yards in the Auckland Trotting Cup. We had ridden our bicycles across town to be part of a massive crowd of 27,000. It was a huge evening and we were part of a boisterous, heaving throng of people. There I was, about half Dave's size, trying to find a place in the crowd from where I could see the track.

Eventually we pushed and squirmed our way to the front of the old stand near the asphalt. The whole event was electric, because you could hear the thump of the horses' strides and the incessant noise all around. Never one to be too shy, I had a huge bet of 10 shillings each way on Cardigan Bay, even though he was a very short odds favourite. It was a two-mile race and when we watched the start it was hard to see Cardigan Bay, who was round the corner off his back marker. Trainer-driver Peter Wolfenden was in the sulky and the pressure on the pair was immense.

Cardigan Bay's advantage was that he was a very fast starter, but in a field which was very strong, he was going to need every bit of that expertise. There were others like Jay Ar, Robin Dundee, Tactile and Gentry – all quality horses in a truly marvellous field. With about seven furlongs to go, Cardigan Bay made his move. The noise was simply deafening. It seemed every person in the crowd was yelling "Cardy, Cardy, Cardy". He stormed around the field and with one lap left he was still three wide. Like many, I wondered whether that effort might tell on him, but Cardigan Bay just surged on past and went into the lead.

I had never been so excited. I was watching history. There was just a magical buzz, almost a surreal feeling about what was unfolding.

But just as everything appeared right in my world, Tactile came out of the bunch. All the way down the straight he gained on Cardigan Bay and the spectators, who had been so buoyant, suddenly went quiet as they went through a range of emotions from disbelief, to uncertainty and then incredulity. Surely this was not going to be the time when the champ faltered.

He did not let us down, but it was ultra-close. He called on all his reserves and managed to scrape home by half a length. The spectators regained their feverish voices, the noise was deafening and it was bordering on pandemonium when Cardigan Bay came back to scale.

It was an inspirational moment watching a champion, against the best and against the odds on an outrageous back mark on a difficult track. He showed all the courage and brilliance of a champion, while his driver stayed ultra-calm and very composed to complete a fine package of talent.

From that day, I decided it would be great to own a horse which won the Auckland Cup. The whole evening had inspired me, impressed me, enthused me and fired me up. It was just magic to be part of a huge occasion and to watch such a champion.

I think it was even more impressive, after he was sold to the United States in January 1964 with 40 wins on his record sheet, that Cardigan Bay should go on to collect another 40 victories. When he came home to retirement, I had to be there again at Alexandra Park in 1970 to salute an exceptional champion.

Cardy's exploits pushed me into trotting and a special moment came when I was Auckland coach and was asked to take part in a celebrity drivers' race. My good mate, Peter Murdoch, was there with his father, Doc Murdoch, who was the trainer and happened to be a great friend of Dave Todd, who bred Cardigan Bay. I was absolutely thrilled to win the race and head off others like Winston Peters, who, I think, came third.

Anyway, Dave Sixton and I were hooked on the racing scene by then. We must have had about 140 victories in our times with various syndicates and horses, but the greatest thrill and one which completed the circle, came on December 31, 2001, at Alexandra Park, when our horse, Holmes DG, won the Auckland Cup.

John Hawkesby

CYRIL EASTLAKE AND OTHERS

John Hawkesby began his broadcasting career in 1972.
He is a former news reader for TV One and TV3.

We lived within spitting distance of the Ellerslie rugby league ground and with jibes like you were heading for the theatre if you did not play league, it was perhaps no surprise that I first donned the club colours when I was five.

I loved the sport – it was fast, physical and tactical – all the elements that kept me involved until I finished playing at 22, when I was starting to get knocked around a bit too much and was siphoned out to fullback or wing in the senior reserve side after stints as a lock or stand-off. Most guys who play league tend to go from the backs to the pack as their pace slows, but I managed to buck that trend.

As a teenager I was lucky enough to be involved in a very good side that was unbeaten for several seasons. We had players like Murray Eade, who went on to play for the Kiwis, while co-coach Bruce Castle was a marvellous help and had been a proud Kiwi as well.

About the same time, I was going to Auckland Grammar and played rugby in the mornings for the school and then league for Ellerslie in the afternoons. I was superfit, with four training runs a week and two games on Saturday. Life was great, though Saturdays could be a bit of a tight struggle to fit in two matches.

I remember playing rugby on the No 3 field and then having to change into my league kit in our Austin A30 car while my father drove me to my next sports appointment, at the Mt Wellington Reserve.

One game at school sticks in my mind. I was asked to trial for the First XV as a centre. I had never played there in my life and specifically asked the teacher, Mr Elder, why he wanted me to play out of position. His reply was quite specific. The guy I was going to mark had been in the First XV for two years, but was quite greedy and they wanted me to rattle him with some of my tackling, to force him to distribute the ball

CYRIL EASTLAKE (with ball) was a nimble and elusive runner who took some stopping.

more to the wingers. I was told to shake him up.

The moment the ball arrived I was to hit him hard. The coaching staff gave me the licence to loiter offside and the referee was also in on the plan for me to rough up this centre, all in the name of encouraging him to pass the ball more.

About 12 minutes into the game this guy had scored five tries and I was subbed off. My antagonist was Grahame Thorne, who just a few short years later was picked for the All Blacks even before he had played for Auckland.

My only revenge against Thorne, who was older than me, came when we ended up in the same sixth form class and I achieved my only academic success at Grammar. I had managed to shed difficult subjects like chemistry and physics and had topped the class in English and history, and received my end-of-year prizes from Wilson Whineray, who was the guest speaker.

For someone like me, who had a great love of sport, this was a moment to savour. Meeting the All Black captain, even if it was only fleeting, after the side's successful 1963-64 tour of the Britain was a magical moment. I received several books for topping the class, but it seemed far more important to shake Whineray's hand and later declare I had not washed that limb for some time afterwards. We had a couple of words, he offered his congratulations, I mumbled something in response. He was a lovely man, extremely gracious and to have such a sports god in my sights was a special moment and one I have never forgotten.

We all had a mix of heroes and around that time my father took me to Eden Park to watch Auckland play a midweek rugby match. We were sitting right next to the tunnel and when the teams ran out I couldn't help myself and yelled out "Waka". The flanker looked up at me and just winked.

I had never seen anyone play quite like Waka Nathan that day. He was built like a Greek god, was all over the ground, and just flowed through the game. He was always near the action, the Michael Jones of his day. Nathan was magic and was so aptly named "the Black Panther".

My league hero was Cyril Eastlake, who played for my Ellerslie club. His mother-in-law lived two doors down from us and I would often see him down there playing cricket or kicking a ball around with some of his younger relations.

Cyril was known as "the Silver Fox". He was a short, slight, wiry man, someone who seemed very quiet, almost withdrawn off the field, but on the paddock was incredibly nimble, smart and elusive. He captained the Kiwis.

One day we were watching the seniors at the Domain, and Ellerslie were 12-10 behind with a minute to go when they were awarded a penalty. It was about 40 metres out, not a gift but well within Eastlake's range to tie the match. He took his time, digging the hole, placing the ball carefully on the mound and measuring out his run-up as the Otahuhu team, rather resignedly, gathered near the posts.

Eastlake then walked up as if to check the ball position one final time, then tapped the ball and scampered to score untouched in the corner. To top that bit of chicanery, he then converted from the touchline and all I could think was what a clever dude he was.

Graham Henry

JOHN REID

Graham Henry, a former secondary school headmaster,
has coached the All Blacks since 2004.

A swag of us growing up in Christchurch were fanatical about cricket. I still am and
think it is a great sport, one to be ranked alongside my other great sporting love.

We used to operate the scoreboard at Lancaster Park under the watchful eye of
Ted Delahunty, who was the Canterbury and Old Boys club scorer for many, many
years. I guess I was about 11 or 12 when I first worked on that scoreboard. Eventually,
a number of my mates managed to get in on the deal and we had many great summers
helping to run that board.

During one of those years, I remember being fascinated as J R Reid took the
South Africans head-on in a tour of the republic in 1961-62. I listened to all of those
radio broadcasts, imaging myself there with Reid as he put the South Africans to the
sword. He was a burly, powerful batsman who scored a power of runs and scored them
quickly. He was my idea of a sports hero, one who led from the front, who was by a
long stretch New Zealand's mainstay on the world cricket stage, someone who would
cut it in modern times and had a real presence and great aura about him.

At one stage I managed to get his autograph, but when I moved to Auckland
in the early 1970s, I gave that autograph book away with thousands of cricket and
rugby programmes I had collected down the years. Remarkably, when I moved to
Wales in the late '90s someone over there told me how they had acquired my original
autograph book.

One of my favourite signatures was J R Reid. He could do everything on the
cricket field, and he was my sports equivalent of Roy of the Rovers. He batted, bowled
fast, could change to cutters or spin, he kept wickets and captained the side. Some
cricketer, some guy, too.

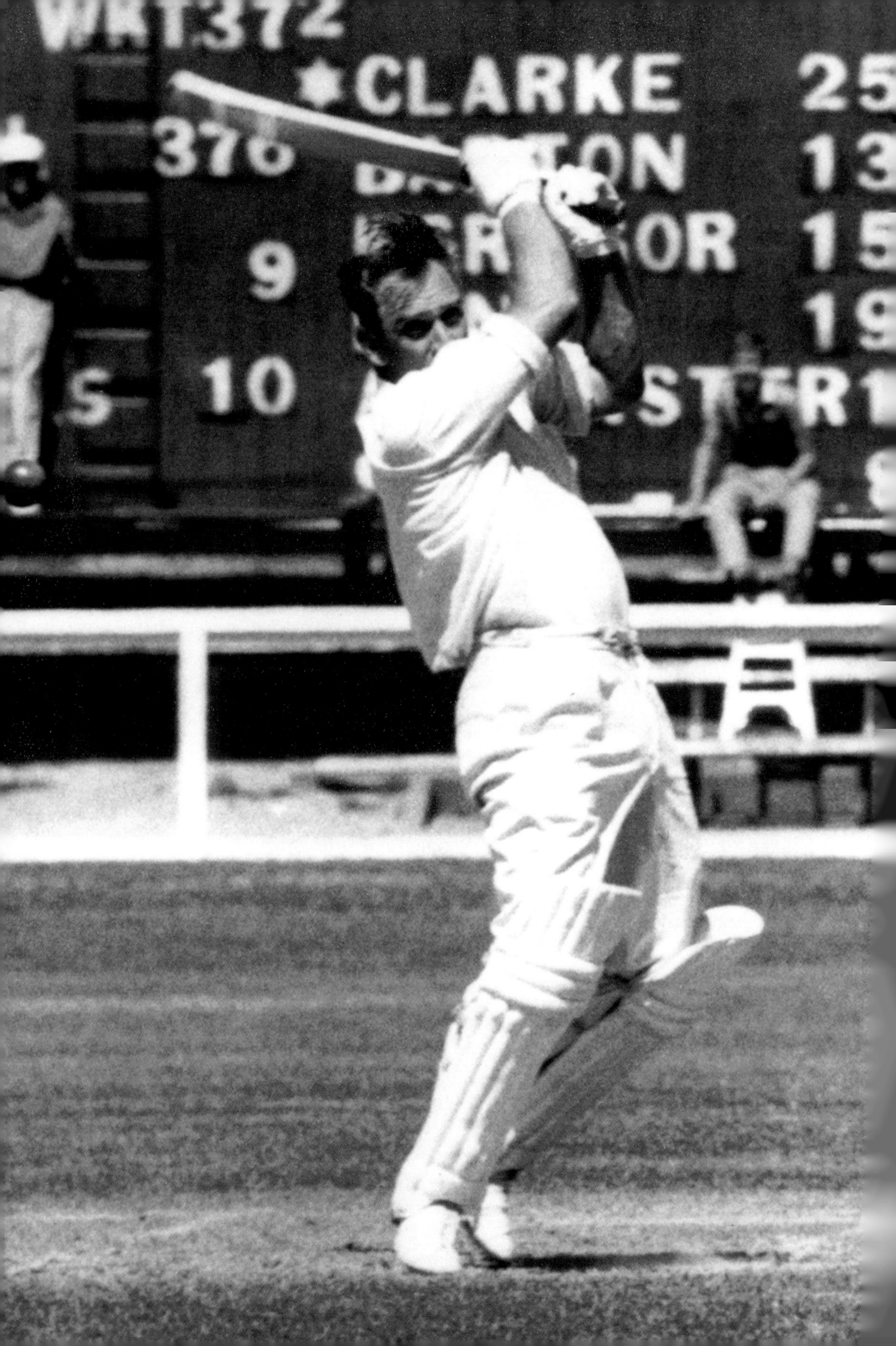
CLARKE 25
13
9
15
19
10

Reid had a fearsome reputation and I just loved the way he played because he hit the ball so hard. He attacked bowlers all the time, and livened up every game he played in. He had those special magnetic qualities and in his prime would have waltzed into a World XI.

He top-scored for New Zealand in their first official test win, in 1956, against the West Indies, he was part of a drawn series in South Africa five years later. He was just such an influential player in those sorts of results, which started to alter the way New Zealand felt about their cricket team.

I loved my cricket, whether it was batting or keeping wickets – indeed I was better at that sport than rugby. My only sorrow was that I played before the introduction of limited-overs cricket, because I'm sure I would have loved to have been involved in those matches.

Neither of my parents were cricket fanatics – my love of the sport just happened. It began when I was very young and was helped by the fact that a number of my close mates felt the same way.

Things like practising at the Hadlees' place helped. That famous cricket family lived not far from us and they had a fantastic net set up in their back yard. I was quite good mates with Martin, Dayle was a year younger than I was, while Barry was about five years older and Richard was younger than all of us. But we all got on and had some great contests there.

My love of cricket continued through Christchurch Boys' High, where we played in the second tier senior B competition.

We were spoiled in the First XI, where my team-mates included Robert Anderson, Alan Hounsell, David Trist, two Hadlees, Cran Bull, Ian Walter, John Christensen and Ken Baker, who all made it to the top in one of their chosen sports. I batted about five or six in my final year at school and remember being very proud of scoring 78 against Auckland Grammar that season and a 60-odd against Christ's College.

Whenever I can these days, I go along to watch test or one-day cricket. I love it. I was there when we beat the Australians in 2007, when Ross Taylor scored a magnificent century.

I can watch cricket for ages and some of the credit for that must go to J R Reid, who fired my interest so strongly when I was a youngster.

Down the years our paths have crossed a number of times and I recall one occasion when I was coaching Wales and he was returning from one of his stints somewhere as an ICC match referee. We met in an airport lounge and struck up a conversation in which his depth of knowledge on a variety of sports topics shone through.

I watch netball, league and most sports events, but there will always be a place for a lot of cricket. It is relaxing, for those of us watching at least, and I am desperate for the Black Caps to do well. They always seem to play above their weight, they always fight hard, and they are combative – all the qualities which endear them and their sport to me.

Michael Hill

JACK GLANVILLE

Michael Hill is one of New Zealand's most successful
businessmen, and owns a chain of jewellery stores.

While I was not much chop at sport, it still played an influential part in my life. Never
more so than when I was going to secondary school at Whangarei Boys' High School.

My maths teacher was Jack Glanville, an immaculately turned out man with a neat
sense of style, a bit of a guru really, who was also a very good golfer.

He carried himself in the manner of someone who knew what he was doing. His
overall aura said much about his confidence, his ability and belief. He had a bearing,
a discipline, while the way he presented himself made a huge impact on me. Life is
very complex, but if you can get some of the basics right, as Jack showed us, then it is
a great start.

My parents were friendly with him because we lived across the road from him,
and though I felt embarrassed at being dragged into that company sometimes, he
was extremely kind to me and, I learned, a very sharp golfer. I would sometimes be
dragged along to watch my parents play a round with him and would marvel at some
of the shots he played.

He was club champion at the Mt Denby Golf Club and I guess that helped fire my
curiosity about the sport which has eventually led me to join up all those interests with
the foundation of the Hills Golf Course in Queenstown.

There was also Jim Gallaway, who ran the Wiseman's sports store in town and was
also a professional in Whangarei. He was, I swear, the best hitter of a 4-iron that I have
ever seen. Goodness knows how I remember that, but I swear he was, as he showed
when he held an exhibition with Norman Von Nida in what must have been another
influential chapter in my growing admiration for the sport of golf.

My parents were members at Mt Denby and while I did not join – I had too many other things to do at that stage in my life – it's amazing how things that lie dormant for a long time suddenly trigger events later in life, like my idea of building a golf course in Queenstown.

When I watched my parents play I would marvel at Jack Glanville, who hit an extremely long ball with what appeared to be so little effort. He used persimmon woods rather than the metal tools of today, and the golf ball was nothing like the quality of the gear these days. From time to time, like any curious schoolboy, I would have a go, but simply could not fathom how Jack could hit the same sort of ball so far and so straight. It is a mystery which I am still trying to unravel these days when I get out the clubs.

I saw little of Jack once I left school, but I guess, in a subconscious way, his attitude towards golf and the manner he conducted himself rubbed off on me when I started to take a more concerted interest in the sport.

He had great discipline and great focus, and showed me that it was a virtuous pastime in which to be involved. He showed me that I could take up golf, then let it lie dormant for some time before reactivating my interest.

Taking up golf is also a great contrast to the other interests in my life, like family and playing the violin. Life is like that, and I am grateful to Jack for showing me how much there is to get out of life everywhere.

Carol Hirschfeld

MY BROTHER CHARL

Carol Hirschfeld is a broadcaster, best-known as a TV3 newsreader alongside John Campbell from 1996-2005, and then as the producer of *Campbell Live*.

The first conscious sporting memory I have was admiring my new tartan gumboots while standing on the sideline one winter morning, watching my brother play lock for Cornwall Park 14th grade. I was eight years old and my sister and I were required to hand out orange quarters at half-time, cheer if play was good and not stray too far over the wooden farm fence, which back then enclosed his team's home grounds near One Tree Hill in Auckland.

Maybe it was because he was five years older, maybe it was because it is the job of every little sister to see her big brother as worldly beyond all comprehension (certainly before you reach the age of 10), but Charl was without a doubt my first sports hero.

It started with an admiration for blokes in uniform. I loved the green and white jerseys with the subtle yellow stripe that he and his mates wore. I marvelled at the way no matter how mud-splattered and wrecked their clothing was from the previous week's game, they came on to the paddock looking a million bucks. Thanks, of course, to the elbow grease of their conscientious mothers.

I would, eventually, move off his sideline and get to throw my own balls around, but even that effort was shaped by his ventures. Charl dispensed with rugby pretty early in his teens (too much head-butting) and picked up a racket for a while, proving to be an excellent badminton player.

He swapped shuttlecocks for a more sizeable ball after his body unexpectedly surged and grew around five inches in a single year when he was 14. Big brother really was big – and so were his dreams, all of which suddenly featured hoops!

Seemingly overnight, Charl joined five basketball teams and the tenor of family life changed dramatically. Our driveway was a scene of continual lay-up practice, the house was regularly jammed with tall, sweaty boys in singlets, my brother's socks had never smelt so bad. My exhaustingly fit brother would drink six bottles of milk a day – the rest of the family consumed a meagre one.

It was probably at the height of Charl's basketball obsession, in 1974, that he persuaded my dad to take us all to a Harlem Globetrotters game. As an early teen, I had no idea who they were or what I was really going to see that night as we sat on outdoor terraces, waiting for them to descend on court.

What I still remember is the thrill of being entertained by this elegant display of athleticism. It was the first time I understood that sports stars could be funny, extraordinarily skilled and beautiful to watch – all at the same time. The Globetrotters were primarily about making sure the crowd had good fun, which they managed to do by employing the languid grace and power that you have to have to be a great basketballer.

So this is why Charl likes the game so much, I thought to myself.

These days, it amuses me to watch another family member lit up with the same kind of fever for a sport as my brother had. He, too, is tall, just like his uncle and wears a green and striped shirt most Saturday mornings during the winter. My son, Will, believes if we were to home-school him and free him up to practise soccer seven hours a day he probably could become a professional footballer.

Whatever his future, I foresee plenty more time on the sideline – watching my new sports hero grow in stature from game to game.

Sir Patrick Hogan

YVETTE WILLIAMS

Sir Patrick Hogan is a horse breeder who has produced a series of champions, including three Melbourne Cup winners, at Cambridge Stud.

If you think about people who inspired you at a young age, people who were magnificent ambassadors for their country and wonderful sportspeople, then great athletes like Australians Marjorie Jackson and Betty Cuthbert spring to mind. They were a pair of incredible athletes, but if I'm to pick one from New Zealand, then it's impossible to go past Yvette Williams, who was at her peak at about the same time.

Yvette was a wonderful lady, a versatile athlete and such a fine person. I was fortunate to be introduced several times and each time was struck by her humility, her manners, her bearing. There was nothing about her attitude to show she had been top of the world in her sport. She was so down-to-earth, so even-keeled, so sensible and just such a nice lady.

I was growing up when Yvette was at the top of the athletics world in the long jump, and she was also a premier talent in her ability to throw the javelin. She was someone who had great natural athletic gifts, but she did not rely on those God-given talents. She joined an unyielding attitude and determination to her sports ability to create an unstoppable package. That mix of talent and drive has stuck in my mind all through the years, and while we have had many magnificent athletes since, like Murray Halberg, Peter Snell, John Davies, Dick Quax, John Walker and others, Yvette was just something special for me as a teenager growing up in New Zealand. She showed us in this small country that we could do things.

Yvette had this incredibly intoxicating mix of talent, discipline and humility and I was at the right age to comprehend her exploits and be inspired by her deeds.

Some of those exploits may have faded with time, but in her day Yvette was a super-athlete, someone who would have excelled these days. She was also a marvellous person who had time for others, something that is not a common trait in the modern sports era.

Each time I have met Yvette at a sports awards evening, she has been the same nice, contained and inspiring person. She has not been in the best of health lately, but has not let those troubles come between her and being interested in others. She is just a wonderful lady, a true inspiration and one of this nation's champions.

Paul Holmes

PETER SNELL AND OTHER ATHLETES

Paul Holmes hosted a popular radio breakfast show on the ZB network for 21 years and the TV One current affairs programme *Holmes* for 15 years.

I was not particularly sporty as a child. If other kids got to pick teams, I was one of the last to be called out. You could never rely on my hand-eye co-ordination. Such is life. I played rugby at primary school and got put in as a prop, so I spent much of my games head down and pushing against big boys on freezing Saturday mornings, not knowing what was going on. Somewhere out in the open, somewhere else on the field, some boys were having a great time running freely to cheering mums and dads. I got out of that lark as soon as I could.

My heroes tended to be astronauts, but I knew how special our Olympic track stars were in those golden years at Rome and Tokyo – Peter Snell, Murray Halberg and John Davies and their mentor, Arthur Lydiard. I thought they were marvellous, I suppose. They were the best in the world and they were ours.

I must have been about 13, in the summer of 1963. During the holidays I went to Napier hospital for an operation and lay there lonely and sad for just over a week. I was terribly homesick. My cousins came to see me early one evening and said they were off to see Snell, Davies and Halberg at an exhibition track meet, those being the days when crowds flocked to those events. Mum gave them my autograph book to take along. Next day my cousins came to see me again and in my book were all three of those great stars. I don't know where the book is now, but I have a feeling that George Kerr signed it as well that night. I was so proud and kept looking at them and showing them to everyone who came by.

I have always remembered what that small effort by those legendary sports greats meant to a young boy in hospital. I will never forget it. In my own life, I would like to think I have never begrudged a child an autograph. I have always been particular about it because of what the autographs of those men meant to me more than 40 years ago.

Later, as an adult, I met them all. It always amazed me that they knew my name. One of my proudest broadcasts I ever did was Peter Snell's *This Is Your Life*. There they all were – Peter, Murray, John Davies, Arthur Lydiard, and George Kerr as well.

I did not mention the autographs. They would never have remembered, of course. But I did. I could see that little book in my mind the whole time I was with them.

Michael Houstoun

TIGER WOODS

Michael Houstoun is an acclaimed New Zealand concert pianist.

I've always enjoyed sport. At Timaru Boys' High School, I played basketball. I wasn't the shortest player in the team, but was close! Later I've enjoyed tennis and a bit of squash.

I'm not a big television watcher, but I have always enjoyed watching the big tennis and golf tournaments, especially in recent years, because of golfer Tiger Woods, who is the person I've most admired in sport.

He really seems like the real deal to me. He does things that only the true greats, the immortals, can do. If there is a chip shot that he has to leave right by the pin, if there's a long putt he simply has to make, he does it. That's a gift bestowed upon very few.

I've never seen a player get himself out of trouble better, and when he's behind, he's especially dangerous.

The thing with Woods is that he's done these unimaginable things tournament after tournament, year after year. Things that other golfers wait a lifetime to do once, he does regularly.

But I admire him for more than just his golf. I like his manner, what he says, how he comports himself.

He seems very genuine. When he shows a bit of emotion on the course, maybe with a fist-pump, it's because he's done something special. He's not like some of these tennis players, who seem to bring out the fist-pump the whole time. If they get a serve in, there's a fist-pump!

Tiger is invariably in the spotlight, but I've never found him gratuitous. He's been very true to himself. Golf has been extremely lucky to have him as its No 1 player. You could see, when he had to take a long break while his leg recovered from surgery, how much the game missed him – crowds and television ratings declined.

He seems to have had a very positive impact on his sport, too. Young players have looked at Tiger – his approach to the game, his training ethic and so on – and known that's what they need to do to keep up, so he's had a hand in lifting the standard of the sport.

I guess the closest modern sportsman to Tiger Woods has been Roger Federer, who was clearly the best tennis player in the world for several years. He has always carried himself well, he plays with artistry and variety and he's been a credit to his sport. It's not that surprising the pair of them became friends.

Just as Woods was good for golf, so Federer has given tennis a big lift. I've enjoyed watching him, but if I had to single out one person, Tiger Woods is the man.

Rachel Hunter

ALLISON ROE

Rachel Hunter is a model and an actress. She was married to rock star Rod Stewart for 16 years.

It had been a pretty tough old winter. I was at intermediate school, at a stage of my life when I was enjoying a whole range of new experiences and starting to question the ways of the world, while New Zealand was in turmoil following the visit of the 1981 Springboks.

I loved my sport, the freedom of being outdoors and New Zealand was such a great place to grow up.

For several reasons my sporting interests had taken a bit of a back seat during the chilly winter of 1981. I had suffered a few injuries and suddenly sport in New Zealand wasn't quite the same as the world watched the fallout from the South Africans' rugby visit.

As a young schoolgirl I didn't grasp all the political implications and was amazed at the divisions that tour provoked in society, in families, work-places and even classrooms. Tour supporters and opponents debated the pros and cons of the Springbok visit long after they played that extraordinary last test with its unforgettable flour bombardment.

The debate was impossible to avoid as newspapers and television screens overflowed with opinion and reports. We would talk about it at school and I wondered how life could have become so complicated. The aftermath of that tour lingered over New Zealand, but in late October that year, as summer peeped into our lives again, for me, there was a magical piece of counterpoint.

I was heavily into my school athletics and enjoying the benefits of a 10km a day training regime as I built up the stamina needed for the middle-distance races that had taken my attention. My favourite distance was the 800m. I found I could mix it with my peers, but I suffered from shin splints and, disappointed with an injury I could feel but not see, I quit athletics and turned my attention more towards dancing before that eventually gave way to modelling.

But back in the spring of 1981... I was happiest outside, running around the roads on the North Shore and carrying with me the dream that one day I might even qualify to run at the Olympics.

Often I would see this tall, blonde woman, with the most elegant and powerful style, striding around the popular running tracks on the shores of Lake Pupuke or powering along Takapuna Beach or Milford Beach. Allison Roe made her training look so effortless. She had such a graceful style and seemed almost to float when she ran. She was such an inspiration for an aspiring young athlete like me.

So you can imagine my joy shortly after when Allison won the women's marathon in Boston and then repeated that feat by leading the field through Central Park in New York, wearing her white gloves, and with her blonde hair flowing. There was that same graceful stride that I had witnessed during her training. As she crossed the finish line, I sat glued to the television broadcast. The celebrations continued when she was crowned the New York marathon winner with a world record time of 2h 25min 29s, a time which would stand up well to this day.

Allison Roe simply strode away from the rest of the field that day in New York. The smile on her face must have hidden the pain she ran with so often. She was a wonderful athlete, but had already been blighted by injury which, tragically, was to cut short her brilliant career.

Though she had already won the Boston marathon, there seemed to be so much more hype about her winning in New York, because she was up against Greta Weitz, who was a colossus in the world of women's distance running at the time.

If she could win like that after training on the same tracks I ran on, it wasn't hard for a young blonde Glenfield schoolgirl to imagine herself doing the same. Injury, circumstance, less desire than Allison and who knows what else all combined to alter that ambition, but for those wonderful months in 1981-82, Allison Roe was a golden inspiration for this girl from Glenfield.

April Ieremia

NADIA COMANECI AND THE 1976 OLYMPIC HOCKEY TEAM

April Ieremia was a New Zealand netball representative and later became a television presenter.

I was seven years old when I told my grandfather I was going to play netball for New Zealand.

We were watching coverage of the 1975 world netball championships in Auckland, where New Zealand finished a disappointing third behind Australia and England, and everyone was moping around, lost. At the time, I had no idea what the girls were playing, but I knew I liked it.

Twenty years later my mother relayed what I had told my grandfather and it caught me completely off-guard. I had no recollection of saying anything of the sort. In fact, I found it ridiculous.

How could anyone know what they wanted at the age of seven and then go on and do it! More to the point, how could I?

Yes, I loved sport, but I had no idea what representing your country meant and at that stage of my development, I didn't care.

Back then, if I wasn't dreaming about white knights on gallant steeds slashing overgrown weeds from ruined castles, then I was fantasising about becoming the world's greatest gymnast.

I was all set to score more perfect 10s than Romania's superstar Nadia Comaneci.

Every girl my age wanted to be her. She had done incredibly at the 1976 Montreal Olympics, winning five medals including three golds, but more importantly, she had received the first perfect score, 10.0, in Olympic gymnastics history. Clearly the star of those Olympics, Comaneci went on to repeat the feat six more times at those games.

For me, the youngest Olympic all-around champion ever was a god. And I wanted to be just like her.

Doing the maths, I concluded that if Comaneci was 14 when she became a sporting rock star and I was only eight then, I had plenty of time to break her record and clock up a few more 10s.

An enthusiastic and diligent approach to my gymnastics career, however, was sadly not enough.

I never made it past my silver badge at primary school level, even though our coach, Mr Fletcher, tried ever so hard to mould me into something I wasn't. I struggled to make my body do basic stuff like a tumble turn, backward walk-overs or even the splits – absolute fundamentals for Gym 101.

In the end, when I failed to perform a simple scissor-jump on the beam, landing painfully astride it then crumbling to the floor in a screaming heap (had I been a boy, I would have been a goner), I decided it wasn't for me.

Admittedly, I was punching well above my weight, but it could have been avoided had someone told me Nadia Comaneci had been doing somersaults since the age of six!

Back home, our national heroes included the men's hockey team, who shocked everyone when they beat Australia 1-0 at the 1976 Olympics.

Their gold medal propelled New Zealand into hockey supremacy... and it propelled my primary school into an absolute frenzy.

Seeing Olympic gold medals and Olympic heroes in the flesh wasn't normal – unless, of course, you knew their dad.

Well, I didn't know him personally, but Barry and Selwyn Maister's father was the principal of our school, Isleworth Primary School. And when I saw their medals, I wanted one.

So, inspired by their visit, their brilliance and their ability to do the impossible, I took up hockey.

Needless to say, it was shortlived, too.

After weeks of sore shins and copious bruises, I unwittingly used my hockey stick like a golf club, ready to unleash the longest drive in history, but instead smashing a poor team-mate in the middle of her head with the backswing.

She was out for the count and hockey was out the door. I thought if I could do that to her, imagine what someone could do to me.

It's difficult to put my finger on a defining moment or special person who influenced my sporting career, changing the course of my life. However, Nadia Comaneci and our greatest hockey team had significant parts.

I learnt two things: I wanted to play among the best and I was going to do that in a team.

Tame Iti

WAKA NATHAN

Tame Iti has become well-known as a Tuhoe Maori activist. He is a social-worker with expertise in combating drug and alcohol addictions.

I was brought up in Ruatoki, near Whakatane, by the same family that raised my father. It was a rural, farming area and didn't have the modern amenities you see today.

For a long time there was only one television in our district. The person who owned it got it even before there was reception available! Then Vic, who lived about three farms down the line – just a short horse-ride – got a television and we kids used to be able to go down and watch it.

I didn't have a lot of time for sport, but I did work out pretty early on that playing sport was a good way to get out of milking the cows in the morning or evening. But what sport? The two options at the time were kapa haka and rugby, and when I was young I thought of rugby as a bit of a poofters' game – 30 players out in the middle of a paddock chasing a ball. So I went with kapa haka.

However, rugby was our national game and I can remember watching test matches in black and white on Vic's television in the 1960s. When the All Blacks toured Britain, the games would be shown on the Sunday following the weekend of the test, and we'd all gather around the television to watch. The NZBC had only one channel back then, so anyone watching television was watching the rugby.

I was always especially proud of Waka Nathan, who was nicknamed "the Black Panther". I didn't know a lot about the fine details of rugby as a kid, but I was drawn to him because he was Maori and because he always seemed to be one of the stars, the way he ran so freely and the tries he scored. People always seemed to be cheering for him, and he was famous. I felt very proud of him.

Later in my life I met Waka. He was a meat boner and I met him out Mangere way, and told him I used to watch him play as a kid. It was good to meet the man who'd been a hero when I was a youngster.

As time went on, I became a bit more involved in rugby. When my kids were young, I got on the Kawerau JAB [Junior Advisory Board] committee and helped to organise rugby in the area. But that all changed in 1981 when the Springboks toured. The kids were moved from rugby to soccer that year.

There were still some rugby players I particularly admired, though. I liked the way Chris Laidlaw spoke out against apartheid in the 1970s. I thought that was good, the way he made a stand. And when the Springboks were here, the All Black captain,

Graham Mourie, made a strong statement by refusing to play against them. I admired him for that.

By then I'd been involved in the anti-apartheid movement for years. It was difficult in New Zealand, because the country was so passionate about rugby, and South Africa were the traditional rivals. I felt we started to make progress in 1967 when the All Blacks refused to tour South Africa because we were not allowed to include Maori players in the team.

The Prime Minister, Keith Holyoake, seemed to support that stand, and maybe it was the first signs of understanding from the Rugby Union.

It all seems a long time ago now. I still follow rugby of course, like most New Zealanders. There are some great players, but no-one thrills me, and fills me with pride, the way Waka Nathan did when I used to watch him on a fuzzy black and white television in the 1960s.

WAKA NATHAN in his days as a meat boner.

Willie Jackson

BRYAN WILLIAMS

Willie Jackson is a broadcaster and commentator with experience in a range of areas from politics to music. He is a strong advocate for Maori.

My old man, Bob Jackson, was a tormentor.

Back in the winter of 1970, just after I'd turned nine, I became besotted by Bryan Williams. I'd spotted Beegee that season on the cover of *Rugby News* in the course of his magical sidestepping tour in South Africa as a 19-year-old All Black winger.

I was smitten. And the more I read of him, the more I heard when I sat up with dad to listen to the games on the radio in the middle of the night, and the more I saw of him bamboozling the Springboks when he was on telly a few days later, the more smitten I became.

He was my hero. Absolutely. Thirteen tries in 14 games on that tour. Sidesteps galore, including two in-goal so he could saunter around, as cool as you like, behind the posts. It was glorious. He could do no wrong. He was perfect. Maybe even better than perfect.

Not according to my dad, though. He couldn't resist taunting this wide-eyed, fanatical, nine-year-old Beegee worshipper there in our Porirua living room.

In those days, dad worked on the wharf in Wellington. And he knew his footie. In fact, he'd been bred to excel in the game.

His grandfather, Fred Jackson, arrived in New Zealand as a member of the 1908 Anglo-Welsh rugby team, and, finding this country to his liking, never went back to England.

Fred Jackson's three boys Tutu, Rongo and my grandfather, Everard, were all Maori All Blacks, as well as officers of C Company in the Maori Battalion in World War II. Grandpa Everard went on to play for the 1937 All Blacks against South Africa.

The talent continued in the next generation. My old man played senior rugby when he was in the freezing works way down at Mataura. And his brothers Bill Nepia, Sid (better

known for his brave battles for Maori rights) and Fred all played representative rugby.

Sadly, the next chapter, if one was written to chronicle the Jackson footie saga, would be about a dead-loss generation – my cousins and me.

We all ripped into it as schoolkids. I was at Windley Primary School and can count among my triumphs making the Porirua bantam under-10s. We gave it heaps when we played bullrush too. And, if you'd looked closely, once I'd become a disciple of Beegee, you would've noticed any number of sidesteps from me. I wasn't half bad either – or so I thought. But there was no rep destiny beckoning.

Although that apprenticeship didn't lead to footie glory, I stayed hooked on the game. And when our family moved north to Mangere the following year, I was nicely placed to close in on my hero. Which I did.

I'd go and watch him play for Ponsonby, and I'd catch him at Eden Park when he was on deck for Auckland or the All Blacks.

Whenever I could, I'd rush on to the field and thrust out a programme for his autograph. I must've collected a dozen or more through the years. All gone now though. Chucked away, I imagine, as my faith fizzled. Not that it did so quickly, because I enjoyed some wonderful Beegee moments at Eden Park or on telly even after some of the magic went from his sidestep and he lost a yard or two of pace.

He could still boom out massive punts and place-kicks, which would have me crowing with delight. He'd bust tackles, too. And sometimes he'd line up an opponent and monster him in a crash tackle. Ooo-eee! Way to go, Beegee!

But there'd still be dad suggesting, for instance, that Grant Batty, not Beegee, was the magic man. ("Only a little fella, eh? But see what he can do!")

Or he'd be drawing attention to a slip-up by my hero. ("Look – there's Gerald Davies stepping your man.")

And anyway, Beegee wasn't Maori, was he? I hadn't realised that at first. As a nine-year-old I didn't know what a Samoan was. He looked Maori to me. That was good enough.

But, as the years went on, my affections drifted more towards Sid Going and his brothers.

When I look back, that was a part of my political education, encouraged by my dad. He, like his brothers (especially Sid and Moana), grew up with a sharp eye for unfairness – and he could see that, too often for comfort, Maori players didn't win the respect or the rewards their talents warranted.

I could see that in the way Sid Going had, at times, to play second fiddle to inferior players (like Chris Laidlaw) – and never got a chance to team up with both his brothers in the All Blacks. Oh boy. Them and their triple scissors. That would've been a revelation.

Eventually, some of my sporting appetite was satisfied when I ran a sports show on Radio Aotearoa. As well as talkback callers, I'd invite guests from netball, rugby league, rugby and so on.

Once I invited Beegee. That schoolboy enthusiasm began bubbling up inside me again at the very thought of talking to my super-hero.

He never called back. And that was the end of my infatuation.

Tony Johnson

SIR JOHN WALKER

Tony Johnson is a rugby commentator for Sky Television.
He previously worked for Radio New Zealand and TV3.

3min 49.4s. A moment in time, the minutes, seconds, and fractions of a second, that it took John Walker to run a mile in Gothenburg, Sweden, on August 12, 1975.

It was the first time anyone had run the distance under 3min 50s and therefore the most significant "milestone" since Roger Bannister had cracked the four-minute mark. Walker smashed the record, held by his nemesis from the 1974 Commonwealth Games, Filbert Bayi, by 1.5 seconds.

It remains one of the great moments in New Zealand sport, an indelible memory from my teenage years.

I think I can admit, all this time later, that not only was John Walker my sports hero, but that he was the Kiwi bloke I most wanted to be like, with that combination of athletic power and a look that was classic '70s.

I fought a constant battle with my parents and my conservative high school headmaster to be allowed to grow my hair to shoulder length, Walker style. I might have eventually won that one, but for all the miles I ran in my thin-soled Skellerup sneakers, the athletic prowess never came, apart from modest success in the school cross-country, when most of the other kids were content to either amble it, detour straight home, or duck into the bush for a smoke.

My early sports idols had been rugby players, like Ian Kirkpatrick, Bryan Williams and the Ranfurly Shield-winning Marlborough rugby team of 1973, or cricketers like Basil D'Oliveira and John Snow of the England side, whose every move in lifting the Ashes from Australia over the summer of 1970-71 I had listened to, as I developed my love of sport on the radio.

But the cricketers had been virtual figments of my imagination, listened to but unseen, and we were afforded only fleeting looks at our rugby heroes because of the paranoia over live TV held by rugby administrators in those days.

John Walker was different. He was a much more visible, accessible champion, something owed in part to the massive advancements in televising live sport in the 70s.

The first time I saw Walker in action was in 1973, in a live telecast of the 1500m at the national track and field champs. I watched to see Rod Dixon, bronze medallist at the previous year's Olympics, and Tony Polhill, who also made the Munich 1500m final. But as Dixon led them into the final stretch, the imposing figure of Walker appeared on his shoulder, before powering away to leave a high-class field in his wake, and a 14-year-old awestruck.

With the 1974 Commonwealth Games in Christchurch came the advent of colour television and suddenly everything seemed so much more real, vivid and exciting – "almost better than being there", as the ads for the Philips K9 used to say.

Well, actually, I was there. Family friends from the Marlborough Sounds had scored some tickets, and I was invited to go with them to Christchurch, which to us in those days was a bit like going to London.

We went to the swimming on the first Saturday afternoon, and I can still recall the frenzy of excitement as Mark Treffers won gold in the 400m medley, and if our Sunday at the track and field came on a relatively low- key day, with few finals, we at least got to see lots of stars in the heats, like Don Quarrie in the 200m, Ben Jipcho in the 5000m, and Walker in the 800m.

I watched the rest of the games at home with a mix of hope that they would never end, and impatience for the last day, and the much-anticipated 1500m final.

New Zealanders were confident Walker would win, that the little Tanzanian, Filbert Bayi, couldn't possibly get away with his rabbit-chased-by-hounds approach at the head of the field.

Well, Bayi did, but not before withstanding a desperate late surge by Walker in what still ranks as one of the most enthralling moments in my sports recollection. Both went under the world mark, long held by American Jim Ryun.

Over the subsequent years I would wait for news of Walker's campaigns, along with Rod Dixon and Dick Quax, in Europe, hoping to hear of world records and rematches with Bayi.

It was supposed to happen in 1976, at the Montreal Olympics, but it didn't, because the New Zealand Rugby Union, with its glib "politics and sport shouldn't mix" stance, insisted the All Blacks should tour South Africa, sparking an African boycott, an eternal blot on New Zealand's sports reputation.

That meant there would be no Bayi-Walker clash, although apparently Bayi had been no certain starter anyway, because he had been suffering from malaria and was in far from peak condition.

I'll confess now that I didn't care too much about Bayi's absence. All I wanted was for Walker to win the gold for New Zealand, and he did not let us down.

Much was also made of the slow time, the slowest Olympic 1500m in years, but again, I didn't care. Walker was not in top form either, having been hampered by a

painful injury in his lead-up, and to win was all that mattered.

It's amazing to think that 14 years after Montreal, he was still good enough to make the 1500m final of the 1990 Commonwealth Games, although it was not a happy day, and I can offer first-hand testimony of that.

My role at the Auckland games was to do interviews at the track and field. This mainly consisted of talking to foreign athletes who had done well, and, too often, to New Zealanders who had not.

England's Peter Elliott was a hot favourite for the 1500m gold, but after the semis, Walker told me he felt he had a good chance of medalling in what was billed as his last big race in New Zealand.

Any chance of that was quickly dashed when, early in the final, Walker got caught up in a tangle caused by the awkward, gangly Australian, Pat Scammell, and hit the deck.

It was an awful moment. The packed crowd went from high excitement to stunned silence, almost drawing one sharp, collective breath, and everything seemed caught in slow motion as Walker got back to his feet, and desperately, bravely, tried to reel in the pack. That he managed, but a medal was out of reach, and as much as the Brits celebrated Elliott's inevitable success, there was an undercurrent of sadness that such a great career should end so cruelly.

My own disappointment quickly turned to the cold realisation that I was going to have to interview him. John Walker was heading straight for me and he had smoke coming out of his ears.

I couldn't imagine what I should ask him, and eventually stammered out the old state broadcasting standard: "How are you feeling?"

"How would you feel if you fell over in front of 36,000 people!" came the snapped reply, before he gave vent to the frustration of all his hard work coming to nought because Scammell couldn't keep his elbows and knees to himself.

My colleagues later assured me it was a riveting interview, but that was no consolation. I hated doing it, because I hated what had happened. Fortunately I can recall other interviews, other encounters with John Walker on much better occasions. He was always approachable and forthcoming, even to a nervous 18-year trainee radio reporter who plucked up the courage to approach him back in 1978.

For all the great images of John Walker winning races and breaking records the world over, the everlasting one to me is the front-on slow motion film of him used in a TV documentary during his prime years.

That shot captured everything that made Walker one of our greatest sports icons and the hero of my teenage years...the stride of the long powerful legs, the broad shoulders, the upright head with its jutting chin, eyes squinting from the sun, the effort, and, of course, the flying long hair.

The documentary was called *The 3:49.4 Man*.

Sir Bob Jones

TOMMY DUNN

Sir Bob Jones is a noted property investor
and a boxing aficionado.

Indirectly I can thank religion for having a major beneficial influence on my life. Here's why.

In the labour-shortage late 1940s, my father, a welder, made ends meet for some years by working seven days a week and four nights overtime. He was gone by the time my three siblings and I woke in the morning and still working a half-hour bus-trip away when we went to bed each night. Thus we saw him briefly, only on Friday, Saturday and Sunday nights.

By 1951, wages had risen and he could have Sundays off. But in a small state house, with my three sisters sharing one bedroom and I in the other with my elderly grandfather, it hardly constituted a day of rest for my parents.

My mother resolved this difficulty by announcing we would go to church. She declared, with absurd working-class snobbery, that we were Anglicans, and to set an example, accompanied us on our first, and as it transpired, last church service. Once was enough and we all returned, my now subdued mother included, as raving atheists, a sentiment that has intensified with the passing years.

Religion was now out, she said, but only subject to us finding something else to do on Sunday mornings. My poor sisters became brownies and were rightly released from this horror a few months later. But what could I do?

Then through a school-mate I learnt of boxing, run from a corrugated tin shed at Taita, three miles from my home, on Sunday mornings and Tuesday and Friday nights. And so, to escape the terrible threat of superstitious nonsense hanging over me, I, a then somewhat timid 11-year-old, entered the alien, but as it transpired, wonderful world of boxing.

Nearly six decades have elapsed, but I still vividly recall that first hesitant approach and the magical Aladdin's cave of leather and liniment boxing gym smells, with 40 or 50 other boys sparring, skipping and punching bags.

But most of all, I remember our principal trainer, a dear man, Tommy Dunn, whose beloved Taita gym was his life. He had equally kindly assistants, who came and went, but somehow, miraculously, he always found time for each of us.

Tommy had won the national amateur lightweight championship in 1939, served in the navy during the war years on the Achilles, including taking part in the Battle of the River Plate, and then after the war, boxed with mixed success as a professional.

His face was battered, his nose crushed and he spoke with spluttering nasal difficulty. In short, he was a little "punchy", a term common enough back then, although out of use today. But like so many old fighters so afflicted, he took a benign view of life and saw only goodness in us all.

For us small boys, he was, of course, Mr Dunn, and for many like me, with rarely-seen dads, he became an inadvertent substitute father figure.

Soon Tuesday and Friday nights and Sunday mornings became the most important times in my then fairly spartan life.

My first-ever journeys beyond the Hutt Valley were in crowded old vehicles Tommy somehow managed to borrow, for boxing tournaments as far afield as Taihape and, on one magical occasion, a trip across Cook Strait to Picton.

Any overheard remark of disrespect, be it for our schooling, school-teachers, sisters and memorably, once, of derision for school choir participation, would lead immediately to all activity being brought to a stop.

"All boys here," Tommy would bellow, and we would gather round the ring and be subjected to an oration on the merits of schooling, choir participation or whatever mockery had induced the lecture. We took aboard these homilies, which would not have been the case had they been rendered by parents or teachers. That reflected our respect for Tommy, whose primary role as a boxing tutor extended unwittingly to that of a life mentor.

Occasionally a policeman would visit over some act of mischief after a previous training session's journey home in the dark, boxing being confined to the winter months.

Tommy's distress was palpable. We had failed him. We would be mustered ringside. "Who threw the cabbage through Mrs Murphy's window last Tuesday night?" he would croak. Silence! Tommy would then cast his eyes over the throng and invariably cry: "Where's Jimmy?" and someone would be despatched to the toilets where Jimmy, for it was usually he who had offended, was hiding. He was ultimately to become one of our senior Foreign Service diplomats.

A regular highlight was visits by a professional middleweight, the late Jack O'Leary, who would spar six rounds with a scientist, Bob Street, who was the New Zealand universities heavyweight champion. Tommy would bristle with pride at their attendance, which was usually accompanied with a lecture to us boys that if we studied hard we, too, could go to university. Few of us did, but I can recall his great joy when half a dozen years later I, too, was to capture a New Zealand universities championship in Dunedin.

A rare treat was to be one of two boys chosen to accompany him to the Wellington Town Hall for professional contests, to fill the position of bucket boy in the professionals' corners. These coveted roles were rationed around the numerous regional boxing gyms. I experienced it twice – a small boy awestruck in the presence of gods.

There are thousands of Tommy Dunns out there; unsung heroes every one, who thanklessly devote their time and passion mentoring other people's children in different activities. Sadly, it is not until we are much older that we fully appreciate their efforts and sacrifice and the positive influences they had on us.

From my perspective, looking back nearly six decades, those Taita boxing gym years under the guidance of Tommy Dunn were the strongest character-shaping influence in my life, notably in teaching independence and self-sufficiency, and, though it is irrational to many people, giving me an abiding love of boxing that has intensified with the passing years.

Lloyd Jones

MUHAMMAD ALI

Lloyd Jones is an award-winning novelist. His latest successful book was *Mr Pip*.

I inherited a book of sports autographs from my older sister.

Another sister, Pat, managed to get Mick Williment's signature for me. He managed to breach the distance between our worlds by adding "best wishes". That was special. One of the rugby gods knew about my existence. Why else would he have written "best wishes"? It was remarkable and sort of baffling.

Williment was an elegant and well-groomed player. His forté was taking the ball on the full and sliding elegantly across the touchline on his knees. The crowd would go wild. At school, though, not all of us contenders and pretenders were into that.

Bryan Williams came along just in time to remind us we had two feet and we might try to beat a man on the inside and out.

My childhood coincided with the arrival of television into our living- room, so at an early age I got to see Peter Snell make his run from the back and mow down the field in that heart-breaking way of his; he'd hit another gear and glide past the clenched faces.

I loved McEnroe for his precision and artistry and the soft touch that sat uneasily on a volcanic temperament. I especially like the *Saturday Night Live* skit of a teenage McEnroe screaming at his mother for over-boiling his boiled egg. ("You cannot be serious!")

I came to cricket late, as one inevitably does. I could watch Martin Crowe bat all day. He was so good. New Zealand athletes are generally about power. But Crowe had the same fluency and craft that McEnroe did on the tennis court.

There's a whole production line of rugby players I've admired over the years. I tend to warm to those players who break the mould. Of the current crop, Ali Williams is one of those. Is there another lock in world rugby who would take the tap himself and place a cross-field chip off the boot for his wing to collect and crash over? (ABs-Lions, third test, 2005.)

Then there are those players whose genius separates them from the rest. There aren't many of them. Richie McCaw is a special talent. Andrew Mehrtens was another. The game seemed to be played for his personal benefit. He could speed it up or slow it down as he saw fit. The game's energy level would appear to pass through his hands and feet.

Dan Carter is the same and more. The way he uses defenders for balance, allowing them to come to him and then accelerates, bouncing off them like a pinball.

In my lifetime two athletes stand out. Ed Hillary – yes, for climbing Everest, but more than that. It's what he did with the rest of his life.

The other is Muhammad Ali. He demanded his place in the world and grudgingly it made room for him.

Ali gave so much pleasure and in so many ways, with his extraordinary speed and unorthodox and sometimes foolish defence, then, finally and tragically I suppose, with his courage. I shall never forget his coming off the ropes in the seventh round against George Foreman – this after he'd offered up his body as punch-bag to wear out the younger man; the way he moved around his bigger opponent and brought him down. Even then, with his ribs damaged, no doubt exhausted, he still found his style and elegance.

Barbara Kendall

DAME NAOMI JAMES

Barbara Kendall has competed for New Zealand in boardsailing at five Olympics and has won gold, silver and bronze medals.

Settling on someone who inspired me was easy. I was only young – about 10 – when this amazing person, Naomi James, became the first woman to sail solo round the world via Cape Horn. It was even more extraordinary because she had not done much sailing at all before she headed off on this great adventure.

The fact that she was a Kiwi also seemed to give me extra interest and pride in her feats. I thought it was incredible that this woman, with so little sailing experience, took off with her cats and went round the globe.

Her feat struck a real chord with me. It sent me a strong, clear message and inspired me to live out my dreams. Her example said to me that you don't have to be ordinary, you don't have to follow others or do what they do.

Naomi followed her dreams, which is what I have done for large chunks of my life. She opened my eyes to adventure, to expression, to pursuing my passion and goals. It was incredible how this woman could contemplate, let alone succeed, with her dream. She showed the beauty of thinking and living outside traditional boundaries.

A few years later, I was sailing in the national P-class championships and was considered a bit of a favourite for the title after winning three Auckland titles. I guess deep down I thought I would do well, but I came 13th overall and second in the women's section, which meant, sadly, that I did not collect the Naomi James Trophy that I had my heart set on. However, it was an extremely good learning curve for me.

My respect for Naomi had also increased because about the time she sailed round the world, our family had sailed to Fiji. On the way back, we got caught in a storm and were very lucky to survive. It was a life-changing experience for mum, dad and we three kids when this massive cyclone hit us as we hove to for a few days. It was pretty terrifying because we did not have any fancy navigation equipment and my father and brother suffered badly from seasickness.

I remember my mother shaking when she came off her shift one day and I was giving her cuddles in our one big bed on the yacht. I thought she was just cold, but she was frightened, although she never let on to me at that stage. I have never had any nasty flashbacks or fear about the episode, although it gave me a renewed respect for the sea.

The ordeal put my parents off ocean-sailing forever. While I never hankered to do a great deal more, it did not put me off the idea. That experience certainly made me far more aware of the power of the ocean and gave me a renewed respect for its beauty and ferocity. I later lived in Hawaii, where the surf would have five-metre faces and I would go out in that stuff, but I would do so with great admiration for the power of Mother Nature.

But those things did not compare with the issues that Naomi James faced and I am still amazed at her feat. It was outrageous and it inspired me. It would be superb to meet her one day, to share some stories and just thank her for her influence on my life.

John Key

SID GOING

John Key is the New Zealand Prime Minister and leader of the National Party. After a successful career in finance, he became a Member of Parliament in 2002.

My childhood sporting hero was Sid Going.

Super Sid was a brilliant halfback for the All Blacks, the New Zealand Maori, and North Auckland. There was something about the way he grabbed the ball and ran, and the way that, when he took off, the commentators would yell "Going, going, gone!" that seized my imagination and made him a hero for thousands of kids my age.

Sid was the bee's knees when I started playing rugby. I was about eight and was a hooker of limited skill. I shifted to halfback, partly because it was the best place to be on the field and partly because that was where Sid played.

Like every halfback my age, I thought I had some of Sid's skill and flair. And I hoped that one day I'd be pulling on a black jersey with a number 9 on the back and putting the ball into the All Black scrum. Of course, it didn't take long to realise that this was just a dream, and I'd be better pursuing a career off the field!

Sid's flair, his great breaks, his ability to run with the ball, his unpredictability, and his try-scoring record, made him, in my mind, rugby's greatest halfback. He was also a brilliant tackler and even kicked goals when he needed to.

I can remember Sid going head-to-head against the famous Gareth Edwards on the 1971 Lions tour. And Sid was a key part of the great 1972-73 side that toured the UK and Ireland, and went so close to winning the Grand Slam.

I was very disappointed when, as happens with nearly every All Black eventually, Sid Going was dropped.

Despite Sid having hung up his boots years ago, I still harbour a lifelong ambition to meet him and I hope one day our paths will cross.

Jayne Kiely

JIM WESTLAND

Jayne Kiely was a leading New Zealand athlete who later became a television presenter and sports commentator.

Living in a small town with a population of only 3000, I could easily have been overlooked, even though I was fast, co-ordinated and smart. My folks were the local funeral directors. Needless to say, the boyfriends picked me up in the main street rather than at the front door!

I was blessed with athletic talent and by having a certain gentleman named Jim Westland looking over me. Jim was retired, about 65, and I was 12 and jumping out of my skin.

He watched me at the various local school athletics meets and saw something that gave him a sparkle, which he passed on to me. I was the only kid who trained before school with the aim of producing my best while at my freshest and to escape the scorching Central Otago summers.

Jim had a European philosophy – he proudly dressed in his St John Ambulance uniform to train his athletes. He was unique. Under his guidance from 13 to 17, I prospered.

The locals thought I was mad getting dragged behind his Mitsubishi Galant to increase my cadence. I dodged many a beer can as I sneaked in a training session after a successful one-day cricket match at Molyneux Park in Alexandra, respectfully declining dinner invitations from jovial provincial representative cricketers coming out of the changing rooms in their jock straps.

I had already eaten anyway, and much preferred looking at the hills and pine trees as I toiled.

Jim has long since passed on, but his work ethic and incredible insight into modern training methods put me in good stead to head to the North Island. I went on to win seven national secondary school titles and eight New Zealand track and field titles, and secured four New Zealand records.

In 1991, I not only got to meet my athletics heroes, but to compete against them (minus the steroid-induced pimples and five o'clock shadows – it was the 90s!).

Heike Dreschler and Jackie Joyner Kersee were the queens of long jump then, and I was up against them at the 1991 world champs in Tokyo. In all seriousness, I was the skinny white chick (with boobs) from New Zealand and these girls were, well, something else.

I was so overwhelmed in my first competition in the United States, where all the girls competing were black and gorgeous. Looking at all those beautiful black athletic bodies and crazy hair-styles, it was all so new to me. It got to the serious business of the competition and everyone pretty much looked down their noses at me as they had no idea where I had popped up from. Anyway, skinny white chick was leading the comp after round two, and this one girl came up to me and said: "Girl, where you from?" I said: "New Zealand." She said: "Girl, where the f*** is New Zealand?" I ended up second, made a couple of new athletics friends and handed out a geography lesson.

Training hard and making a name for yourself nationally is very special. It motivates you to keep going. But making my first true New Zealand track and field team on a world stage was something else.

Walking into an opening ceremony wearing the silver fern erases the memories of those winter beach sessions where you throw up against the tyres afterwards, the weight sessions where you cross the road, put your keys into the car door lock and collapse on to the road.

It is what we all aspire to as kids (well I did). It was like playing in the driveway with the netball hoop and saying to yourself: "If I get six in a row I will get to the Commonwealth Games one day."

Those sorts of memories are so, so vivid for me.

Being an athlete in the 80s was very exciting. Track and field was a popular sport in New Zealand. We had the Pan Am track series, which brought world-class athletes from all over the world to our country. A lot of that occurred because of the relationships that Dick Quax, John Walker, John Davies and Rod Dixon had with top middle-distance runners.

Let's face it, it wasn't worth bringing in anyone else because we didn't have the sprinters who stacked up and only a few elite field athletes.

I love the fact that I can look back and say that as a junior athlete I was in the New Zealand squad with Walker, Lorraine Moller, Mike O'Rourke and others.

Those where the days (violin music) when crowds of up to 10,000 would come and watch. I competed at Crystal Palace in London and various venues in Europe with those same numbers of spectators and I swear that the injection of hype you get is worth another 20cm on the tape measure in a long jump.

The best thing about being a New Zealander in the black singlet, and a field athlete, was that you got starts in meets in Europe. Unlike track events, which are restricted by the number of lanes, you could always squeeze in another jumper.

Quite often being the unknown and with no pressure, I pleasantly surprised myself (and my London-based promoter) and came away with wins in the smaller European meets.

I loved my time in the New Zealand track and field team and the whole era. Although I could hang my coat on the Adams apples of some of the women I was competing against, I did well, making those world champs in Tokyo, the world indoors in 1991, two Commonwealth Games and claiming various national titles and records, plus the wonderful opportunity to commentate at the 2000 Olympics and 2006 Commonwealth Games.

I don't have a shelf in my "pool room" for my memorabilia (and we do have a pool room). Instead I have a bag full of tangled medals and headless trophies.

But I look back with pride, bringing out my musty-smelling New Zealand singlets for my boys to wear as dress up and remembering that gorgeous feeling of being fit and dangerous.

I am glad I worked full-time, trained full-time and had a life as well. It has made me more appreciative of what I achieved. But I would never have got where I did without the guidance of that one man in Alexandra, Jim Westland, who saw something in me.

You wonder how many other talented young kids are out there who never get the chance to shine because of their location, so I am forever grateful to him for my passage in life, a life surely changed through sport, travel and good ethics from the St John Ambulance driver from Alexandra.

Oscar Kightley

BRYAN WILLIAMS

Oscar Kightley is an actor, television presenter and writer
with a special bent for comedy.

Forrest Gump didn't know what time it was. Life is not like a box of chocolates at all.
It's more like a K-Bar that's been left in the fridge – quite hard.

I can't remember how hard life was for Samoans in New Zealand in the 1970s, but
it was probably harder than it is now. Nowadays, Samoan folk are pretty welcome in
New Zealand. We're still at the wrong end of too many bad stats. But these days most
people know someone who knows a Samoan. If they don't, they may know someone
who hangs out with one, works with one, goes around with one, plays touch rugby with
one, has a kid with one, was bullied by one at school or was even let into a nightclub
by one. We're pretty much everywhere.

In the 1970s, though, we weren't so welcome. The National Party that swept to
power in 1975 featured as part of its advertising campaign a cartoon about Pacific
Islanders coming over in their droves, getting drunk and becoming violent and lawless.
Islander was a dirty word. We were the scapegoat du jour until different scapegoats
were to arrive later.

Around that time, the Labour department decided to use police and dogs to burst
into people's homes before dawn to look for people who'd overstayed their visas, a
crime that was virtually overlooked in the prosperous 1950s and 60s, when the country
needed workers for its factories.

While Pacific Islanders made up a third of the number of overstayers in the country
– because they were easier to spot I guess – they were about 80 per cent of those
prosecuted and deported.

Things were way worse for darker-skinned people living further along the southern
hemisphere in South Africa. There it was written into law that black and coloured

people could be treated badly. When you look back at that time, it's weird the stuff that was tolerated in the world.

For this young brown kid who arrived fresh off the plane from Samoa in 1973, at the age of four, New Zealand in the 70s could be an occasionally bewildering place. Sometimes the best way to cope was to put your head down and try not to be noticed.

And then I got my first glimpse of my hero on our family's stink old black and white TV.

A colossus of a man who was brown and Polynesian, thundering down the wing in a black jersey, striking fear of the silver fern into opponents, all the while moving with a combination of power and grace. Mr Bryan George Williams.

I couldn't give you a detailed breakdown of glorious moments in his career. I cannot recall precise details of games, or the stats or the figures, so I had to look them up.

Bryan Williams debuted against the Springboks in Pretoria in 1970. He was only 19.

From 1970 to 1978, he played 113 times for the All Blacks, which included 38 tests, during which he scored nine tries. His 66 tries in all matches for New Zealand stood as a record until John Kirwan broke it over a decade later. He also played 132 games for Auckland before retiring in 1982, the year he helped them win the national championship division one title for the first time. He was also a stalwart of his beloved Ponsonby, the oldest rugby club in New Zealand.

He had success as a rugby coach for Auckland, then as an administrator, and was a major figure when Manu Samoa announce their arrival on the world stage in their glorious 1991 World Cup campaign.

He's continued to be a passionate supporter of the game and a staunch advocate for the game's development in smaller nations.

Those are just a few of the highlights on his CV, but like I said, I can't remember all the details.

What is burned in my mind is the image that transfixed me, rooted to the spot in front of the TV when I was a young brown kid in the suburbs of west Auckland. I couldn't believe what I was seeing. One of the mighty All Blacks was Polynesian! And he was really good, too!

That sounds pretty normal now, but back then it wasn't.

Bryan Williams was the first Samoan face I saw on TV. It was the first time I ever saw a public reflection of my community in this country. And what's more, he was so good at what he did, it wasn't just Samoans who liked him.

It helped make me feel better about being Samoan at a time when Samoans were looked down upon. It helped me stand a little taller at primary school. It helped me to try a little bit harder with the hope that maybe you can do cool things in this country and people will let you. That it didn't matter where you came from.

Of course, Bryan Williams probably wasn't thinking about that while he was doing those things. He would have just been operating on that heady mix of instinct and focus as he demonstrated the art of the sidestep, while exciting a whole new generation of rugby lovers.

The All Blacks website says of Bryan Williams on the 1970 All Black tour to South

BRYAN WILLIAMS was an elusive runner and sometimes he beat not just the opposition.

Africa: "He had an important part to play in history as one of the first players to demonstrate on the field both the injustice and stupidity of apartheid."

Other All Blacks of Polynesian descent followed and they have all thrilled and inspired in their own way. Michael Jones, Inga Tuigamala, Joe Stanley, Frank Bunce, Jonah Lomu, Christian Cullen, Tana Umaga... the list goes on.

I believe it was the success of Polynesian sports heroes that started breaking down barriers for Pacific Islanders in New Zealand.

The current stars with Polynesian heritage are creating their own legacies, and no doubt more will follow.

But at that time in the world, when being a minority occasionally made for some interesting experiences, Bryan Williams was the hero that history thrust forward. He stepped up and represented his people simply by being the best at what he did.

One of the things I love about sport is how sometimes something as simple as a game can mean so much more than just the final score.

He may have been just playing a game of rugby on TV for the national team, but symbolically that helped give my life here so many more possibilities. And I'm sure I wasn't the only one.

There have been many great All Blacks – players who came from all over, from farms to freezing works, players with astounding skill and heart, who all contributed to the All Black legend.

And amid all these great players, the All Blacks official website says: "It would be hard to think of anyone who made a more monumental contribution to New Zealand and world rugby than Bryan Williams."

Thank you, sir. You are the man.

David Kirk

MEMORIES, BUT NOT SENTIMENTALITY

David Kirk captained the World Cup-winning 1987 All Blacks.
He has been a doctor and a successful businessman.

When Wynne Gray, the editor of this book, asked me to contribute I was wary. The brief was for contributors to remember a sportsperson or event that helped shape their lives or had been an inspiration through the teenage years for what they later achieved.

I have no difficulty recalling people I know to be admirable, even inspirational, in what they have given and achieved. I also have no difficulty recounting people, moments and events that have been important to me in my efforts to make the most of my talents and opportunities.

My difficulty is in putting the two together.

I can honesty say there are no people or events that I can remember, in my teenage years or at any other time, that have inspired me to achieve the sorts of things that have resulted in the invitation to contribute to this book. This is not to say that I don't have a history. Things happened to me, people were important, but none inspired me in the way I suppose the publishers of this book have in mind.

I therefore had two options. One, decline to contribute – and for a while I did my best to ignore Wynne in the hope that he would give up on me. Alas, that was not to be. He has been the proverbial dog with a bone.

The second was to relate some interesting events and people along the way that are important to me, not because they inspired me to climb every mountain and ford every stream, as the song goes, but because they were there and they still matter to me.

What lies at the heart of my unease, really, is a pathological dislike for mawkishness or sentimentality when it comes to sports success or other stories. As entertainment, *Rocky* is fine, but as a truth about what it takes to succeed it's a crock.

It is an admirable human trait to want to see the underdog win through. But for me this book is not primarily about entertainment. It is about successful people telling the truth about what it takes to be successful. For me, linking stories of inspirational people or events to later achievements as cause and effect is untruthful. And in so far as some part of this book is about inspiring others to achieve their goals, sentimentality is positively unhelpful.

This then is it, some of the things that I remember today as milestones, markers along that 20-year road that led to June 20, 1987...

Mum driving me to Saturday morning rugby, bare feet on frosty fields. A long diagonal run at aged eight – not me, mum. I had stayed the night before at a school friend's place and after staying up late, I was weary and lethargic on the field the next morning. It was half-time. Mum and dad were both there and I was mooching around, uninvolved, ineffective. Half-time and the long diagonal run. I saw her coming and wondered what it could be.

As the coach finished, mum, standing next to me, tugged on my jersey and, when she had my attention, gave me my first rocket. In motherly vocabulary, she began a long train of half-time advice amounting to get-off-your-arse-and-do-something. Make an impact! Give your best or get off the field!

I have very vivid memories of the major All Black test matches played when I was nine, 10 and 11 years old. In 1969 I remember Wales playing the All Blacks in New Zealand. Wales were the all-conquering Five Nations team and in grainy black and white on our recently-acquired first television set, Brian Lochore, Colin Meads, Ken Gray and some backs who didn't count for much (except Sid Going, who was fantastic), absolutely killed them.

The next year was 1970 and the tour to South Africa. A great All Black team off to finally win in South Africa. I had a picture of the touring team on my wall and I would wager I could still name at least 25 of the 30 players. My scrapbook covered every match.

Alas, too old, too slow in the backs, inconsistency in selections and poor goal-kicking. My first real, deep-felt disappointment in rugby. Gods were mortal after all. Thank heavens for Bryan Williams, who was the best player on either team.

And then came 1971, and Barry John, Gareth Edwards, John Dawes, Mike Gibson, Gerald Davies, JPR Williams and on and on it goes. Extraordinary players all. Particularly in the backs, they were so much better than the creaky All Blacks it wasn't funny. A good bit of biff and Ian Kirkpatrick in the second test kept us in it, but we were simply outclassed. My first realisation that there was another level of skill and talent, another world to conquer.

High school, teenage years, someone who will help you be what you can be. Jim Wallace was that person for me. Housemaster, coach of the First XV, former player, subsequent Wanganui and North Island coach and selector. A rugby brain, endlessly curious, focused on the basics – passing, running with the ball in two hands, kicking with both feet. He was uncompromising – I criticise you because you can do better, if you couldn't, I wouldn't.

Three years after leaving school I went back. Marooned as I felt I was in club rugby,

I drove to Wanganui for I don't know what really. I dressed it up as skills analysis, how to pass better, but really it was self-belief. The answer: keep working.

After school you are more than ever on your own. Every coach taught me something, the players I played with taught me a whole lot more.

A prop at club rugby scrummaging practice asks the hooker for help on Saturday defending against a massive opponent. The answer: "I've got my own job to do; it's up to you" – self-reliance.

When we're under pressure and uncertain where to attack next, JK's answer: "Just give it to me" – self-belief.

Mark Shaw trapping his fingers in the springs of a scrum machine in France and saying nothing until the scrum was over and asked why, his answer: "Because the boys had a good hit on" – toughness.

Sitting next to Michael Jones on the bus after a trial match, deputised to ask him if he would play on Sunday if selected for the All Blacks. His answer: "No, never" – strength.

Foxy holding his hands out in front, saying: "There, there, I want it there" – obsession.

Drakey, three scrums into an expected torrid session on the scrum machine: "That's it, three good ones, no point leaving it here" – it's all in the mind.

Brian Lochore finishing a team talk with: "If today each one of you outplays your opponent we will win" – simple truths.

And finally, Brigit, who taught me balance and perspective, a time for everything, including rugby.

And so it goes on, the more I remember, the more the temptation is to sentimentality and that, as I have said, is not for me. Not today.

Cindy Kiro

ARTHUR LYDIARD

Cindy Kiro was the Children's Commissioner from 2003-2009.

A sports hero? I should say Sid Going. I'm from Northland and in Northland when I was growing up, Sid Going – all the Goings, actually – were heroes. We all admired them. I'm sure up in Northland there was a general belief at the time that Sid Going was the greatest All Black ever. He was the whole province's sports hero.

But if I was to single out one particular sports hero, on a more personal note, I would go for Arthur Lydiard, the famous athletics coach.

I had a first cousin, Darrallin Burns, who was a long-distance runner when she was young, and Arthur Lydiard offered her exceptional encouragement.

We grew up in extreme poverty in Otara, in south Auckland. Sport was how Darrallin achieved; mine was more school.

Darrallin used to run in all the school and junior championships and one day Arthur was watching. After she'd run, he went over to her and asked her if she wanted to train properly. He offered to coach her and took a real interest in her.

This was quite amazing, really. This was a man who had coached Murray Halberg, Peter Snell, Barry Magee and other world-famous athletes, yet here he was at an inconsequential kids' meeting in south Auckland, making time to help teenagers he didn't even know.

I remember how kind he was to Darrallin when she needed it, because really she had had the worst kind of life.

Arthur did that for a few young athletes who might not have got any official help otherwise. He did not seem concerned with status, or money.

He was an inspiring person and he was interested in athletics, but what stuck with me was how kind he was, and how interested he was in people, no matter whether they were famous or not, rich or poor, or where they lived.

The stopwatch tells the story - **ARTHUR LYDIARD** (right) and marathon king Jeff Julian seem happy with the time at the end of a training session.

John Kirwan

WAYNE LYNCH

John Kirwan, a world-rated winger, played 63 tests for
the All Blacks from 1984-1994. He has since coached
the Italian and Japanese national teams.

Things stay with you from your childhood and there was no greater thrill for me than
watching some of the early surfing documentaries. Centre, left and right, the star was
Wayne Lynch.

He was Australian, but his nationality was irrelevant. All that mattered was his style
and expertise. He was just so smooth on the water. He seemed to be tied to his board,
and did some of the most daring moves you could imagine – he was just such a class act.

There was a radical backhand 360, which he completed with such ease. And then,
to show his courage matched his peerless skills, Lynch jumped off a 100-foot cliff to
get into some massive surf in Australia. He was such a dominant character that he
made it really difficult for me to decide whether I wanted to try for the top in rugby
or surfing.

My parents bought me a board when I was about seven and I would go and do
my athletics first, then head for the beach at Waihi and into the surf, where the
exhilaration of learning that craft was very powerful.

As I got older it made me want to travel as well, to see some of those great breaks
round the world. In the meantime, I used to head out to the softer breaks on the east
coast, then some of the more gnarly breaks at Piha or Muriwai, which really used to
scare you.

I remember burning out to Piha on one of those beautiful long summer nights
after work in Auckland and losing my board in the six-foot surf when my leg-rope
broke. That was pretty intimidating, but thankfully I survived.

I have had some similar experiences in Bali, where I once wiped out and was washed
on to the coral rock. I was struggling with little energy and then suddenly popped out

on to a reef. You need to be sensible out in the ocean, but the thrill of being out there is immense.

Lynch was able to show me that emotion and euphoria through his documentaries and that feeling has never left me.

He was a goofy-footer, with a power-surfing style. He was very aggressive and his backhand re-entries were something. When he was working his magic, surfing had a bit of a bad rap, but he helped change that image, and showed the benefits of that sort of lifestyle, as well as the skills, courage, fitness and vision needed to be a champion in the surf.

I have never met him, though I hope it might happen one day.

These days I get around the world a fair bit and always have a chance to get into the surf somewhere. There is nothing quite like it. Home is near Venice, and a hard-core group of Italians go to Venice Lagoon, where they latch on to a windswell from Africa.

I first went there in 1986 to give it a go and it was three-foot rubbish and freezing. I was not impressed. However, I have been persuaded to return about three or four times a year and you can get really sharp three or four-foot waves that do the business.

A few other weeks in Bali each year help out as well with my surfing cravings because, as Lynch showed me, there is nothing quite like being out there with nature, challenging yourself to deal with the beauty and power of the ocean.

Tom Larkin

LANCE CAIRNS

Tom Larkin, an acclaimed drummer, was one of the founders of popular rock band Shihad, which is still going strong two decades later.

I was always interested in sport. I was brought up in a cricket and rugby culture. My dad had been a representative player at both sports. I didn't really connect with rugby as much when I was young, though I follow it avidly now.

For me, cricket was the sport. I was just an average schoolboy batsman and bowler. Like all schoolboys I tried to be a fast bowler, but when I found I couldn't bowl fast I tried spin. I batted okay, but I was never a big hitter.

When I began following cricket in the 1980s, it was all about the New Zealand team. Being only a schoolboy, I didn't realise what a good team we had then. I suppose I imagined we were always that good, that that's the way it was. But when I look back now, the team was full of world-class stars, with Richard Hadlee leading the way and lots of quality players backing him up.

My hero was Lance Cairns. I'll never forget the thrill I had when he went out to bat in a one-dayer. As a kid, it was an awesome feeling, watching this big, burly man with his famous bat – Excalibur – heading for the crease. His manner, his build, his bat – it was all very exciting to a schoolboy.

I loved the explosive way he batted. With hardly any effort he'd lift the ball into a nearby street.

Of course, he was a really good pace bowler, with that unusual in-swinger's action, and that was his major value to the team.

But for us kids, his batting, and the promise of the big hitting, was what held the most appeal.

I can remember going to the Basin Reserve one day and seeing a banner that summed up how I felt. It read: *"666664 – ask for Lance Cairns"*.

Richard Hadlee was more clinical. He was astonishing and the idol of many.

But Lance Cairns was my man. Dad used to often drag us down to the cricket, and sometimes we were more willing than at other times. But it was never a chore when Cairns was playing.

Peter Leitch

SIR COLIN MEADS

Known nationally as "The Mad Butcher", Peter Leitch owns a chain of butcheries. He is an avid rugby league fan, and has worked hard promoting and fundraising for the sport.

All the assumptions, no doubt, were that I would choose someone from the rugby league world or someone connected with the butchery business who had inspired me to live my life as I do. Fair guess, but in this case well wide of the mark.

The guy who has been such an influence on me comes from neither arena, although he did carve his way through the sports world.

Ever since I first met him, and that was more years ago than I remember, Colin Meads has been my inspiration. I know it sounds a bit lame to talk like this about a person who may have been one of the toughest guys to ever play for the All Blacks, but he is such a loveable bloke. He is a Kiwi icon, and simply tops.

There are no airs or graces about Pinetree. He is an ordinary bloke who likes to have a drink, loves talking footy and gives the modern game a bit of a shake or two. He was a "steak, eggs and chips" man before a match, with a lot of beer afterwards. He wasn't the sort of bloke who needed a special diet to be able to play. And the way he played was just an inspiration.

I have the utmost admiration for guys like Reuben Wiki and Stacey Jones, who have adorned rugby league, but Pinetree has something extra. He is one of those rare people who has been blessed with the x-factor. It didn't matter whether he was playing footy, talking to the crowd afterwards, working on the farm or helping out the many charities he is involved with now, he has just got it.

One time when we were doing a promotion for the field-days in Hamilton, we got involved in a cooking demonstration. I thought this was a bit more my department, that I'd be able to sort out Colin. I was going to get him. I gave it my best shot and he killed me.

He had the crowd eating out of his hand in a very short while. He has the driest sense of humour, or maybe it's timing, because he never tells jokes. He just draws the people in. It's a combination of him being such a down-to-earth bloke and such a hard bastard at the same time that people love.

He is an uncomplicated man, and doesn't have one snobbish bone in his body. He has time for everybody and is very humble.

We do a few charity things together, like speaking at the Mad Butcher's Suburban Newspapers Community Trust, and I'm in awe of him – and I'm 64!

There are many times when Colin doesn't charge a fee, although there is a price on his evening – his beer glass or jug has to be topped up, otherwise he stops talking. People think he is joking, but I've seen it happen and I've had to scuttle over to the bar quickly and get some beer so he would carry on.

In my life I have met a great cross-section of people across a variety of sports codes. But no-one has quite the aura that Colin has. There are many other special people, but he is above all those, a man of the people.

Those of my age were brought up in an era when the All Black jersey was gold, the epitome of sporting achievement. It does not have that effect now, but in those days being an All Black, and being a great one, made you far more important than the Prime Minister. Pinetree was the best of them all.

I have heard Piney speak many times and I could listen to him again and again. He has had some tough times, and has copped his share of criticism – he is a straightforward man who at times does not think things through. But he has that aroha, that karma, that very few people have.

Over my life there have not been that many role models for me, but he would be one of the few.

He is a bloody great joker and I am so proud to have known him.

John Lister

PETER THOMSON AND OTHER GOLFERS

John Lister is a former professional golfer who competed on the United States tour during the 1970s and '80s.

My parents were sports enthusiasts who also excelled in their chosen fields. I was fortunate to inherit those genes, which brought my father, Tom, a national boxing title and helped my mother, Peggy, become a useful hockey player before she turned to golf and represented South Canterbury in the Russell Grace tournament.

We moved from Temuka into Timaru when I was about 11 and lived across the road from the Highfield Golf Course. The club had moved its headquarters out of town to the links course, but the original course remained as a public sports arena.

I took up golf then because I wanted to get involved in a sport other than rugby, at which my older brother, Tom, was making his mark.

The club across the road was very encouraging and even allowed us to form a schoolboys' section with our own starting times, coaching clinics and areas where we could sit and socialise. Eventually we had 173 members and at that time, in the mid-60s, we led the world in junior numbers and the way the club operated.

Harold Coxhead, the founder of Mutual Rental Cars (which was later sold to Avis), was a major force behind the scheme and worked tirelessly to make it function.

About the time I started to take a real interest in golf, the area hosted an exhibition featuring Peter Thomson, Harold Henning, Dave Thomas and Gary Player. This was something else for a teenager like me, who was sports-mad and developing a passion for golf. On our back doorstep we were treated to the sights and skills of Thomson, who had a magnificent swing and was possibly the best player in the world at that stage, and the others, who were very fine players.

I was not savvy enough then to understand many of the intricacies about swings, but I remember being drawn to Henning's style. He was a tall man with a slow, easy swing and for the next month or so I tried to emulate the great rhythm and tempo he had shown during the exhibition.

The appearance of those stars confirmed my decision to follow this new sport. It all seemed such a good fit.

Golf was extremely rewarding, although it could be equally punishing if things went awry. But I liked the game because you knew where you stood. The numbers on the board or on the scorecard told you what had happened, whereas in a game like rugby, you could play well but be buried in the middle of a match somewhere and get little reward.

In golf, though, it was up to the individual, and the only person you had to answer to was yourself. It was up to you to sort out your mental and physical strengths, weaknesses, limits and styles. Out on the course it was you against the rest. That sort of challenge was a magnetic force for me, one which was ignited when that fearsome foursome showed off their skills in Timaru all those years ago.

Australian **PETER THOMSON,** who did such a lot for New Zealand golf.

Jonah Lomu

MUHAMMAD ALI

After bursting into prominence at the 1995 World Cup, Jonah Lomu became the world's most famous rugby player. The big wing played 63 tests from 1994-2002.

No question about my choice. I never got to see him fight, but it has been the greatest thrill to have met Muhammad Ali when our paths have crossed.

My parents and uncles were always talking about him, how inspiring he was, how brilliant he was as a fighter, what he stood for and what he believed in, so his greatness is sort of rolled into that one package.

Ali's exploits instilled in me the importance of having the drive to succeed and his words encouraged me to achieve as much as I could, to reach for the sky with the gifts I had been given.

I have seen all his fights on tape, including that group of spectacular fights with Joe Frazier and the "Rope a Dope" special with George Foreman in Zaire. Ali had the class, skill and finesse to operate a range of styles and also that mental sharpness and conviction, which every champion needs, to work out what he had to do to win any fight.

If it meant he had to switch to southpaw or had to take his time, or even take a pounding, then Ali was prepared to do it. Some of the fights took their toll, but Ali always found a way to get the job done.

When he wanted to, he had the flashiest glovework. He was a sizzling puncher, and had great timing, speed and precision. But he was prepared to shelve those skills while he worked out an opponent before he moved in to finish him off.

Basically Ali sacrificed everything to find weaknesses in his rivals.

He was classy, cool, had great charisma and was black, so all those things were like a magnet to me. He said what he thought. He did not care what others thought – he stuck by his beliefs and he backed them up.

I ran into him a couple of times. The first was in London, when we were there for the BBC Sportsman of the Year awards in 2000. We were both adidas athletes. The first thing I did when I found out Ali was going to be at the same function was to go out and buy all these Muhammad Ali t-shirts and memorabilia.

When he walked into the room you could feel the aura of the man, the air of greatness, just like the legend of All Black rugby, which is carried forward by each generation. He walks into any function and everyone whispers that Muhammad Ali is in the room.

It was a huge thrill to talk to him at the awards dinner. Chris Eubank, the English boxer, was part of the evening and it is pretty hard for anyone to ever slow him down. He has always got something to say, but the first time I ever heard him stutter was when he went to shake Ali's hand. He was gobsmacked and the presenter even remarked on it. As Eubank later said, there is nothing to say in Ali's presence because he is the greatest of them all.

I was okay, although I was buzzed out a bit because you are meeting such a great man. He is still pretty sharp, even though he has been affected by Parkinson's disease for some time. His speech is slurred, but he is on to it. I recall Ali got up on stage and just stood there for some time before someone went up to ask him a question and he went "boo" and then "gotcha" in lightning sequence.

He looks a little frail, but everything is still working upstairs. He is a tall man and naturally has lost some of the fabulous condition he had in his boxing prime.

It was a huge thrill to meet him, though, and something that will last through my lifetime. From my young days, Ali was always someone I wanted to meet and to actually have a chance to shake his hand was something else, something you would never have thought would happen.

I asked him for his autograph. I got it on a boxing glove. I carried the glove into the dinner because I knew Ali was on the guest list, so I wasn't going to miss what I thought might be my one and only chance to meet him and get his signature.

He was the one guy I wanted to ask for a signature. It was a thrill, a high that I rode for some days and an experience I will never forget.

Ali had that aura, that wow factor. His deeds always matched or surpassed his words. He endured, and he had physical courage as well as his beliefs.

When people told him he could not do something, he did it. Like the time he opted out of boxing instead of going to Vietnam and then returned to the ring and rose to be champion again. He was something else and always will be to these eyes.

Midge Marsden

JOSH KRONFELD

During a career spanning nearly 40 years, Midge Marsden has become one of New Zealand's most acclaimed and popular musicians.

If life is a series of moments, then one that stands out for me was a barbeque in Northcote in 1990. Buck Shelford, John Kirwan, Joe Stanley and John Wright were there. Buck was the All Black captain, and Wright was the Black Caps captain. My profile as a musician was high at the time, but I was humbled by the company I was in. It was a genuine thrill to be among my sports idols in an intimate setting.

Nowadays sport and music seem intrinsically linked in the media-entertainment package. It wasn't always so. Growing up in New Plymouth in the 1950s and 1960s, when Taranaki held the Ranfurly Shield under the watch of local rugby greats like Neil Wolfe, Peter Burke, Ross Brown, Roger Urbahn and Kevin Briscoe, the domains of music and sport were worlds apart.

Life in New Plymouth in the 1950s was very sport-orientated. I played rugby and swam at Ngamotu Beach. We were always playing bullrush and last man. I was good at that stuff – I was quite small, and could run like the wind. It was about then that my schoolmates started calling me "Midget". At high school I played rugby and regularly went to Rugby Park to watch the Yellow and Blacks.

That barbeque in 1990 was an eye-opener. The lines of communication were open and free as the sportsmen and the musician sought out each other and swapped yarns.

John Wright, who was fagging up, scruffy, unshaven and keen to talk, enthusiastically informed me he owned a Marshall amp and a Fender Stratocaster guitar – iconic bits of rock and roll paraphernalia. And the barbecue's host, the inimitable Phil Gifford, was not only waxing eloquent about sport, but regaled us with well-researched stories about rock and roll, blues, soul and country music. In this personal setting, away from the public and the media gaze, the lines between the worlds of music and sport were blurred, and almost imperceptible.

Being on the road with the band had given me many opportunities for random meetings with other sports stars. Among the most memorable was running into Graham Mourie on the inter-islander ferry coming back from the South Island. We had a long chat as the ferry made its way to Wellington.

Other meetings included a neighbourly relationship with renowned cricketer John "Mystery" Morrison while we lived in Ngaio. We had become acquainted while we were at New Plymouth Boys' High School and now, so many years later, he was living next door.

As I chased the musical dream, I followed the All Blacks' fortunes with a passion, and still do. During my years on the road I read newspapers, watched the sports news, and followed the rise and rise of new sports stars.

As rugby moved into the 1990s I began to follow phenomenally-talented young flanker Josh Kronfeld. He surfaced playing for Otago in the National Provincial Championship and was fast-tracked into the All Blacks.

Josh was different. I noticed his character, his individual on-field personality, his unique approach to the game. Quirky, unpredictable, committed, he stood on the shoulders of the great No 7s, Kel Tremain, Mourie and Michael Jones.

Sitting in Raglan one evening with my manager and fellow rugby-head, Jim Rowe, we watched Josh being interviewed on television. He was talking about the fairly common phenomenon of All Blacks sitting in the tour bus playing guitars and singing. But Josh talked about how he loved to play harmonica – my main instrument. In one swoop he had confirmed for me his individuality, not just as a sportsman, but also as a budding musician. "Everybody plays bloody guitar. I wanted to be different, so I took up the blues harp," he said.

We decided to get in touch with Josh, and Jim got his phone number through the New Zealand Rugby Union. I gave him a call. I was nervous. We were going to London with the band and the All Blacks were on a northern hemisphere tour. Would Josh be interested in playing a gig with us in London?

When Josh picked up the phone he didn't believe it was me. Turned out he was a fan of blues music and had been watching my career as a journeyman musician. Mutual admiration led to collaboration. He was suitably self-effacing and ummed and aahed. "Aw mate, I dunno if could do that... I'm not that good." We hadn't met, but the repartee was established.

The first gig with Josh was in 1997 at the end of the tour of Ireland, Wales and England.

We agreed that, once his AB duties were fulfilled, we could advertise his name on the gig bill and he would play with the band at The Walkabout in Shepherd's Bush. It was a large, converted picture theatre-cum-bar – two bars and a mezzanine. The Shepherd's Bush gig had hosted other Antipodean rock and roll bands, including The Exponents, and was a hangout for New Zealanders and Australians on the loose in Europe on the big OE.

We met for the first time on the day of the gig. The ABs had drawn 26-26 with England the day before. For Josh, the prospect of playing to 1000 rugby and music fans made him more nervous than playing to 80,000 people at Twickenham. There was no rehearsal as such. I was pretty nervous myself. I was about to meet one of the most popular and great All Black No 7s face-to-face, and teach him some basic blues

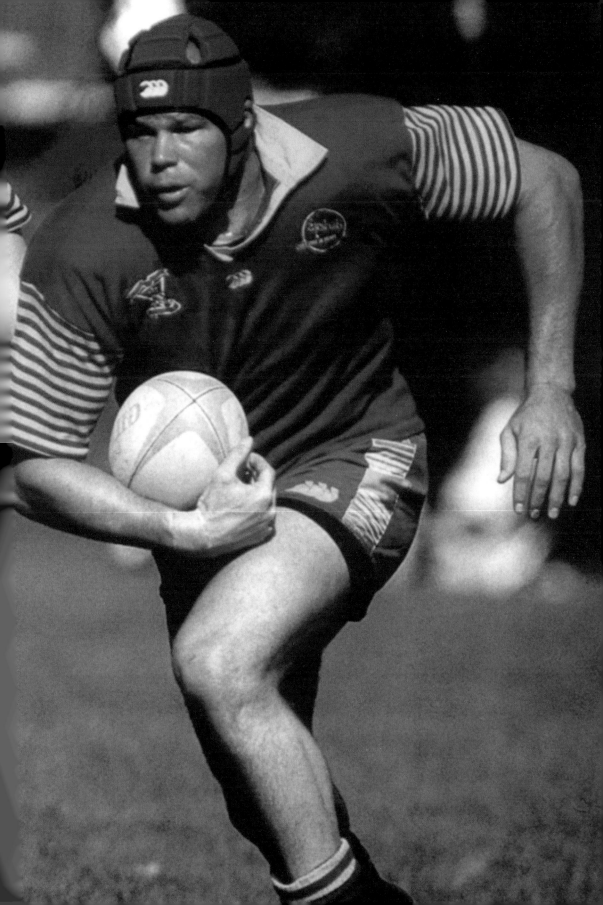

licks for the songs we were going to do together.

The well-used expression "level playing field" was exactly where we were at. We quickly ran over the tunes in a dank concrete stairwell beside the gig, while the temperature rose in the audience in anticipation of Josh taking the stage. To be honest, his harmonica technique was limited, but I knew the fervour of the crowd would see us through. Josh was worried. I said: "Man, just follow me. When I point to you, just bloody blow the hell out of it!"

The band romped through our set, cranking out renditions of rockin' rhythm and blues, finishing with *Burning Rain,* while Josh nervously paced the side of the stage waiting for his big moment. When he took the stage, the crowd went nuts. We dueted, trading harp licks, and Josh was immediately in the zone. Like his rugby, he played out of his skin. A great moment of sport and music colliding.

Carried along by the energy of the crowd, he played with unbridled enthusiasm and his limited technique rose to the occasion. The crowd loved him. On the rugby field, he was hundreds of yards away or on a TV screen. Here in Shepherd's Bush, he was right in front of an adoring crowd, who connected with the All Black and musician in an emotional close encounter. Josh blew them away.

Fellow ABs Mark Cooksley and Aaron Hopa (the gifted young Waikato lock who sadly later died in a diving accident) were on stage the whole time, waving their arms to encourage the high-spirited Shepherd's Bush crowd.

As the encores died away, Josh was swamped with fans. They wouldn't let him go. He was surrounded by admiring fans toasting The Man. There was also a fair smattering of Josh's AB team-mates in the crowd, and the punters were in rugby heaven. It was a great night, one of the most memorable gigs in my entire career.

Our friendship grew from that first encounter to the point where he began to stay at my house in Raglan quite regularly, mainly to pursue his other passion, surfing.

Those visits often coincided with his return from Super 12 games in South Africa or Australia, or local NPC games. I remember him slowly walking up my path with his bags, then plonking himself down on the couch, hardly able to move at times because he was in so much pain from the game. I'll never forget the first time he walked out of the shower in a pair of shorts. His body was covered in sprig marks and bruises and scars from previous encounters, the result of being at the bottom of countless rucks.

He would cook up a storm and over a few wines would talk about the game. The next day he'd be up early and out to Manu Bay or the Indicators for a surf, and he'd come back rejuvenated. Then I'd run him to Hamilton airport so he could be back in time for training in Dunedin.

He really loved Raglan and finally bought a piece of dirt in Whale Bay. He called me from Johannesburg one night to say his bid had been successful and that we would celebrate when he got back.

After he built his new house, I kind of missed those times when we shared music, food, wine and rugby stories. I felt privileged to have had those one-on-one conversations with Josh. Being a fan of sport, especially rugby, I got all the info about what was going on in the inner sanctum of the All Blacks – the politics, the coaching, the players who weren't pulling their weight! We established a great friendship that endures to this day.

A year later I had a call from Josh. "I've been asked to play Gershwin's *Summertime* with the Dunedin Symphony Orchestra. Can you give me a hand to learn it, mate?"

Two hours later we were in my friend Liam Ryan's Hamilton recording studio. Josh was in training gear and jandals, lunging and stretching with a Hohner chromatic harmonica cupped in his hands.

I had to lend it to him because you can't play a tune like that on a diatonic blues harmonica. Also, it was not an improvised blues piece, but a specific melody. A famous All Black struggling over a famous minor key melody. The fish was jumpin' and the cotton was high.

For the record, Josh approached learning the piece the way he did rugby training: repetition, discipline and responding to coaching. His cameo performance with his hometown orchestra later that week was a triumph. As a footnote, he has never seen the filmed concert, or heard the recorded version of his piece. And he still hasn't returned my $250 chromatic harmonica!

Bullfrog Rata and my band repeated the London trip again for the 1999 World Cup. The ABs were unexpectedly knocked out by France, and we thought our gigs with Josh would be in jeopardy.

There was a great shot of Josh on the sideline after being subbed. Totally disheartened, he turned to the camera and shrugged his shoulders with a resigned look on his face.

I wasn't particularly looking forward to facing him, but the shows we had lined up had to go on.

He seemed to handle it okay. In fact, he didn't really talk about it much, but he definitely had the blues. The final gig we did was for a function on the top floor of New Zealand House for an invited, mostly Kiwi, audience. It was one of the best gigs we ever did together, and he played out of his skin. By now he was a far more confident harmonica player.

The following year we did one more trip to London for a few gigs. By then Josh had quit the All Blacks and came over with us in a more relaxed space. His body was recovering from all the hard years of rugby and he was in a more relaxed, non-rugby mode, although he had just signed to play with Leicester.

Our trip included a stopover in Rome, where even at the airport he was constantly recognised and greeted by fellow travellers, including Lionel Richie, who was there to play some concerts.

Josh had become a seasoned performer and we cruised through the gigs. Once again we had sell-out crowds of mainly ex-pat Kiwis. Josh's enduring popularity meant he was in constant demand and he spent hours patiently chatting to everyone who wanted a piece of him.

We keep in regular contact and it was like turning the clock back during a recent New Zealand tour when Josh got up on stage with us in Dunedin and wowed the audience again.

Ivan Mauger

**RONNIE MOORE, SIR EDMUND HILLARY AND
SIR ROGER BANNISTER**

Rated the finest speedway rider ever, Ivan Mauger won
six individual world titles from 1968-79, plus nine others
in long-track, pairs and team.

I've had three heroes in my life – Ronnie Moore, Sir Edmund Hillary and Sir Roger
Bannister.

Ronnie was New Zealand's first world speedway champion, and was also speedway's
first boy wonder. He was the reason I, and many others in Christchurch, wanted to be
riders. When he went overseas he was a teenage sensation. In 1954 he won the world
title for the first time, and became a hero throughout New Zealand.

For the technically minded, he rode slow-revving long-stroke JAP engines, with
spindly frames and a 22-inch rear wheel – this at a time when tracks had plenty of grip
on the rear wheel and were very hard to turn at speed.

His successors generally rode high-revving engines, 19-inch rear wheels and on
tracks that were very slick and with not much grip. In laymen's terms, the bikes and
tracks were 70 per cent easier to ride in later years than when Ronnie started.

In 1950, he went to the famous Wimbledon team in the British first division, having
turned 17 on the voyage to England. He was sensational, and qualified for the world final
at Wembley that same year. Ronnie is still the youngest to qualify for the world final.

Back in New Zealand, in those pre-television days, he was like a rock star, a
predecessor of Elvis and the Beatles.

I have many times been asked how I got started in speedway and I always give the
same answer: when you're young, you want to be like your hero. Kids in Spain wanted
to be bullfighters, whereas Kiwi kids would go to an All Black test once a year and
there would be 45,000 or more at Lancaster Park. The All Blacks were a bit special.

But there were 10,000-odd going to the Aranui Speedway every Saturday night
from October to March. That was the biggest thing happening in Christchurch and
Ronnie was the star, so of course we all wanted to be like him.

My mates and I rode on cycle speedway and used to ride our bikes to the corner
of Pages Road and Rowan Avenue in Aranui by 3pm, because the riders had started
to arrive by 4pm. We were really only waiting for Ronnie to arrive. He would always
have the latest big flash English car, with a trailer and two beautiful bikes. When he
turned the corner, we used to rush into the Aranui Stadium and go to the bridge that
overlooked the pits. We never took our eyes off him all night – we watched everything
he did in the pits and on the track.

If there was no Ronnie Moore, I doubt very much whether there would ever have been a Barry Briggs or an Ivan Mauger in speedway.

Ronnie won his second world title in in 1959 and when I won my first championship in 1968, I thought I would be a bit of a star with my mates in Christchurch, but they were not overly impressed! I won it in 1969 and again in 1970, which impressed them a bit, but I was still Ivan from the cycle speedway team and the Olympic Harriers, and nothing like Ronnie. However, when I won the world pairs championship with Ronnie in 1970, that impressed them. I had won with our hero, so at last I was accepted as at least an equal of Ronnie.

I rate that pairs win second in importance only to my first individual world title in 1968. I felt like King Kong standing with him on the podium in Sweden that night.

I was at Newcastle speedway in New South Wales in 1974, when Ronnie had a career-ending crash. I was leading one of the races at the world series meeting and Ronnie was in fourth place on a borrowed bike when he crashed. The red lights came on immediately and I was the first rider to get to where Ronnie was lying on the track. He had swallowed his tongue and a paramedic was trying to get it out of Ronnie's throat and had an oxygen tank with what looked like an end to put in someone's mouth to help breathing.

The paramedic was struggling to free Ronnie's tongue, so I reached into his throat, pulled his tongue out and administered the oxygen.

Briggo and I have often discussed that situation. I don't think I could do it again. Fortunately, on the spur of the moment it was just a natural thing to do. Ronnie had

Happiness is winning a world title with your hero. Ivan Mauger (left)
and **RONNIE MOORE** after they won the world pairs title in 1970.

serious head injuries and was taken to the Newcastle Hospital. Briggo and I abandoned our last rides and went in the ambulance with Ronnie.

About midnight they told us to go to the hotel and that they would call if there was any change. Briggo, his wife Junie, and Raye and I could not sleep. We were in our room and at 2am the hospital called us. A man said in a matter-of-fact voice: "If you guys want to see your mate alive you had better get here quick."

We jumped into the car, didn't stop at red lights and arrived at the hospital in record time. I told the surgeon: "Ronnie is a special person and a fighter, so get back in there and fix him up."

The surgeon came out a little later and told us Ronnie's only chance was to go immediately to the main head injury hospital in Sydney, 100 miles away.

Briggo and I tried to hire a helicopter, but there was none available until 7am. The surgeon said an ambulance would take a couple of hours, so it was decided to transport him that way in an air-bed. We were all down at the Sydney Hospital by 8am. The surgeon there said it was just as well we couldn't get the helicopter because Ronnie would have died because of his serious head injuries if he was above 500 feet.

Happily, Ronnie recovered in the next year or so and is okay now.

The most amazing thing about Ronnie is that he is still a hero with kids at the track named after him – Moore Park in Christchurch. Most of their parents were not born when he had his big accident.

There is much more to Ronnie than his world championships. He is a very nice person, quite unassuming and with a friendly word for everyone.

Ronnie has been my hero from when I was 10 and remains so today.

There is no doubt in my mind that Sir Edmund Hillary was the greatest ever New Zealander. He took over temporally from Ronnie as my schoolboy hero when he became the first person to reach the top of Mt Everest. I was at an impressionable age and remember it as if were yesterday how proud I was that he was a New Zealander.

I was always very proud to represent New Zealand and I'm sure that feeling came from the day Edmund Hillary "knocked the bastard off".

It is an incredible feeling to stand on the No 1 position after world championships and have the national anthem played and the flag raised and realise it is for you after all your efforts and sacrifices. With no crowd to salute him, the young Edmund Hillary must surely have felt that pride when he was the first to plant the flag on the top of Everest on May 29, 1953.

I met Sir Edmund at a function at New Zealand House in London, in about 1971. He was very easy to have a conversation with. Of course, I asked him questions that he had been asked hundreds of times, including what the most difficult part was. I don't remember what part he said, but his answer to my question was that at one stage he was faced with about 400 feet of ice that was virtually straight up!

I can't remember exactly how it came about, but at one stage I asked him what the weight of his backpack, oxygen bottles etc had been. He said about 70 pounds. I reflected that that was about the same weight as one of our speedway engines.

In the early '90s I began running international academies and introduced many new training methods for modern types of machines and techniques, mind-power training and motivational aspects. At one point, I put some plastic markers in different parts of the track and tell the pupils to weave in and out of them and gradually speed up until they can do it at full throttle.

At every academy a few of the guys tell me that it's too difficult. I quote Sir Edmund and tell them to imagine having their engine strapped to their backs and then climbing 400 feet of ice straight up.

I stress to them that that's difficult and that what I'm asking the pupils to do is not. I don't get any arguments from them after that message.

My wife, Raye, and I were so very proud to be two of the 600 people to be invited to the service on January 22, 2008, at Holy Trinity Cathedral for Sir Edmund's funeral.

I particularly liked the piece in the funeral booklet which typified everything he stood for. It goes like this: "I have had the world lie beneath my clumsy boots and saw the red sun slip over the horizon after the dark Antarctic winter. I have been given more than my share of excitement, beauty, laughter and friendship. Each of us has to discover his own path, of that I am sure. Some paths will be spectacular and others peaceful and quiet – who is to say which is the most important? For me the most rewarding moments have not always been great moments – for what can surpass a tear on your departure, joy on your return, and a trusting hand in yours?"

Last but not least, my third hero is Sir Roger Bannister, who inspired me to do things most people in speedway thought were impossible.

On May 6, 1954, Bannister became the first person to break the four-minute barrier for the mile. He broke the record at the Iffley Road track in Oxford, England.

It was an achievement which to a teenager was on a par with being the first person to climb Everest.

There are always very special humans and Roger Bannister was certainly one of them. He broke the four-minute barrier when I was running for Olympic Harriers in Christchurch and following athletics closely.

In that era, there were many great milers, all trying to be the first to beat four minutes. I followed all their attempts in our local Christchurch newspapers – no Sky TV channels in those days!

From the mid-1960s I began to be invited to Sportsman of the Year dinners in various countries and soon learned that if I arrived an hour or so before the scheduled time I could look at the table plan and pretty much choose who I wanted to sit with. It was quite easy to change the seating plan.

I wanted to sit with individual world or Olympic champions, from whom I could learn training methods, ideas on psychology, and mental and mind-power techniques. As a result I sat with Roger on numerous occasions – and sometimes he would comment that we were on the same table again. I never confessed to him that I had arranged it most of the time!

As with Sir Edmund Hillary, Bannister proved that what previously had been thought impossible could be done and it wasn't long before lots of guys believed they could do it. At the highest level, belief is one of the strongest assets an athlete can have.

Richie McCaw

MY GRANDFATHER JIM

Richie McCaw is the All Black captain. Regarded as the world's best openside flanker, he made his test debut in 2001.

As a teenager, I spent a lot of time with my grandfather Jim at Wanaka. He would take me fishing in the evenings. While I enjoyed that pastime, it was also a great chance to quiz him about his times as a fighter pilot in World War II. He was part of 486 squadron, based in Britain, and told me how he had shot down 19 VI flying bombers during some of his missions. He told me stories all the time, not in a boastful manner or in any attempt to glamorise those events, but because he knew I was really interested in aviation and anything associated with that industry.

I just loved sitting there, listening to all these stories that I thought were pretty cool.

I grew up on a farm and each weekend as a young fella, I remember going to the airstrip on my grandfather's farm, where my father and his brothers would all be indulging their passion for aviation. It was in the family's blood, I guess, and I was no exception.

My father was a tow-pilot as well as a glider pilot, and I would hang around the airstrip for long periods. The passion grew from there.

I'd have the odd ride in his two-seater, and when some of my mates came and stayed, they would also get a flight, which they thought was pretty cool. It seems flying has been around me since I was born and I count myself very lucky for that.

We had a spell where my father sold his glider and bought a boat, but he kept his aviation licence and in the last five years when I have got back into gliding as a mix of recreation and therapy, dad has picked it up again. We talk a bit about rugby, of course, but there is also an awful lot of discussion about weather forecasts, climate patterns and flying conditions, especially in the best months for gliding, before and after Christmas.

We'll go down to Omarama, which is only about 40 minutes west of where the family farm was, and we will holiday there. It's funny after all these years away, to be returning to somewhere that is so familiar.

It's a great environment because all the people there are so passionate about gliding, and we get into some pretty robust discussions about all sorts of theories. I can just go there and relax. I am just one in a group of aviation fans. Rugby gets a mention, but it's a side-issue during those times.

Gliding is a great challenge because you are learning something new on every flight. Each one has its own subtleties. You are never quite sure how much lift you are going to get, or how far you are going to travel. Trying to get home is often quite a thrill.

Being up in the air is both peaceful and demanding. And it is freedom, an escape. Nothing is ever quite what it seems, either. Sometimes you end up back at the airstrip in 20 minutes from a flight you thought might have lasted a couple of hours, while at other times you might be away for five or six hours and cover 400km.

I have flown more than 100 hours in a glider now, and the scene has changed markedly from the time I was first involved, watching my father.

The people have not altered, but there are kids as young as 14 or 15 who are flying solo now. I first went solo in 2002, and have pushed that more and more in the last few years.

It's an interest and a passion, but the real challenge is the technical part. A lot of people can fly and get a glider off the ground and back to the airstrip. But the good pilots stand apart because they make the most of every bit of lift and have the ability to sniff out all the best places to find that lift. This is where my competitive nature kicks in.

The idea of racing gliders with all the extra bits, like map-reading and gauging the weather, is the part that fascinates me. Every cloud means something and gives you clues about lift and direction.

People get the idea when you are sitting there in the cockpit that it's all serene, but a glider can be very noisy, especially when you're travelling quickly. You have to concentrate all the time, thinking about where you're going, planning where you might land if there is no lift and always working out where the wind is coming from. It's stimulating, busy and a refreshing escape from my regular rugby routine.

Back in 2001, when I became involved in my first six months of professional rugby, I was also studying at university. It was difficult, but each discipline was a release from the other, and while I did not realise it then, they counter-balanced each other. By the end of 2002, I was even more heavily involved in rugby and had stopped going to university.

When I was able to step back, it was obvious there was an imbalance there – my life was skewed too much towards rugby.

So I went and sat my aeroplane licence, did some flying and my life seemed to have much more balance to it again. It was a good lesson and one my grandfather would have been proud of.

Gary McCormick

KEN GRAY

Gary McCormick is a television star, raconteur, corporate speaker, radio commentator, comic, published poet, author and veteran surfie.

Growing up in Titahi Bay, Porirua, during the 1960s, sports heroes seemed a million miles away. I was a side-drummer with the Mana College Military Band and we (all 80 of us in the band) got to lead the procession through the streets of Wellington before a rugby test and spell out the words LIONS VS ALL BLACKS, or SPRINGBOKS VS ALL BLACKS before the tests at Athletic Park.

But heroes, or indeed celebrities of any kind, never touched our lives. We lived celebrity-free lives!

I followed the Porirua Rugby League Club because they were tough, man! When they played Wainuiomata or Petone, it was out-and-out war.

In about my fifth form year, when I was 15 or 16, and coming into my own as a surfer, I needed to earn some money for a new surfboard.

Someone at Mana College told me that Ken Gray might have some work on his farm. I don't know where I got the courage to go over and ask him, but he gave me a job cleaning up and helping in the woolshed for a week or so.

I remember his massive hand when he shook mine and those deeply recessed eyes with the strongest stare in the world.

Working with him, he appeared to be the perfect gentleman. I cannot recall him ever swearing in the shed and he could toss sacks of wool around like dice.

I had imagined I was fit because of the surfing, but it was impossible to keep up with Ken. He had a great laugh. It was very affecting, because he had a naturally serious face and when it broke into a smile, it was like an Easter Island statue breaking up.

Ken was the first man I recognised for his sheer strength and measured manner. A man who knew his strength and exercised it with humility.

Of course, he went on to make his stand on the Springbok tour. In a quiet, dignified way.

We don't get many leaders like the late Ken Gray. He was intelligent, perceptive and a giant of a man in every sense.

Suzanne McFadden

MARTIN SNEDDEN

Suzanne McFadden is a journalist who established her reputation as a sports reporter for the *New Zealand Herald*.

Never has there been a more golden, glorious summer in my life than the New Year of 1983, a summer of lemonade popsicles, bronzed skin and beige pyjamas. I was 15, yet to be beguiled by boys or Elvis Costello, and I remember it being hot, and having my best tan ever.

Richie Benaud thought it was blistering too, so much so he wrote a book he called *The Hottest Summer: World Series Cup Cricket*. For me, too, that summer and cricket melted together.

My sister and I spent the school holidays at my uncle's motel and camp ground on the dazzling white-sand spit at Taipa in the Far North, running as part of a mob.

It was the only gang of kids I'd ever been in, and the worst things we did were eat too much sugar, ride untethered in the old Trekka – 12 kids, no seatbelts – and throw rocks at naive John Dories swimming under the bridge.

We waterskied, played beach volleyball before it was cool, fished, did the tuatua twist, used the camp's steel rubbish bins for cricket wickets, and got gobbled alive by sandflies.

On Saturday, January 13, the day before the three-hour drive to the beach, we ate dinner in front of the TV during a one-day international between New Zealand and England in Brisbane – the last 10 overs bowled after the news.

At the time I had more than a passing interest in cricket, simply because I loved watching any sport with my father, Ray. He was a natural all-round sportsman, and he had played rugby for North Auckland, but he was blessed with two daughters and no sons, and I felt somehow guilty about that. So from the age of eight, I would get up in the middle of the night for All Black tests played in the northern hemisphere.

In this ODI in the Benson and Hedges World Series Cup, New Zealand (long before they were the Black Caps) had set England a chase of 241, and the English needed 17 runs off the last three overs on a sluggish pitch.

The hunt was excruciating, I kept running from the room or tugging the lounge cushions down over my head. Vic Marks need to smack three off the last ball for England to win, but Martin Snedden bowled him, and victory was New Zealand's. I think Snedden's final ball was a yorker, because I'd never heard the word until that game.

There could have been so many heroes from that victory – Richard Hadlee, Lance Cairns, Glenn Turner on his return to international cricket. But it was Snedden who from that moment became my sporting idol.

Not like a girl with pin-ups, who fancied the cut of his brown polyester trousers. No, there was something about his head-down, gritty Kiwi battler style, his honest medium-fast deliveries, and his persistence through some pretty up-and-down times that year (remember the world's worst one-day bowling record, conceding 105 runs off 12 overs in the World Cup?), that struck an impressionable 15-year-old.

During that long summer holiday at the beach, we would constantly have a transistor radio outside a tent, tuned to New Zealand's fortunes in that drawn-out series in Australia. A thin sheet of cloud overhead would be enough excuse for me to sit in front of the motel's TV all day and score the innings with dot balls and Ws.

I cut out every newspaper article from the *New Zealand Herald* and the *Auckland Star* that had anything to do with the New Zealand side and kept at least three detailed scrapbooks with statistics, the players' middle names and even, I'm almost too bashful to admit, songs and poetry I'd penned about the seemingly great feats of '83.

Through the winter, when I was reluctant to get out of bed in the mornings to go to school, my father would open my door and would describe Snedden's skills in less than complimentary terms to raise my hackles and my head.

I am hardly embarrassed about my teenage fixation for cricket, that New Zealand team and Snedden. It led to good things. The following year I captained the girls' XI at school, and wrote sports reports for the school journal. And ultimately that idyllic season set me on a path to becoming a sports journalist – not so straightforward in a male-dominated domain, I came to discover, but that's what I became, through a bit of Snedden-like doggedness, I'd like to think.

About a decade later, when I was a reporter on the *Herald*, I accidentally bumped into my hero in the doorway of the bakery across the street. He won't remember it; I'll never forget it. Another 15 years passed before I got to say more than "oops, sorry" to Snedden, when I interviewed him after he left his chief executive's role at New Zealand Cricket to head Rugby New Zealand 2011.

Even then I was too shy to reveal to him the role he had unwittingly played in my career. But on each of the occasions I've had to sit and talk with him since, it has only reinforced one thing. I chose the right hero that golden summer.

Sir Colin Meads

BOB SCOTT

Sir Colin Meads is often cited as New Zealand's greatest All Black. He played 55 tests, mainly as a lock, from 1957-71 and was named Player of the Century in 2000.

As young men, making our way into the rough and tumble of the rugby world, my brother Stan and I were slightly isolated from what was going on in the rest of the sporting arena. We used to follow as much as we could about our favourite sport in the newspapers and on radio, but it was nothing like the instantaneous news and updates you get these days through television. We always collected much more information when we were on tour with King Country or the All Blacks. We were not so cut off then.

However, the news always filtered through when you talked to others who had played in various games or you eventually saw footage or reports on what happened in tests, high-pressure Ranfurly Shield or provincial matches.

There were any number of heroes for me, men whose play and calibre I really respected. Tiny White was a big raw-boned bugger from Poverty Bay who I played against in the All Black trials in 1956, and he was the epitome of New Zealand's uncompromising forward play.

Fred Allen was another rugby figure who had a big impact on me, although I never got on that well at the beginning with "the Needle". We are good friends now and he was a great coach, but we were never really close when he was in command of the All Blacks, because he was the boss and we were the pupils.

There was never that sort of divide between players.

I always drew inspiration from a player like Bob Scott, a remarkably gifted fullback who, when he finished playing rugby, became involved in all sorts of charity work in which he would help out children and many others less fortunate than himself. He gave his time, his wisdom and his expertise and I have always felt that was marvellous.

He provided inspiration to me as I was coming through the grades, and he still has that effect on me. I run into him a few times every year at rugby reunions, bowls functions or at matches, and he is such a great man, a terrific old fellow. And he is still bloody good at bowls, tough to beat, a heck of a competitor and still an inspiration to me.

Bob was ahead of my time, but I was fortunate enough to be involved in a charity match with him when I was a teenager. I was invited down to the West Coast for the game. Bill Freeman coached one side and famous players like Ron Jarden and Scott were involved. It was a stunning experience for a kid from the King Country to be involved, and it made a huge impression on me.

About the same time, Stan and I were listening to the radio while our parents were overseas, and we heard Bob explaining the importance and techniques involved in kicking during rugby games. He was adamant that all players, not just backs, should be able to kick with both feet. I'll tell you what: that had Stan and me out there in the backblocks on the farm whenever possible, practising kicking with either peg so that in time both of us were fairly proficient and would have passed any of Bob's kicking exams.

Down the years I'm sure I kicked a few left-foot punts during matches, especially provincial games, but it was about 1963-64, when the rules allowed you to mark the ball from a kick-off, that this skill came into its own. Wilson Whineray and I used to fight for the call and the ball – it was a part of the game then for the forwards.

I also remember drop-kicking a goal for King Country, the only one I ever did, in one of my very first games for the province. North Island selector Jack Finlay happened to be at the match in his official capacity. I was about 17 and there was this kid, playing at lock, drop-kicking a goal. I was out of position, trying to get to a ruck and there were not many backs around when the ball squirted out, so I grabbed the pill and dropped it over from about 20m, a wobbly old thing, but it went over.

Kicking by forwards became part of the game in '63-64 because you could mark from the kick-offs and it was a useful tactic on the provincial rugby scene. Lineouts were a bit of a shambles then, something of a lottery, but we were able to arrange things better from kick-offs, and often found ourselves kicking the ball well enough, I hope, to have satisfied that master technician and true gentleman, Bob Scott.

Bernice Mene

MY PARENTS MENE AND SALLY

Bernice Mene was an athletic goal keep and goal defence who represented the Silver Ferns from 1992-2001, playing 78 tests. She was the captain for two years.

I feel like my story has probably been told already and is very cheesy, because I grew up in a household where sport was very much the norm and a lifestyle. I do not remember having sporting idols as such, but mum and dad had the most influence shaping me into the person I am today. We really did not do much sports-watching because we were "in" it or out doing it when we could.

As far back as I can remember, QE2 Park in Christchurch was our second home. On Saturdays, mum would pack a chilly bin or "food bag" and we'd get dressed in our athletics gear first thing in the morning. Children's athletics meetings ran in the morning and often we scoffed down lunch and raced indoors to the pool for a swim before returning to the track to sneak in to bounce on the high jump mats, paddle in the steeplechase water jump, play in the greyhound starter cages or simply watch mum and dad compete.

During our teenage years, we migrated into the afternoon competition and often there was a twilight competition or even social drinks after the final relays were run. The days at QE2 were long, but we never seemed to tire of entertaining ourselves. As we got older, Sundays, too, were taken up with athletics or other sport as our range expanded.

As a family, we all went down to the park to train together or in the winter we would often all head to Hagley Park in the yellow Ford Falcon and would drop off at either the netball or the rugby first, depending on the timing of each game.

Things were not always smooth sailing though, particularly with the very competitive nature of the family members, and our parents coaching us all in various codes.

I recall mid-week training at the athletics ground, finishing at the shot put circle and the sun starting to set as dad kept saying, "Ten more", then shaking his head, "Not good enough", and me getting grumpy, with myself mainly, but grumbling at him. In my mind it was his fault we were not at home eating dinner!

Understandably, he was tougher on us because he could be and because, he maintains, he could see the potential in us. He wanted us to keep improving and pushing ourselves, training harder and aiming higher.

At athletics, dad trained my two brothers and me, as well as an entire stable of athletes (who were like extended family), while mum had a few key athletes and coached many of my netball teams, as well as running the household, cooking meals, doing washing (all things I only now appreciate as a mother).

Mum was teaching full-time and dad worked shiftwork as an aircraft engineer for Air New Zealand.

As Chris, Nathan and I reached representative honours, we always had support. We would all travel long distances to compete or watch one another compete, and if overseas sports trips were an option, then the mortgage was extended to get us there. There was always a way and life was for all of us rich in experience owing to our parents' enthusiasm, can-do attitude and commitment to us all.

Even now when we get together, it's chaotic – mum and dad are racing off to golf and my husband [Dion Nash] is selecting or watching cricket, my big brother is coaching, or we are running around with our own families.

One Christmas we had a doubles tennis competition after breakfast and presents opening – dad and I were randomly pulled out of the hat as a pairing. I am not too flash with a bat on the end of my long levers, so there was lots of laughter, lots of flying limbs, and a few strains on our side of the net, but we really did not even feature in the fiercely competitive games happening around us.

FOOTNOTE: *Bernice's father, Mene, and mother, Sally, were both champion athletes. Mene Mene represented New Zealand in the 1974 Christchurch Commonwealth Games, finishing sixth in the decathlon. Sally Mene, represented New Zealand in the discus and javelin at the 1970 and 1974 Commonwealth Games, finishing seventh in the discus both times.*

Peter Montgomery

PETER JONES

"The voice of yachting", Peter Montgomery has been a leading New Zealand sports broadcaster since the 1970s and has covered eight Olympic Games among a host of international events.

"And on the halfway mark he throws it in. In it goes, in the front of the lineout. Hemi comes through with the ball at his toe. Going to it he knocks the ball out of Dryburgh's hands. And Jones is coming down. He takes it and he's running to the goal-line. It's a try to New Zealand, it's a try to New Zealand. Peter Jones has scored..."

The Peter Jones try is *the* moment in New Zealand sport seared in my mind like nothing else. The try and its impact made a huge impression on me. I was with my parents in Dunedin listening to Winston McCarthy on the radio commentating the fourth test of the 1956 Springbok tour.

This was more than a try. This was more than a game. This had significance beyond sport. For many New Zealanders this was much more than the last test of a rugby tour. National identity and pride were at stake. The try and the series win gave New Zealand a lift away from the long shadow of the war and enabled us to shake off some of the demons and injustices of the 1937 and 1949 series against the Springboks.

New Zealand was a different country then, a different world. Rugby clubs were the centre of communities across New Zealand.

Tours were years apart. The planning, anticipation and expectation were as important as the games. Rugby tests were occasions people planned for months ahead. In a good year there would be only four tests. So much was different. No reserves were allowed. Sometimes seriously injured players returned to the field. Most male spectators wore hats. There was no television.

There has never been anything like the build-up to the 1956 Springbok tour.

I was too young to know about settling old scores. But my father often told me of the injustices of past years. When the '56 Springboks arrived in New Zealand, the

When he wasn't putting fear into opposing players, **PETER JONES** was a fisherman in Northland.

country was consumed. I was at Carisbrook for the first test, on July 14, 1956, sitting on top of the Craven A sign to see the All Blacks win 10-6.

On September 1, 1956, New Zealand was under a spell of test match hype that has never been repeated. If you were not at Eden Park, then radio and the outstanding broadcasting of Winston McCarthy was the only way to know what was happening.

His brilliant commentaries were a magnet and an inspiration.

The try by Peter Frederick Hilton Jones was the decisive moment in the grim, tough test won 11-5 by the All Blacks.

New Zealand beat South Africa for the first time in a test series and South Africa were beaten in a series for the first time in 60 years.

For those who did not experience the '56 tour, it may be hard to comprehend the effect of the try by Peter Jones. It was much more than the decisive moment of the test and the winning of the series. It had a social knock-on effect as well.

It helped change the way New Zealand thought of itself. It helped New Zealand grow up. A try, winning a test, winning a test rugby series, had an effect on New Zealand society that would not happen today.

After the match Peter Jones said he hoped he never played in a tougher game because he was "absolutely buggered".

Today "bugger" is accepted in everyday language. But in 1956 it was definitely not acceptable for broadcast. The honest summary from the Northland fisherman enhanced his folk-hero status. New Zealand was proud. New Zealand was smiling.

At Christmas 1965, on a visit to the far north, I popped into the Waipapakauri pub with some friends and there right in front of me was my hero, P F H Jones, wearing a life-jacket. He had just come ashore from fishing off Ninety Mile Beach. He was so unassuming and friendly, and very happy to chat.

Many years later, my broadcasting duties took me several times to Okara Park, Whangarei. There I was able to talk to Peter Jones without his halo.

One day I told him we had a family joke after 1956 and that he was one of the Three Great Ps of New Zealand rugby born in Kaitaia.

He wondered what on earth I was on about. So I explained.

Peter Frederick Hilton Jones, Patrick Timothy Walsh, who was also a hero of the '56 series, and Peter John Montgomery were all born in Kaitaia.

Peter Jones chuckled and a huge smile crossed his face. He was not surprised to hear of the tenuous link of associating our birthplace and first initial. Peter was humble and modest, but aware that his famous try had made an impact on so many people in many different ways.

Don Neely

SIR DONALD BRADMAN

Don Neely is a sports historian and author. He was a first-class cricketer, and then, for 14 years, a New Zealand cricket selector.

Eighteen months after I was born in 1935, my Scottish immigrant parents were fortunate to receive one of the first state houses built for rental by the State Advances Corporation.

It was in Miramar, and in the midst of these houses was Crawford Green, which became Twickenham, Wembley, Lord's, Yankee Stadium and the Melbourne Cricket Ground for all the youngsters growing up in the area.

The heart of New Zealand softball was in the eastern suburbs of Wellington, with Miramar Aces, Broadway Demons and Jenkins Gym all winning the national club competition in its first 10 years. So naturally, until the age of 12 I was a promising softballer.

Then I became an avid reader and at a time when you were allowed to borrow only one book at a time, I was forever running to the Miramar Public Library in Chelsea Street. There was a miniscule section given over to sports books, and there was nothing on softball. A small beige-coloured book, little bigger than the *Readers Digest,* caught my eye. The spine read – "Bradman – Moyes – Angus and Robertson". I must have borrowed that book once a month for the next six months, until the librarian asked me to borrow something else.

Ian Peebles, an England test cricketer from 1927–1931, once wrote that there is no cricket fan like a 13-year-old boy. His ambition to play test cricket was lit when he saw the Australian team play in Glasgow in 1921.

The bug settled in my bloodstream – where it has ruled ever since – while I was reading Johnnie Moyes' book on Don Bradman.

It covered not only his exceptional career to date, but also his place in the history of

A PLUCKY BATSMAN

Don Bradman's pluck and quality of adaptability lead Australian critics
to expect much of him during the coming English tour. The advent of
the breaker of many records is keenly awaited in England.

cricket in Australia, and the great players who preceded him. Thus I met my sporting hero and was introduced to the history of cricket.

At 13 I cycled to the Wellington Central Library and devoured all the cricket books that I could find. I was in my element at Rongotai College, where a place in the cricket First XI became my long-term goal.

In the fifth form (year 11 in today's terms), our English teacher suggested to six of my classmates that they should enter the junior oratory contest, the subject being "A person or event of importance in history". These boys were the brightest in the class or had a history of entering elocution contests or were budding actors with Nola Millar at Unity Theatre. The competitor in me drove me to enter. My subject? Don Bradman.

I had never addressed a group of more than my classmates and was extremely nervous speaking to a full assembly hall. It was one of the most exhilarating moments of my life when the adjudicator, Professor Joan Stephens of Victoria University, awarded me second place and told me that what I lacked in poise I more than made up for in the intimate knowledge that I had of my subject. Once again I was grateful to my sporting hero.

In 1994, my wife Paddianne and I wrote *The Summer Game – The Illustrated History of New Zealand Cricket*. I sent a copy of the book to Sir Donald, because on page 130 there was a photograph taken in 1937 of Don and Jessie Bradman sitting on a grass bank in Adelaide with Curly and Phil Page and Jack and Edna Kerr. On their way home from a tour of England, the New Zealand team played three Australian state sides, the first of which was South Australia, and this happy photograph had been taken on Jack Kerr's box brownie camera on the rest day, Sunday, when players socialised.

I promptly received an aerogramme of thanks by return mail congratulating Paddianne and me on such a quality production. I still treasure this letter today.

During the last few years I have been asked to deliver many eulogies at cricketers' funerals and I am always reminded of my indebtedness to Sir Donald Bradman.

Sam Neill

PETER SNELL

Sam Neill has starred in more than 50 movies since his first, in 1977, in addition to appearing in a number of television classics.

There was a time when New Zealand seemed to own middle-distance running. We took it for granted. So many greats – Halberg, Davies, Quax, Dixon, Walker. But head and shoulders above them all was the greatest, Peter Snell, hero of all of us when I was at school.

His achievements seem even more staggering now, nearly 50 years later. A gold in the 800 metres at the Rome Olympics in 1960, and then an astounding double-gold in Tokyo in 1964 – 800 metres and 1500 metres. At one stage in 1962, Snell broke no less than three world records in a week. Astonishing. And boy, did we walk tall in his reflected glory.

And then it was over. After an international career of only five years, he pulled the plug and walked away from it all. It took our breath away.

Fascinating really, and part of the enigma of Snell. Why leave the stage so soon? Why has he lived so apparently determinedly in exile since then? And why is he not more lionised at home? I've never understood this – why is Snell not *loved* in New Zealand?

How was it that he was so completely dominant at middle-distance when he didn't even look like a middle-distance runner? Snell was built like the proverbial brick breakaway.

Have a look at some of those old photographs. He looks like a god, for heaven's sake. But at the same time, he looks like a boy from the dairy country. Kind of goofy; always bad haircuts. Only from New Zealand. One of us, but superhuman, too.

Fascinating. Peter Snell.

Tracey Nelson

WARWICK TAYLOR

Cantabrian Tracey Nelson has turned her love of rugby into a career. She has run a website dedicated to rugby and broadcasts the game.

I grew up during Canterbury's glorious Ranfurly Shield tenure in the mid-1980s, so it goes without saying that my sports hero was a rugby player. With names like Wayne Smith, Robbie Deans, Jock Hobbs, Victor Simpson, Dale Atkins and various others in the side, there was no shortage of great players to pick your hero from.

But for me, one player stood out, simply because he didn't stand out in that obvious, in-your-face kind of way. That player was Warwick Taylor.

"Tayls" was the unsung hero of that Canterbury backline, and while there were plenty of plaudits going around for the poster-boy of the time, Robbie Deans, I always felt that the importance of Taylor's role at second five-eighth was largely unrecognised. Perhaps it was because he was sandwiched between the playmaker, Wayne Smith, at first-five, and the effervescent yet sometimes erratic Victor Simpson at centre, that his work went largely unheralded.

There was nothing flashy or show-ponyish about his game, he didn't score loads of tries like the wingers did, and nobody ever sang songs about him. He was simply a player who performed the basics of the game better than most, whether that was putting his outside players into space, threading his arms through the tackle to make the offload, his perfectly-weighted wipers kicks, or cutting down the opposition with copybook tackles.

Off the field, he was modest. He wasn't one to swagger about just because he was a top rugby player. On the field, he was the quiet achiever – the pivot in the backline you could always rely on to throw the correctly-timed pass to someone running into the backline on the cut. He was so accomplished at the draw-and-pass that you knew he could probably perform it with a blindfold on.

When Taylor was on the field, you never felt worried. You knew you could rely on him, and that he'd never let you down. You always felt secure, safe in the knowledge that he wouldn't miss that crucial tackle, that he would do his bit in that backline move so we could score the winning try, and that we just couldn't lose a game when he was at second-five. Your expectations were always met. What more could you ask from a hero?

I remember when he was named in the All Blacks. It was a whole new feeling to have your hero elevated to the black jersey. It wasn't just the bragging rights, but also the excitement because it meant he got to play the British Lions in his first year as an All Black. It was the only time I ever bunked school – so I could watch "Tayls" and Canterbury beat the midweek Lions team on a sunny, winter's afternoon. The crowning glory a few years on was the All Blacks winning the inaugural Rugby World Cup in 1987, in which "Tayls" played in five of the six matches, including the final.

When I stop and think about it, I guess the thing that made Warwick Taylor stand out as a hero to me was that he had that rare commodity among rugby players – a rugby brain. He could read play on the field and vary his game as things unfolded. If a move broke down or the defence came flying up, you could rely on him to not panic and throw a hospital pass. He never let his team-mates down, and therefore he never let his fans down, either.

Years later, I am now fortunate enough to sit alongside Warwick as part of the ZB radio rugby commentary team in Christchurch. In some ways it seems surreal to be sitting next to your childhood hero, something I could not have foreseen in my wildest imaginings all those years ago – and there are still times that I almost need to pinch myself. Yet just as it was back in his playing days when he had the ball and you knew it was going to be something worth watching, now when "Tayls" opens his mouth to say something about the game, you know it's going to be worth listening to.

His insight into the game is impressive, the speed with which he can read play and describe what is happening never ceases to amaze me, and his ability to remain calm even when I'm literally leaping off my seat beside him is beyond admirable. The humility he displayed as a player has remained a constant in his personality as he has moved into commentary and coaching.

I consider myself to be one of the very lucky few who once had a childhood sports hero and can now count him as a respected colleague and friend.

WARWICK TAYLOR leads an All Black attack, supported by Michael Jones (left) and Sean Fitzpatrick.

Grant Nisbett

DON CLARKE

After a long career with TVNZ, Grant Nisbett has established himself as Sky Television's No 1 rugby commentator. He is also the TAB's rugby bookmaker.

If you've stood on the pavement outside the ground since seven in the morning waiting to watch your hero, you need him to perform when the time comes, and some nine hours later he did just that.

The scene was Athletic Park, the year 1959, the opposition the British Lions, and the hero – D B Clarke.

Don "The Boot" Clarke had single-handedly beaten the Lions in the first test at Carisbrook by landing six massive penalties, but in the second test the All Blacks, although scoring two tries, found themselves behind with just minutes remaining. Standing on an apple box at the northern end of the famous old ground, I watched nervously as the All Blacks explored ways to crack the Lions defence. One final backline movement and suddenly this huge figure appeared out in midfield – the big man had the ball with not a single tackler in sight and D B Clarke had won another test match.

To an impressionable eight-year-old, D B Clarke was far bigger than the game itself. I simply had to be like him. I had to kick the ball for miles. I had to kick penalties from my own side of halfway. I had to win games for the All Blacks.

In my great rush to achieve all of these goals I spent hours and hours on the spare section next door honing those skills that would eventually propel me into that No 1 jersey that the great man wore. Broken windows were testament to the fact that I could place-kick the ball over the fence that divided our place from my training paddock, while many hours searching in dense gorse for my lost leather ball must have meant that I was achieving good distance with my punting.

Donald Barry Clarke had come into national prominence in 1956, but I was a little too young to appreciate his impact. Two years later I saw my first test and it was a day that, ironically, the great kicker was off form with his boot. The All Blacks scored seven tries, but Clarke could convert only two as the Wallabies were cast aside 25-3. Graham, Meads, Whineray, Jones and company all scored tries.

In terms of hero worship, 1959 sealed the deal for me – put quite simply, without Don Clarke the All Blacks would not have won the series and so 12 months later I looked forward to the same man bringing us our first series win in South Africa.

History, of course, tells us that it wasn't to be, but to my young mind D B Clarke was simply amazing and went up even further in my estimation.

The penalty, conversion and dropped goal that won us the second test and the sideline conversion in Bloemfontein to draw the third meant that Clarke had kept the series alive until the fourth. Like most Kiwis listening to Bob Irvine's crackly commentaries from South Africa, I was devastated that the Springboks won the series, but nobody could speak ill to me of my special hero.

Ten-year-olds forget very easily, and by 1961 the All Blacks were back in vogue and my hero achieved legendary status, in my mind anyway, when he landed an unlikely conversion in dire conditions to beat the French at Athletic Park. These match-winning performances carried on to the point where it was expected that whenever D B Clarke lined up for the All Blacks, the game was in the bag. So it came as a great shock to me that in 1962 his two penalties were only enough to ensure a draw against the Wallabies at the park.

Having D B Clarke as a boyhood hero meant that I could follow his progress throughout the sports year. In the summer, the All Black fullback was a medium-fast bowler for Northern Districts and a very good one at that. When the great John Reid smashed the Northern bowlers all over the Basin Reserve in 1963, scoring 296 and hitting a world record of 15 sixes in the process, Don Clarke emerged with the respectable figures of 3-82 from 27 overs.

I never got his autograph - I simply didn't collect them. But it was a great pleasure to work with him at an All Black test match in Cape Town 2001.

I never let on that 40 years earlier he was everything I wanted to be.

Bernadine Oliver-Kerby

LINDA JONES

Bernadine Oliver-Kerby is a television and radio
news-reader, having previously been a sports reporter
for Television New Zealand.

I blame my nana Tess for my fascination, and yet my incredible fear, of all things
equine.

She'd tell magical stories of riding Mary Lass to school, leaving her to graze in a
nearby paddock until the slow plod home, which one evening left nana sprawled on
the ground after Mary Lass was spooked by glow worms in a nearby stream.

The horsey theme naturally progressed down the family line. I spent many weekends
and school holidays exploring the nooks and crannies of the Waipa Racing Club in Te
Awamutu, where my uncle, an owner/trainer, was secretary for many years.

Imagine an eight-year-old with an "all seasons/all areas" pass on race day. Magic.

Tweed coats, cheese-cutter hats, binoculars slung around necks and housed in
brown leather cases. It was very much a man's domain – not a natural gathering place
for woman or child. But it's where one day, under the member's stand, I had my first
brush with a female sporting great who, to this day, I deeply admire.

Punters would gamble a dollar each way based on a jockey's silks, a lucky number
or belief that you always back the grey in the race. I would scan the race book hunting
for the name L Jones.

I would watch Linda Jones ride – and win – and one cool Waikato morning, I
watched her move through the grandstand looking every bit a beauty queen –
impeccably groomed, complete with Farrah Fawcett hair.

I swiped a pen from some poor, unassuming race-goer studying *Best Bets* and
charged after Mrs Jones. She had already made a great mark with me, but I wanted
the real thing, her mark in black and white. And I still have her autograph on the back
of my race ticket, safely sellotaped to the inside cover of her book.

The Linda Jones Story was my constant reference. Her book documented her struggle to be accepted in a male-only sport, and her meteoric rise to become one of our great pioneering athletes. I'm undecided whether the resistance to females riding as professionals was due to a fear of letting a woman compete in a deeply traditionalist sport, or the fear of having a woman actually win.

Jones eventually did both.

After her initial unsuccessful attempt at gaining a licence in 1976 (the first woman to try), women finally won the right to ride as professionals in New Zealand in 1978-79. During that season, Jones was a standout, riding more than 50 winners in her apprentice year.

She also became the first woman in Australasia, Europe or North America to ride a derby winner (Holy Toledo, Wellington Derby).

There's no doubt this talented woman made a big impact on a little girl from the Waikato. She proved she could not only conquer the seemingly impossible by competing, but that she could be one of the very best in the field.

Any aspirations of donning the silks for this wannabe were swiftly dismissed after I watched one of our country neighbours mow his lawns in woollen jerseys and oil skins to sweat off the kilos and make weight for his ride. Madness.

Plus the regular after-school double-scoop of orange choc-chip ice-cream would have to go. Further madness. Thankfully, being 5ft 7in and cracking 50kg at 15 didn't help. And I could never whip a horse.

It would be many years later that my path would again cross with Linda Jones. I began anchoring Television New Zealand's racing coverage, which took me to all the big meets around the country. I was secretly thrilled to see that joining me for comments would be none other than the great Linda Jones. The childish buzz at meeting her decades later was just as powerful as it was that cold, grey day in Te Awamutu – and I told her, though, I admit, it was very hard to recall a story like that to someone who was now a colleague, without sounding like a groupie.

So, a career in racing? No. But a chance meeting under the grandstand with a sporty, strong, successful woman who was following her dream helped shape another one.

So thanks nana Tess, thanks Mary Lass, thanks uncle Mark. And thank you, Linda Jones, for your drive, commitment and refusal, in what was a man's world, to accept the word no.

Lance O'Sullivan

DAVID PEAKE

Lance O'Sullivan was arguably New Zealand's most successful jockey. He won a record 2479 races from 1980-2003.

I was a teenager when I really became interested in pursuing a career as a jockey, and at that stage there was really only one rider I admired, one I wanted to emulate. That was David Peake, who was in his prime then, riding winner after winner. He was light, but he was strong. To me he was the ultimate professional, someone I looked up to and who inspired me to go as far as I could in the racing world.

David became my benchmark, someone I aspired to emulate for the way he went about his work and the successes he had. He rode out of Takanini at that stage, so I was restricted to watching him live at race meetings. But what a rider! And what a pleasure it was to see how he coped with all sorts of rides and conditions. He had what I consider the perfect physique for a jockey. He was small – he would ride at about 50kg – but immensely powerful, and had that wonderful ability to understand the track and his horse.

David was also generous with his help and advice for someone like me, who was making his way in the racing world. It was a different era, but all the characteristics that helped him through his career remain true today. He was a very hard worker and never shirked trackwork, even when he got older. He was a true professional, a stickler for fitness and he had a massive amount of determination.

When I got into the game, David seemed to ride all the winners. He won several premierships and it was always a pleasure to watch him and his mount. He could use his stick in either hand, he could nurse his ride through sticky patches, he could smell and taste the racecourse. He was simply a great jockey in his era.

He taught me about always soaking up information and I recall on the last day that I rode, even though my last three rides were all winners, I kept thinking about David's

advice and agreeing with him even as I headed into retirement.

The only issue on which I would question David was the length of his career. I felt he rode for perhaps a decade too long, riding into his 50s. While that was his choice, strangely it also offered me another lesson about my career.

Most jockeys stay in the game too long, probably 99.99 percent of them, because they don't know when to stop or how to change careers. They have all the courage in the world and many of them continue because of financial necessity. But when they look back on their careers, they know they should have got out and done something else.

David was old-school and, in partnership with trainer Ray Verner, made a formidable team. Many found David gruff and that may have been because they were too familiar with him. I remember showing him the utmost respect, calling him Mr Peake for more than half my competitive years, until he told me to call him David. The first time I rode I managed to spend a little bit of time with him and while he put fear into most of us, he was also a terrific tutor. Whenever he whistled me over to give some advice about a track or a style of horse, it was a real highlight.

He rode so many good horses to victory, like Blue Blood and Good Lord, that it's hard to pick out one as his best ride. What he did have, though, were attributes every jockey envied: fitness; determination, especially on wet tracks; and ability to go and go. Often people would be left saying not many would have won from there after David had sneaked through on the line.

These days he is still someone people sound out for all sorts of advice about piloting horses in every condition.

Keith Quinn

WINSTON MCCARTHY

Keith Quinn was for nearly three decades New Zealand's No 1 rugby broadcaster. He has covered eight Olympic Games and a vast variety of international sport.

When I was a skinny kid growing up in the King Country, the national radio rugby commentator, Winston McCarthy, was as well-known in our country as the All Blacks or other newsworthy personalities like the Prime Minister, the Governor-General or Olympic athletes.

In the 1950s, there was no TV and all our news came from a large "wireless" radio in the corner of the living room. My dad was a bit of a hard case and at dinner he'd tell stories about mythical places in funny voices. One of his voices impersonated the radio rugby commentator we used to listen to, Winston "Scotty" McCarthy.

I remember many a dull match was made exciting by the way Winston "talked it up". He was the first commentator to use crowd noise as part of his excitement. When a kick for goal was being taken from the other side of the field and he was unable to see the ball's flight-path, he would say: "The crowd noise will tell us [if the kick was going to go over] ...so LISTEN!...it's a goal!" It became his trademark call.

From the King Country we shifted to Wellington and lived near Athletic Park. Like so many kids, I used to go free to club rugby every winter Saturday. Watching the games, we soon recognised Winston McCarthy was the voice we'd also hear on the public address. He would give out the team changes and the scorers. He was so famous that no-one complained when he would sometimes call out to the match referee on the PA: "Sir, sir! There's an injury back at halfway, sir!" Imagine a commentator doing that today!

The Kiwis Army tour of 1945-46 started the game in Britain after the horrors of World War II. Winston was there for the NZBC. His style of raised-voice, excitable sports commentary was completely the opposite of the dignified "old school tie" style of the BBC. When British radio audiences heard Winston they soon asked the BBC for his commentaries rather than those of their own chaps. In 1953, when television was in its infancy, the telecast of the All Black game at Twickenham was interrupted so that the TV could cross over for a while to a take a 10-minute burst of what Winston was saying on BBC radio!

In Wellington, I used to be fascinated watching Winston in his commentary box. I even used to wait behind until he had recorded his post-match summary. I remember the thrill of whistling and crying out, and then running home to hear myself behind Winston's voice on the local radio replay. That didn't last long, however, because the following week he told me and my mates to "piss off!" before his next recording.

They reckoned that at his peak Winston could influence the All Black selectors' thinking. Winston had favourites all right. Ron Jarden, the lightning-quick Wellington winger was one, Johnny Smith, the sleepy-looking Maori centre from the far north, was another. Also, Peter Jones, the fiery flanker from up there, too. And not to forget Fred Allen and Bob Scott, from the Kiwis. Those blokes could do no wrong.

I suppose you could say that it eventually formed in my mind that I wanted to become a rugby commentator. After leaving school, I joined the old New Zealand Broadcasting Corporation as a cadet and used to meet Winston regularly. What a thrill! He would come into the office on a Friday for a chat about rugby and to record his previews. Then he and the senior blokes would head off to De Brett's Hotel to talk some more. Or to listen to Winston some more. He sure knew how to hold court.

The first things I remember about him were his loud and salty language, his outrageous views on everything, and his indifference when someone mentioned to him that this "Young Quinn" had ambitions to be a commentator. Years later, he told me that such aspirations were mentioned to him all over the place every day and he tired of hearing them. In pubs, men used to come up and broadcast to him into empty beer glasses, mimicking the sound of a radio commentary, or they would just shout loudly: "Hey Winston! LISTEN! – It's a goal!" Winston could talk, but he didn't suffer fools gladly.

In time, he and I became good friends. He had seen rugby played 40 years earlier,

A young Keith Quinn (right) and his broadcasting hero, the incomparable
WINSTON McCARTHY, at a farewell function for McCarthy in Wellington in 1978.

in the 1920s. I enjoyed him passing the stories on to me. He gave me some very sound advice about commentary. He really understood how a good broadcaster should use the rise and fall of his or her voice, and its modulation, and he really understood timing, when not to talk over crowd noise, that sort of thing. His call of "Listen! – It's a goal!" was a classic example of using crowd noise. And I have never forgotten his sharp advice about how to deal with public criticism: "Sonny, it doesn't matter what they say about you. As long as they spell your name right."

Even though there was no television in those days, Winston was easily recognisable to the public. Most affectionately called him by his first name. The NZBC used to put out long-playing records of his radio commentaries and they became best-sellers. I still have my copies. I also have his personal scrapbook from the 1945-46 Kiwis Army tour of the UK. It was given to me by a friend, whom he had passed it on to. It is priceless to me. It has his hand-written summary notes of each tour game with each one beginning: "Hello New Zealand..."

In 1956, when the Springboks toured for their epic series, Winston was so popular that the NZRU allowed only the four tests to be broadcast live. He was affecting gate-takings around the country. Club games in all cities had to be played in the mornings so that everyone could rush home to thrill to his call in the afternoons. Apart from the tests, all other afternoon tour game broadcasts were delayed until 5pm.

Winston's glory years as a commentator lasted only from the Kiwis tour to the 1959 British Lions tour. Thereafter he wrote books and newspaper columns. I was really wild when I heard that members of the 1970 All Blacks on their tour of South Africa didn't rate his reports for *New Zealand Truth* very highly. One time at a team barbeque, some players grabbed him and swung him back and forth over a blazing bonfire. Then they dropped him on the ground and broke his arm. Winston was then 62 years old.

Mind you, the 1949 All Blacks on their way home from South Africa had dangled him feet first over the side of the boat. His comments didn't always meet universal approval. But one thing I gained from hours of listening to him was that he deeply loved the game. And his affection for the All Blacks was total.

I last saw Winston in 1983, sitting by himself at Eden Park having a cup of tea before a Lions tour game. Most people were just passing by, not aware perhaps of the role that the old bloke sitting there had played in New Zealand. For 15 years he was the eyes and ears of the national game. I stopped and chatted and he offered encouragement for my work.

Winston McCarthy was a great broadcaster and a powerful on-air personality. I always appreciated that. He lived by the Oscar Wilde credo that "the only thing worse than being talked about is not being talked about".

These days I'm sometimes asked if his radio style would have survived in today's television world. While it was often said he could make a dull game sound exciting, I am certain his personality would have made him as significant on television in today's world. Winston was a performer. He swept me along in his style and had a hero's influence on a young lad from a tiny post-war town.

In fact, after hearing Winston I only wanted to be like him.

Christine Rankin

JONAH LOMU

Christine Rankin was the chief executive of the Department of Work and Income from 1998-2001. She is now a Families Commissioner.

There are millions of things to like about Jonah. I do a lot of public-speaking and my work is about developing leadership in New Zealand. It's not something that I feel we New Zealanders are passionate about – we put everyone down, we want to put everyone on the same level and to be unsuccessful together. Anyone who stands out and is different, we put down, and I think Jonah Lomu is a perfect example of that.

There is something about him, a vulnerability which as a mother I connect with, but there is a hell of a lot more than that. I look at him and there is just something about him. He feels like one of my children. I look at that boy and look at the way the world sees him. You know if he is a guest in a stadium somewhere, that arena is filled with people who just want a glimpse of him and consider him the greatest rugby player ever. And we in New Zealand put him down. We give him hell, we make jokes about him.

When he was 16 or 17, he was very shy, not very articulate, and we gave him hell. For God's sake, how many people, when they have a television camera in their face, are articulate? I would like to see the people in the street who criticise him being able to cope in terms of that.

Look at what he has done – this young Tongan boy who found himself in an environment where there were some issues. He walked a fine line between making a decision to use his wonderful, amazing skill or going into crime. He is very open about that. It was a fine, fine line, and he had the courage to do something which was very, very hard and was going to take an enormous effort, and he did it. That was the first sign of huge courage and determination.

Later on, he was very ill. Most of us could not have walked down the street, yet he played international rugby with that pain. And we gave him hell. When people found out he was very sick there was no real sympathy. Some of the talk I heard was that Jonah should have walked away from his sport. But he didn't because he had courage and determination, he had that operation and he has never given in. He has been incredibly determined, and while lots of people thought it might be pie-in-the-sky, he has been the most fantastic example for our children. He was able to play rugby again – a New Zealand hero demonstrating everything we could want out of our heroes.

His personal life may have been a bit messy, but that is nothing to do with us. We should be more concerned about his absolute determination to succeed and never give in, and be inspired by what he went through with his kidney transplant, and afterwards how he trained and trained and trained. Others would have thought they were lucky to be alive and would then have chosen to lead a quiet life. Most people would have that opinion, but it is not one I share.

What an amazing role model, what an incredible man. I just admire him so much. I have spoken to him twice and because of the way I feel about him, I was very silly. He was at a café in Ponsonby when I dropped in and blurted out: "Oh God, there's Jonah."

He was sitting there with arms the size of most people's thighs and my embarrassed reaction was not very becoming. I promised myself I wouldn't go and speak to him, and then I couldn't help it. I went up to him, rubbed his arm and said: "I just want you to know that I talk about you [and I'm sure he didn't know who I was] and I think you are one of New Zealand's great men." He politely thanked me.

One thing I notice about New Zealand males is they don't like too much emotion. I remember the first time I saw Jonah on television on the *Holmes* show when he got married. He cried – great big tears rolled down his face. I just wanted to get a handkerchief and wipe him down. At the same time you could feel New Zealanders, as a whole, cringe, because this huge All Black, this 6ft 6in man, was crying. But for me that increased my admiration for the man. Here was a young man who was hurting at every turn and New Zealanders were giving him hell, and I just felt for him.

So whenever things get a bit tough for me, I think about what Jonah has been through. I think that if he can do it, if he can survive all that has been out in front of him, then by God I can stand up to anything.

I worked near Radio Live for a time in Auckland and he used to live close by. One day several of us came out of work and there he was washing his car on the footpath. We both thought: "Oh my goodness!" He was lovely, but what do you do with two middle-aged women reacting like that? It must be a maternal thing, because he reminds me of my youngest son.

But most of all New Zealand needs its heroes and we need to celebrate our wonderful people like John Walker and Jonah. He stood there with the All Blacks while the national anthem was being played with his hand on his heart and that said it all. Imagine being his mother and having a boy like that. You would just be so proud.

I read his book and cried and cried. I watched him on television talking about his fight with that disgusting disease and he is an inspiration to me. He has come from a tough background. What do we expect? Do we think everyone has a straightforward existence? Most people have complicated lives. People with huge talent do not have ordinary lives.

The Australians would die for a Jonah, someone they could celebrate. But we are a nation that likes to put people down, to put everyone on the same level. When I worked for WINZ, I ran a major programme to get people back to work, and we used heroes to help. I contacted Jonah and they sent us photos and posters, which we used to encourage people to aim to be like him. I love the boy, I will support him forever and I hope he has lots of babies really soon. If I could send him a message, it would be to get on with it.

Sir Paul Reeves

SAM MEADS

Sir Paul Reeves was Archbishop and Primate of New Zealand from 1980-85 and Governor-General of New Zealand from 1985-90.

I grew up in Newtown and went to South Wellington School, which was next to Athletic Park. On a Saturday I could hear the noise of the crowd at the park and, depending on whether it was a shout of approval or the collective groans, you could work out whether a try had been scored or the ball dropped. I played schoolboy rugby at places like Wakefield Park, but never at Newtown Park, which was the home of the forbidden game – rugby league.

Initially my Saturday afternoons were devoted to the De Luxe Theatre in Courtenay Place, but then I joined the crowd on the Western Bank at the park and backed my favourite side, Poneke, and my special player, Vic Calcinai, who could kick goals from anywhere and seemed to get better the muddier it got.

In 1946 I went to Wellington College with some nervousness and trepidation. My elder brother had gone to Wellington Tech, as we called it, and could not get away quickly enough. Wellington College was something else – you had to wear a uniform, including a cap and black stockings pulled up to within a couple of inches of the knee, most of the other boys seemed to have a self-confidence which I did not have, and then there was something called homework.

I played in the school rugby teams mostly as a fullback and, even if I say so myself, I could run and I had a kick like a frisky horse.

When the war ended, a group of younger teachers (we called them masters) came to Wellington College. For all I know, they may have been more than a handful for the headmaster, who struck me as a dour and aloof man. Discipline was a cornerstone in the school and to ram the lesson home, tradition and corporal punishment were emphasised in ample doses.

One of the teachers was a big hulk of a man, short-sighted and slightly bow-legged. After school he would put on his football gear and run around the playing field, lap after lap, and in the estimation of one small boy, hour after hour. His socks were around his ankles and his running style you would describe as determined, rather than fluid or graceful. But he got there and he kept on going.

This was Sam Meads, a man whom we admired and really liked. More to the point, he played senior rugby for University and was a great lineout forward. He would leap and get the ball, and he seemed to spin with his elbows out as he came down. Maybe with age my memory is failing, but I remember him bursting through the lineout with the ball, so I reckon it did happen that way.

Sam was a member of the Wellington team that beat the Kiwis Army rugby team at Athletic Park in 1946. The Kiwis had played wonderful rugby in Britain and had provided cheer and verve to a battered country at the end of the war. It was a great game in Wellington, though I suspect that the Kiwis by this time were bone-weary.

Anyway Sam was a lock for Wellington and I have no doubt he played his heart out. He was never an All Black, but he was a big-hearted, grafting, nose-to-the-ball sort of player.

In fact, I have many memories of Sam Meads. His classroom was always full of noise, and we boys had to raise our voices to be heard above his constant stream of advice and admonition, in equal doses. I am not sure what he taught, but a session with Mr Meads was fun and from him I caught a love of learning.

Sam would read to us and we would listen as this big man sat on the edge of his table and pulled out a book. Sam saw the funny side of life, so not surprisingly he read humorous books. His favourite author seemed to be the Canadian humourist, Stephen Leacock, and when Sam read from Leacock he would cackle or nearly choke himself laughing. It was Leacock who told of the trans-Atlantic liner housemaid whose knee was in need of attention. The call went out for a doctor and the medical doctor who rushed to the scene found that he had been outpaced by a Doctor of Divinity. Sam repeated that story several times with great heaving of the chest and ample watering of the eyes.

Incidentally, I am a Doctor of Divinity, and I can only imagine that Sam, who is now playing that great game in the skies, is laughing his head off.

Sam became a headmaster in the Wairarapa and I lost touch with him. We all move on, but I bet there are hundreds of men who were pupils at Wellington College in the late 1940s who remember Sam Meads with great affection – as a man, as a teacher and as an honest toiler on the rugby field.

Melodie Robinson

DAVID KIRK

Melodie Robinson played 18 tests for the New Zealand women's rugby team from 1996-2002, and became a commentator and presenter for Sky Sports. She is now a regular on Prime TV.

When I was 11, I wanted the Princess Diana hairdo. Short, flicked at the sides. Glamour personified. I begged and cajoled my mother for days to cut my long frizzy mop into the more fashionable style. To get me out of her hair she got the kitchen scissors, and gave me something akin to a number two.

When I looked in the mirror, I bawled for ages. I thought I was the ugliest Maori kid in Christchurch.

My only distraction from lamenting about how unlike Diana and my Barbie Doll I now looked was the Seoul Olympics and Flo-Jo – Florence Griffith Joyner.

In my eyes, not only was this woman the most incredible looking thing I'd ever seen, she was amazing at sport and she was brown! Like me. I didn't really equate the difference in brownness at the time.

I spent quite a bit of time in my one-piece togs, sprinting up and down my driveway that summer. It also got me involved in athletics. A year later I beat my dad in a 100m race. It didn't matter that he was, and is, shaped like a potato on sticks and not streamlined for sprinting.

I was 14 years old when my major sporting influence entered my life. He was short, cute and lovely – he was David Kirk.

At this point, my overactive teenage mind was dreaming up all kinds of romantic scenarios. I was glued to the screen whenever the Rugby World Cup and the All Blacks were on. My best friend, Rachel, and I swooned at every tackle, pass or run. It was love.

It got me out into the backyard to play rugby with Rachel's brother, Jacob, and started a fascination for the oval ball, a passion for the game.

Of course, I got over the captain of the All Blacks by age 15, but I never got over rugby.

It's a lifetime love affair. Thank you David, thank you 1987.

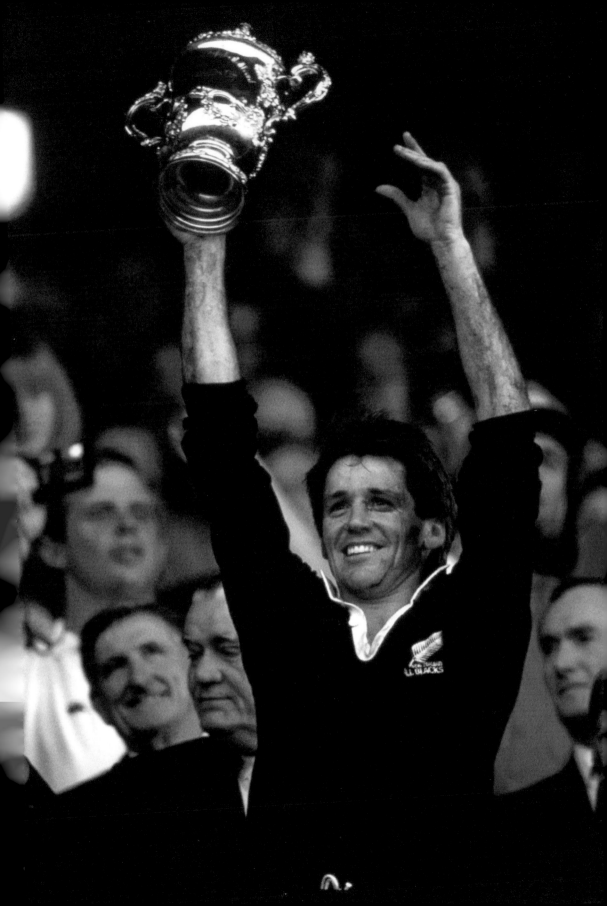

Joseph Romanos

BRUCE EDGAR

Joseph Romanos is a Wellington sports journalist/author. He is the author of 40 books, and the publisher of *My Sports Hero*.

When I was growing up there were lots of sports superstars who were heroes – Muhammad Ali, Geoff Hunt, Heather McKay, Don Bradman, Rod Laver, Bob Beamon, Peter Snell, Grant Batty and many more. But they were all heroes because I'd either read about them, or watched them from afar.

Up close and personal, my sports hero was undoubtedly Bruce Edgar. New Zealand cricket followers who recall Edgar will think of the quiet, business-like, efficient opening batsman who was part of the great New Zealand team of the early 1980s.

But that's not the Edgar I'm talking about. I'm talking about the schoolboy version. What a cricketer he was! Old-timers talk about how dominating John R Reid was at college, and those of a more recent vintage speak of Martin Crowe and Chris Cairns the same way.

Well, at school – first at Evans Bay Intermediate, and then Rongotai College – Bruce was a giant, in stature and ability. He never really grew after he reached about 13, but at primary school he towered over the rest of us.

And he was some cricketer. He had been taught by his father, Arthur, a Plunket Shield player himself, and was a polished wicketkeeper and a brilliant batsman.

I went to Marist Newtown and Bruce's Kilbirnie team used to flog us every time we played them. Bruce always seemed to make a century. I remember one day at Kilbirnie Park he swept the first ball of the match, from our fast bowler, over square leg for six. He used to drive like a man, and cut and hooked powerfully. He was stronger than the rest of us, and even though he ran in a somewhat pigeon-toed manner, he was extremely athletic.

There was a batch of good young cricketers around Wellington at the time, including

Evan Gray, Ian Smith, Clive Currie and Robert Vance, but I thought Bruce stood far above all of them. I felt it was a privilege to be in the same junior rep teams as him, but I was a plodder and he was a star. I was always dead scared of running him out.

He was just as dominating at Rongotai College and everyone said it was only a matter of time before he played for New Zealand. So it proved, but not how I'd imagined.

At school Bruce used to bat at No 3, and he would annihilate attacks.

But once he got into rep cricket, Bruce was turned into an opening batsman. Then he was told to wear down opposing attacks. He proved to be a terrific team player, and would bat for hours, even against bowlers like Lillee and Thomson, Holding and Roberts, Imran and Sarfraz, Botham and Willis.

He would blunt opposing attacks so that those who followed – the likes of Geoff Howarth, Martin and Jeff Crowe and John F Reid – could prosper.

People used to make fun of Bruce sometimes, suggesting he batted too slowly, or didn't have enough strokes. But they didn't know. They hadn't seen him batting as a schoolboy.

Bruce was certainly talented enough to bat at No 4 and play as Martin Crowe did, but a different role was chosen for him. It can't have been very enjoyable, once the initial satisfaction of playing test cricket and helping the team effort wore off.

I wasn't surprised when he gave away test cricket when he was only 29. He carried on playing for Wellington and batted more freely. His play in domestic one-dayers near the end of his career recalled his younger days.

These days Bruce and his family live in Sydney. He's not mentioned much now, and his test record, for those interested enough to look it up, is only good, no more than that.

But he was a hero to me. I wish he'd shown the rest of the country what he could do, instead of letting only a few of us in Wellington in on the secret.

Wynton Rufer

JIM MCMILLAN

Wynton Rufer is regarded as the finest soccer player produced by New Zealand. He played professionally in Europe from 1982-97, and was named Oceania Footballer of the Century.

At 89, Jim McMillan is not in the best of health, but I make sure I talk to him every week. He has always been a very special person for me and I will always remember the part he played in setting me off on my football career.

From as far back as I can remember I always had a ball at my feet. In the very early days in a football-mad family it was my dad and my older brother, Shane, who I kicked around with. Like many kids, we played backyard soccer, but Shane would only let me play if I went in goal.

When I was a little older, I went down to the local park, where I met Jim McMillan, an Irishman who loved his football and was always keen to coach anyone who would listen.

He quickly became my friend and mentor, and I spent many hours kicking a ball around with him.

I soon learned the right way to kick a ball and slowly he taught me all he knew about the game he obviously loved. I wanted to be the best I could be and he encouraged me. I quickly learned how to juggle the ball. By the time I was nine I could juggle it 500 times.

When I was 10 I dreamed about playing as a professional. From those early days I never missed watching *Big Match* on television. I hoped, even then, that one day I could play like those players.

I seized every chance to train with Jim. I was at the park three or four times a week. So was he. There was never a day when I didn't kick a ball. He naturally became the person I turned to.

Later in my career I learned from other coaches in New Zealand, like John Adshead,

Allan Jones and Barrie Truman – all Englishmen – but it was Jim McMillan who had the biggest influence on my career. He watched what I was doing and always offered advice. I enjoyed learning from him and now with the coaching programmes we run, I can quickly tell which players are most likely to do well – those who are prepared to listen, learn and work as hard as I did.

While Jim McMillan was the person who did most for me when I started and set me on my way to a 16-year professional career, Pelé was my hero.

As a youngster growing up, he was my god but, for some inexplicable reason – I think I was still out on the pitch doing the tourist thing – when he came into our dressing room in Seville when we played Brazil at the 1982 World Cup in Spain, I was the only player in the New Zealand team who didn't meet him.

I have been lucky enough to spend a lot of time with him since, though, because we have sat on the same Fifa committees.

The other person with a big influence on me is my wife, Lisa. I wasted a few years of my life until Lisa came along and helped me get my act together. People like Jim McMillan, Lisa and my children make me realise how fortunate I have been.

Ric Salizzo

BRYAN WILLIAMS

Ric Salizzo is a former journalist who turned to television production and created and wrote the popular sports comedy series *Sports Café*.

My first sports hero was supposed to be somebody else. At the beginning of 1970, I was eight years old and just starting to appreciate sports achievements outside the plastic-booted world of my Cornwall rugby team.

I remember quite clearly my first rub with greatness. I was fast asleep at my grandparents' house when a strange hand belonging to a strange man woke me up. Not fully aware of the dangers of the stranger in those carefree days, I awoke to his offers of a little present.

"I thought you might like my autograph," said the stranger.

To clear things up, he presented me with a card with his name and photo on it, along with his soon-to-be-treasured autograph.

Grahame Thorne, All Black... had burst into my world on the eve of the 1970 trip to South Africa. This became my first All Black encounter at a time when I was just becoming aware of what they were.

It was that year that I really become aware of the sports world. My earliest memory is of my father screaming "goal" at the top of his voice as we ran around the house together celebrating Italy's goal in the World Cup final. Things got a bit quieter when some pesky Pelé bloke helped Brazil to a 4-1 victory over our Italians.

But no-one at school really cared about soccer. It was just rugby and the All Blacks. Fortunately I had met one and had his autographed card to prove it.

So I was set to follow Mr Thorne's journey through South Africa when my affections were suddenly won over by another – my new-found hero, Bryan George Williams.

I suppose I should have worked out he was going to be special when he made his debut at Bethlehem, but there was something about him that pushed all other rugby players into mere mortality.

He had everything. He was strong, fast, fearless and every now and then even lined up a penalty goal from halfway to show he had every skill required

My admiration for him became almost total when he scored a try against the South

African enemy and rubbed it in by stepping past half the team behind the tryline so he could dot the ball down under the posts – goal-kicking wasn't exactly a strength in the '70s.

Williams rose to hero status when he returned home to play for Auckland, leaving the other contender for my sports hero spot, Grahame Thorne, behind in South Africa, sort of like Luke Skywalker leaving Hans Solo behind on the Death Star because he fell in love with a stormtrooper.

For the next couple of years, "Beegee", as he was known, was everything. While the rest of the world kept comparing him to the player he was at 19, I was simply enjoying his greatness of the moment.

All the talk of the 1972-73 tour was of Murdoch and disaster, but I was enthralled by Beegee on the wing, with his pals Grant Batty and Bruce Robertson showing we had brilliance out wide also. Batty getting the ball on one wing and then kicking it across field to Beegee, who stepped and powered his way to score on the other was my highlight.

Then I saw Bryan Williams actually walk on water in 1975, scoring a try against Scotland on the tide which flowed above Eden Park that day. It has been called the "water polo test" and Eden Park was absolutely flooded that day, but it didn't slow down Beegee.

There was one game in particular I enjoyed. He was playing for Auckland against Marlborough at Eden Park, and I eventually got there by myself for the first time, managing to work out the 17 buses needed to travel from Mangere to Eden Park. Everyone was saying Beegee was finished and Brian Ford was the man, and indeed Ford played well that day, but nothing like the incomparable Bryan George Williams, who seemed to be playing on a different level.

There wasn't a big crowd, but we rose as one each time he scored, realising that we were privileged to be in the company of greatness.

As my cynicism grew with my years, Beegee was the one constant source of wonderment, though I thought it was all over in 1977, when he was stretchered off against France in Toulouse.

But the next year, the man who started in Bethlehem performed his own Lazarus trick with an amazing comeback try against Australia. In reality, he caught the ball, stepped and went over all in the space of about two metres. But that was enough. Our hero was back.

It was coming to an end though, and in that amazing game against the Barbarians in 1978, when we used the haka as a free kick move, Beegee Williams played his last game for the All Blacks, scoring a try, of course.

It is a sign of the man that the road from Mt Albert Grammar to Ponsonby to Auckland and then greatness is still a road he travels to this day, working so hard with his old school, club and province.

And that's not to mention his awakening as a Samoan legend as he took Western Samoa to their first glory days.

But it was from that one moment in South Africa in 1970 when he burst down the touchline and then stepped his way past deadball defenders to put the ball under the black dot that I knew I had my hero.

Sir Anand Satyanand

SIR MURRAY HALBERG

Sir Anand Satyanand became the Governor-General of
New Zealand in 2006. He previously worked as a lawyer,
judge and ombudsman.

For someone who has strong connections to rugby league – and is also known to
have a soft spot for cricket – it might seem a surprise that I should choose Sir Murray
Halberg as my sporting hero. The reasons are many and varied. Some reflect personal
knowledge and connections, some reflect his athletic achievements, and others his
accomplishments beyond sport.

New Zealanders are great fans of team sports. We love playing in team sports and
watching, whether it is the All Blacks, the Kiwis, the Silver Ferns or the Black Caps. We
also love it when they win. But we have also had a fascination with solitary medium and
long-distance runners and have enjoyed their successes. For earlier generations, that
person was Jack Lovelock, and for those younger than myself, it was Peter Snell and,
later, John Walker. But for my generation, it was Murray Halberg.

Sir Murray entered my consciousness as a teenager when he won gold in the 5000m
at the Rome Olympics in 1960 and repeated that performance at the British Empire
and Commonwealth Games in Perth two years later. I can bring to mind the sonorous
voice of Lance Cross, commentating his Rome victory. As I now know, his exploits
predated both events. Sir Murray had already won the three-mile event at the British
Empire and Commonwealth Games in Cardiff in 1958 and he had become the first
New Zealander to run a sub-four-minute mile, at a race in Dublin later that year.

Even before his Olympic performance, he was named New Zealand Sportsman of
the Year in 1958.

There would be many who would happily and quite justifiably rest upon these
laurels. But Sir Murray chose to use the influence that comes from sporting success to
work for the community in a charitable capacity.

He launched the Halberg Trust – originally called the Murray Halberg Trust for Crippled Children – in 1963 after attending and being guest speaker at a fundraising function in Toronto. He was so impressed by the concept that he approached his employers to see if they might back a similar event in New Zealand.

The response was positive and, as it is said, the rest is history. While the trust's name has changed, its mission of honouring sporting excellence and linking those with a disability to sport and active recreation remains a constant. Thousands of New Zealanders with disabilities have been given the opportunity to enjoy not only the health benefits, but also the personal freedom, that sport and active recreation offers.

Sir Murray is my sporting hero because of the way he has built on his successful career as an athlete to also contribute to the community that helped him get there. The best in any sport do not reach the heights they do without the support of many others, often from a young age.

In this regard, Sir Murray has never stopped giving back to the community. It was with great pleasure, then, that on September 24, 2008 at Government House in Auckland, I had the privilege of conferring on him New Zealand's highest honour and investing him as a member of the Order of New Zealand.

While most people know that the Order is limited to just 20 living recipients, what is often not realised is that unlike every other New Zealand honour, the Insignia must be returned when the holder dies. When they say it is "for life", they mean just that.

In Sir Murray's case, only one other person had worn the Insignia I placed around his neck on that spring day. Quite appropriately, it was the Insignia which had been worn by the late Sir Edmund Hillary, probably one of the greatest New Zealanders of the 20th century, who had died earlier in the year.

Like Sir Murray, Sir Edmund did not rest on his laurels. He could have lived comfortably off the guest speaker's circuit as the conqueror of Everest. Instead, he not only dedicated himself to further expeditions, but also to a prodigious amount of charitable work.

Sir Murray is my sporting hero, not only for his many achievements, but also for the inspirational leadership and the role-modelling he has provided for other New Zealanders.

Governor-General Sir Anand Satyanand confers on **SIR MURRAY HALBERG** New Zealand's highest honour by investing him as a member of the Order of New Zealand in 2008.

Wayne Shelford

JIM MANIAPOTO

Wayne "Buck" Shelford played for the All Blacks from 1986-90 and captained the team unbeaten for three years. The big No 8 became a cult figure and his axing in 1990 caused national consternation.

Growing up in Rotorua, we did not have a television. If it was raining and we could not get out to play, we might listen to rugby commentaries on the radio and identify with our local stars.

We were right into the Hori BoP concept, because the Bay of Plenty was predominantly a Maori community and club rugby was certainly filled with forestry or manual workers, who were incredibly hard men. We all played for our local club side and that was what we were all about.

One of the local legends was Jim Maniapoto, a tough, uncompromising lock who was one of the pillars of the Bay side and also represented the Maori All Blacks. When his wife came to teach us at Western Heights Primary, word soon got around about her husband, and we would always be on the lookout if he came to school.

Our paths crossed a couple of times. When you are a kid and meet someone of Jim's reputation, the thrill stays for some time. He wore walk-shorts in the fashion of the day and I remember being staggered by the size of the muscles in his legs. When you are young, you are impressionable and we were in awe of Jim Maniapoto.

We were only about 10 and it seemed very special to us that a local rugby legend was often at our school grounds. I was also very conscious of the talented loose forward, Alan McNaughton, who was starting to make his way in local rugby.

Both guys had a huge aura about them then as they were not only imposing physical specimens to us youngsters, but were also provincial and New Zealand Maori representatives.

I probably saw both men play only a few times on television because we did not get to go to the provincial matches. My carpenter father worked on Saturdays and we were usually out playing in those days when the rep footie was on, and anyway, he probably did not have the spare cash to take all the boys in the family along to provincial games.

During most of my primary school years, I played first five-eighth, only really moving into the forwards when I was at intermediate. Maybe I knew something about that likely shift because I always admired Jim Maniapoto for what he brought to the Bay side.

Stories about his rugged play and his leadership were the stuff of legend and were often part of household discussions or chats out on the school playgrounds where we tried to emulate our heroes. That was good enough for me, and when his wife came to teach at our school that just topped off my choice.

I never played any senior rugby in the Bay because I shifted to work in Auckland, so I never got the chance to play against Maniapoto, though I had one festival-type game against McNaughton. Even though I had moved north in early 1975, it took me a long time before I switched my allegiance from the Bay.

That Bay fervour stayed with me, especially when they won the initial national championship in 1976, under Tuck Waaka. I remember watching some of those games on television, admiring the way they played and thinking about those men like Jim Maniapoto, who had inspired me in the game we love.

Peter Snell

JEFF ROBSON

Middle-distance runner Peter Snell, who now lives in Texas, was voted Athlete of the Century by the Halberg Trust in 2000. He won three Olympic gold medals from 1960-64, and set a clutch of world records.

Once I was in my late teens and beyond, I was not really the hero-worshipping type, and never really tried to emulate anyone. I did regard Murray Halberg as a mentor when I began running internationally. Murray was a very seasoned athlete by then, and was well-known by most of the top overseas runners. It gave me a sense of belonging and confidence when I was with him, and certainly when I got to my first Olympic Games, in Rome in 1960, having Murray around was like a security blanket for a novice international athlete like me.

At 19, when I started running with [coach] Arthur Lydiard, Barry Magee loaned me his copy of Emil Zatopek's *Marathon Victor*, which was inspirational and extolled hard work and dedication.

When I was younger, perhaps about 14, I was a serious junior tennis player, and my hero was Jeff Robson. Jeff was a New Zealand champion badminton and tennis player, and was always a hard-working, consistent type of player.

I used to imagine I was him, trading shots on the volley board with some imaginary or real opponent, such as John Barry, one of New Zealand's leading tennis players at the time.

Dame Kiri Te Kanawa

SIR EDMUND HILLARY

Dame Kiri Te Kanawa is a New Zealand soprano who has had a highly successful international opera career stretching back to 1968.

Imagination is a large part of my business. I have to transport myself into character, take on another persona and use my creativity. For me, there was special significance in 2000 when I sang in the new millennium. It was wonderful to be part of the celebrations as New Zealand led the world and I had some warm feelings about my contribution and the special part I was playing in history that morning in Gisborne.

Later I could reflect on that special moment and the greeting of the first light in my home town, and try to compare it to the feelings Sir Edmund Hillary must have had all those years ago when he cracked the mountaineering frontier and scaled Everest. We spoke a number of times about that moment in his life, when he really awakened the world to the deeds of people in this part of the globe. But while we spoke about his deeds, only Sir Edmund really knew what it was like to accomplish that feat, what it meant to him, how he felt on that remarkable day in 1953 when he put not only Everest on the map, but also New Zealand.

I was only young when he ascended the world's highest peak with Tenzing, but Sir Edmund's remarkable feat made a huge impression on me. Here was a humble young Kiwi, full of the pioneering spirit which was so potent in all our forefathers, who had achieved something the rest of the world could only marvel at. Yet for all his skill, bravado, resilience, purpose and results, Sir Edmund was an extraordinarily humble man. He never let fame sway his judgement, and he had his feet firmly planted on terra firma, where his demeanour was inspirational.

There have been many moments of privilege in my life, but I count myself to have been very blessed when I met Sir Edmund for the first time. I was even more fortunate that we connected and that friendship led to many more marvellous meetings.

Distinguished company - Dame Kiri Te Kanawa and **SIR EDMUND HILLARY.**

He showed me what it was like to be a proud New Zealander without trumpeting his success. With Everest conquered, he continued to do amazing deeds for others, and his generosity to the world never diminished. His demeanour was inspiring, and he had that wonderful blend of ambition, drive and self-deprecation. Sometimes you felt Sir Edmund was being too humble, but that was his manner, and was part of his compelling nature.

Without realising it, Sir Edmund taught me many lessons and I counted myself as a very fortunate person to have met the great man. It was truly special when we could bond as fellow recipients of the Order of New Zealand and we would get together at the special investitures for the select group.

Call it hero-worship or whatever term you like, but I made sure he autographed all the books he had written and, in return, I was only too glad to supply him with recordings of my work, because I'd heard he used to love to sit back in his chair and soak up the music.

There have been many other special private moments when we would share our thoughts, ideas and experiences. In public, it was wonderful to sit with him at the concert at Craggy Range Winery, when he described to the audience the final days before and the moment he and Sherpa Tenzing conquered Everest. He was one of the first people I approached to endorse my new foundation for young New Zealand singers and musicians at a gala concert, along with Prince Charles, Jackie Stewart, Placido Domingo and Neil Finn.

I was greatly saddened to hear of Sir Edmund's passing. He was an extraordinary man and an inspirational ambassador for our country. On a recent visit to Windsor Castle, I sought out and sat in the chair in St George's Chapel that Sir Edmund occupied as a Knight of the Order of the Garter and reflected on what a great man we had lost.

Sir Edmund was one of the great men of this nation, an inspiration, a true legend and my hero.

Brendan Telfer

CHASING THE THREE GREATEST FULLBACKS

Brendan Telfer has been one of New Zealand's leading sports broadcasters since 1974. He began a long stint as a Radio Sport host in 1998.

"Fiery Fred" Trueman must have presented a truly fearful image, which many of the world's leading batsmen would have attested to, as he charged into the bowling crease, ball in hand. His thunderbolt deliveries were usually accompanied with a menacing scowl and a sharp tongue.

Shortly before he retired from the test arena in 1965, Fred became the first player in test cricket to take 300 test wickets.

Happily, I avoided the misfortune of having to face Trueman in full flight – well not from 22 yards on a cricket pitch. But, as a shy, star-struck 12-year-old in 1963, I did feel the full brunt of one of his famous verbal volleys on the steps of the old stand at the Basin Reserve in Wellington.

Trueman was in New Zealand with MCC, as they were known in those days. During a test in Wellington, I approached him, seeking his autograph. I had carefully stalked him around the Basin on the Saturday of the test, waiting for an opportune moment. When I saw him standing on the steps of a landing in the main stand, conversing casually with his manager, the Duke of Norfolk, I struck.

With much apprehension and intrepidation, I approached the great man and politely asked for his autograph while handing him my well-worn autograph book. I needn't have bothered. He took one look at me, broke away briefly from his conversation with the good Duke and told me in a very matter-of-fact sort of way to "f*** off, son", and with that returned to his conversation. I stood there shamed and humiliated. This wasn't the first time I'd been fobbed off by a sports star while seeking an autograph, but never so brutally, and so publicly, by one so famous.

As a consolation, later in the day I did get the Rev David Sheppard to sign my book

– the only England player to do so.

Chasing autographs had become a sort of passion of mine during those formative early years. As a product of a working-class family growing up in the Hutt Valley in the 1960s, sport became an important part of my life.

We didn't have too many treats or fancy trips as mum and dad struggled to make ends meet most weeks, so sport, for me, happily filled the void.

Sport was my main priority, really my only priority, and also my fantasy. I desperately wanted to be a famous All Black fullback. Schoolwork, housework and family affairs were all distant seconds. Every Saturday afternoon in winter, for example, I would head to our local rugby ground, Fraser Park, in Taita, to watch our senior team do battle for the Hardham or Jubilee Cup, and tucked away safely in my pocket, my sacred autograph book.

Year after year, from about the ages of 10 to 15, I would fill it with the illegible scrawls and scribbles of senior rugby players in winter and senior cricketers in summer. After each match I would very carefully and neatly print the name of the autographee under the signature.

As every new page filled, so my pride would swell. How I cherished that increasingly tattered little multi-coloured autograph book.

The greatest single day in my autograph-seeking career came at the Basin a year after the Trueman rejection, when the brilliant 1964 South African cricket team (arguably their best-ever side) were here playing a test. On this occasion, I secured the signatures of some of their greatest cricketers, Graeme Pollock, his brother Peter, wicket-keeper Denis Lindsay, Colin Bland, the finest fielder and thrower of a cricket ball of his generation, and all-rounder Peter van der Merwe. And for good measure I landed one of the umpires as well, a gentleman by the name of D P Dumbleton, according to my handwriting.

I sought not only the mighty, but also the minnows.

There was the time (May 21-23, 1963) when the Freyberg Rosebowl interprovincial golf championship took place a few miles from home at the Hutt club. Each afternoon after school I would cycle furiously to the golf club, only a mile or so from school, whereupon I would track down any golfers in sight and ask them to sign my book. For the unknown amateur golfers of Northland and Poverty Bay, among other parts, it may well have been the one and only time these obscure club players were asked for their autographs. But I got them and still have them.

Even members of the 1963 Featherston senior rugby team found their way into my little book. They were, from memory, playing a pre-season warm-up game against Taita at Fraser Park, so I chased them down and signed them up either before or after the game.

Quite why I pursued so many anonymous sportsmen for their autographs is difficult to explain. Part of growing up, I suspect. There was always a certain thrill approaching some huge rugby player, famous or not, and getting him to sign my book. And with it came a touch of pride every time I secured another signature.

The year of 1963 was certainly a vintage one – and not just because I landed the boys from Featherston. International cricketers, amateur golfers from sundry parts and members of a famous Wellington rugby team all helped to fill the pages of my little coloured book.

On August 31, 1963 Wellington lifted the Ranfurly Shield from Auckland. The following Monday morning the team arrived home at the Wellington railway station to a rapturous reception. It was the school holidays so dad, a dyed-in-the wool Wellington supporter, took the morning off work and, with the whole family in tow, off to the railway station we went to join in the civic celebrations. Naturally my little book came with me and I picked up the autographs of eight members of the team that day, first five-eighth Cam Stewart, prop Dave Bendle, halfback Barry Cull, hooker Colin Currie, No 8 Paul Russo, lock Nev MacEwan, flanker Gary Hermansson, and a couple of All Blacks of the time, winger Ralph Caulton and prop Ken Gray.

It was a truly joyous day – no school, the Ranfurly Shield in Wellington (where it stayed for all of six days before Taranaki grabbed it) and a bunch of famous players in my book.

On another occasion during a Christmas holiday at my cousin's place in Hamilton, I went to Seddon Park to watch a Plunket Shield match and approached the truly legendary Bert Sutcliffe, who willingly added his name.

By now I was really only after famous sportsmen.

My greatest triumph was to secure the signatures of the three greatest All Black fullbacks of all time – Bob Scott, Don Clarke and George Nepia (well, in my youthful opinion they were).

As a budding All Black fullback myself, Don Clarke was my undisputed sports hero, but how could I secure his autograph? Trouble was he lived on farm in a place called Kereone, somewhere out the back of Morrinsville, and I was stuck in the Hutt Valley. Dad had an idea. Why didn't I write a short letter to Don, asking for his autograph and tell him that I, too, was a fullback and wanted to emulate his deeds.

But how would I get it to him, I asked? Well, said dad, probably all we could do was address the envelope to "Don Clarke, Famous All Black Fullback, c/o Kereone Rugby Club, Morrinsville, Waikato", and see what happened.

As added incentive we generously enclosed a stamped addressed envelope. A few weeks later, to my unalloyed joy and delight, the envelope with our address on it in dad's writing arrived back in our mail box with Don's autograph inside and a few words wishing me all the best for my future rugby days.

As an aside, some 15 years later while dining in a restaurant in Whangarei one summer's night with some colleagues from TVNZ after filming a track and field meeting, Don Clarke walked in. He was back from South Africa for a short visit. Our producer, who knew Don, introduced him to me and I could hardly restrain myself. Words tumbled out of my mouth at a rate of knots as I regaled him with the story of his autograph. He laughed heartily. But what a sweet moment it was for me to be able to personally thank him for his fine gesture all those years earlier.

Now that I had secured Don Clarke's autograph, next in line was Bob Scott, another great All Black fullback. R W H Scott, as he was known, was a member of the ill-fated

1949 All Black team to South Africa, but it didn't tarnish his reputation as one of the finest fullbacks the game had known. Dad would tell me tales of Bob's greatest feats, one of which was an ability to kick goals from 60 yards in bare feet.

In the 1960s, Bob ran a menswear store on Jackson St, the main street of Petone. As the crow flies, Bob's shop was only a couple of miles from the college I attended. After school one day I biked down to Bob's shop and there he was behind the counter with his unmistakable bald pate and a tape measure draped around his neck.

The shop had that nice warm smell of new suits, which lined the walls. Dear old Bob. He could not have been any nicer to this shy, awkward college kid as he signed his autograph on the same piece of paper Don Clarke had signed and chatted away cheerfully to me for a few minutes.

I couldn't wait to get home to show dad my latest priceless acquisition. Mum, incidentally, was singularly uninterested in the whole exercise.

The third leg of the treble was George Nepia, still alive and well somewhere up the top of the east coast of the North Island. But buoyed by the success of the "Don Clarke plan", dad suggested we do just the same with George, writing a short letter explaining why I wanted his autograph. This time we decided to include the precious piece of paper with Don Clarke's and Bob Scott's signatures.

Dad took the same approach with the address, sending the letter to "George Nepia, Famous 1924 All Black, c/o Wairoa Post office". This, of course, was an almighty risk. If the letter were to be mislaid or lost I would lose my two precious autographs. But once again another All Back fullback came through for the young lad in the Hutt and a few weeks later George Nepia's lovely reply, complete with autograph, showed up in our letter-box.

My life at the ripe old age of about 13 years was complete. I now had not just the autographs of the three greatest All Black fullbacks of all-time, but all on the same sheet of paper and all accompanied by a personal note.

Could that happen today? Could a young lad write to his three greatest All Black heroes and obtain their autographs? Or would it have to go first through the media and communications division of the New Zealand Rugby Union, which, in the interests of efficiency and cost reduction, would happily send the young lad a cyclostyled letter with three cyclostyled signatures?

But alas! There is a truly sad end to this boy's own dream. While I still have my famous little autograph book, which gives me great joy still when I flick through its pages from time to time, that special sheet with Don's, Bob's and George's signatures is lost.

Privately, I hope it's still sitting wedged somewhere, maybe in a family photo album, or gathering dust in a box of papers in a family member's garage, and one day will miraculously re-appear.

Then the dream of that youngster would just about have come true – to be re-united with my three greatest rugby heroes.

Sara Tetro

OLGA KORBUT AND NADIA COMANECI

Sara Tetro is one of New Zealand's leading model and celebrity managers, and has hosted the television show *New Zealand's Next Top Model*.

Gymnastics is a great sport in which competitors need to be incredibly disciplined, though I always felt they lacked a little warmth or humanity. They kept their emotions in check and that meant there was a separation between them and the audience. That was until Olga Korbut and Nadia Comaneci came on the scene with all their skill and personality in the 1970s.

Fortunately my interest in gymnastics coincided with their involvement, and I was able to watch them during some of their outstanding performances at the Olympics.

Olga Korbut looked so small, but she had a massive presence and an infectious smile. I was sitting in my parents' living room when I first saw her, at the 1972 Munich Olympics. She continued to have an impact at Montreal four years later, but those games really marked the explosive arrival of Nadia Comaneci, who flourished further in Moscow at the 1980 Olympics.

Suddenly, it seemed, gymnastics went from an austere, technical competition to a warm, open, expressive sport that was dominated by younger and more adventurous athletes. They looked as though they truly enjoyed their sport; they were daring and inventive, they engaged the crowds and, certainly for me, growing up in New Zealand, they flicked the switch that connected me to the love of their sport.

Korbut and Comaneci, to me, were champions no matter the colour of their medals. I was happy to wait for them to appear – the television coverage did not run to any precise timetable, but what a treat when they finally came on screen.

They were daring but brilliantly disciplined as they injected their personalities into the sport. They made us feel we could at least attempt their feats of brilliance because they performed their work with smiles on their faces and with grace and warmth. They

broke the mould, giving gymnastics a humanity it had seemed to lack. More than any other competitors they created an interactive atmosphere. Their open, engaging freshness gave us something we could aspire to.

What brilliance they both delivered, topped off by Comaneci when she scored that first perfect 10 at Montreal. Then there were several other perfect scores at the same games. I can still picture the confusion as we watched her magnificent performances while the scoreboards showed her scoring a 1.00 because they had not been programmed to record the maximum 10. My young self loved those moments and the adulation continued when Comaneci graced the cover of *Time* magazine shortly after, with the words, "She's Perfect".

Both Korbut and Comaneci let me believe in my dreams and targets and whenever I competed in gymnastics and subsequently moved into business, I'm sure I took some of their attitude with me.

Besides these two famous gymnasts, another major influence in my life has been my mother, who reinforced to me that if you wanted to do well, you had to make yourself count, you had to back yourself, and that if you did, the glitches would not seem to hurt so much. It has been much the same in my career.

I learned that if you hesitate you're lost. You have got to back yourself with your family and in your business and I back myself 100 per cent.

OLGA KORBUT, who had the gymnastics crowds at the 1972 Munich Olympics in raptures.

Paul Thomas

SIR TERRY MCLEAN

Paul Thomas is a successful novelist, newspaper columnist, and sports book author.

Back in the days before all sports events of any significance and some of no significance at all were accorded live television coverage (or, in my case, before television itself), the young sports fan had to make do with books.

This was the heyday of the tour book. Most were formulaic and pedestrian; some were little more than recycled, padded-out newspaper reports. But I was fortunate enough to come across two notable exceptions, which not only cemented my relationship with the respective games, but also sparked an interest in and appreciation of the art and craft of writing.

One was *Australia 63*, an account of the 1962-63 Ashes series, which I found in a little bookshop in Newmarket run by a stately European lady. I was familiar with the subject, having spent many hours in close proximity to what was known in my family as a transistor radio, although it was the approximate size and weight of our cutlery drawer.

The dust-jacket insisted the book was an "exciting and well-informed account", which was good enough for me. I handed over my birthday takings and hurried home to relive the exploits of Richie Benaud and Ted Dexter and their respective supporting casts.

It soon became apparent that *Australia 63* didn't conform to the conventions of the tour book sub-genre. Large chunks of it were, in fact, cricket-free zones. There was even a poem. Entitled *Watching Benaud Bowl*, it began:

Leg-spinners pose problems much like love,
Requiring commitment, the taking of a chance.

The flyleaf shed some light, revealing that, in addition to being *The Observer's* cricket correspondent, the author, Alan Ross, had published four volumes of poetry, three travel books and in his spare time edited a literary magazine.

My initial reaction was a resentful feeling of having been sucked in by false advertising. Only a reluctance to risk offending the stately European lady dissuaded me from demanding my money back. Seeing I was stuck with it, I ventured into the cricket-free zones, where I learned there was a type of writing which did more than just convey information ("Her eyes were an unnaturally pale shade of blue") or tell a story ("Carruthers took a deep breath and flung himself into the path of the charging rhino").

I also learned a few things about that vast land mass squatting over the western horizon, at the very edge of our mother country-fixated consciousness. How lucky we were to live in a temperate land without lethal insects or sinister reptiles, a land whose inhabitants co-existed in relative harmony with nature.

"Weekend in Sydney," wrote Ross. "*The Sydney Morning Herald* records deaths by redback spider, snake and shark, a reminder that nature in Australia, moving violently from drought to flood, is essentially hostile. On the surf beaches beyond Manly, the dumpers thunder in and rips whirling the unwary out have life-savers in continual action. Half-a-dozen are drowned in New South Wales over the two days."

Mind you, it didn't sound all bad: "With darkness, Sydney becomes magical, the headlands and bays flickering with reflection and the electric blue lights of the bridge arching over the estuary. The sky is like black velvet inlaid with diamond, the night an illuminated Cartier's window. At Kings Cross the espresso bars and night clubs give off an aroma of coffee, buried jazz and foreign accents far into the dawn."

As for the cricket-writing, it brought a drawn series already fading from the collective memory vividly back to life, as in this description of a match-winning innings by the Rev David Sheppard, an amateur who'd emerged from semi-retirement for one last hurrah before devoting himself to higher matters:

"For four hours Sheppard played with the assurance of one who had heard an old nostalgic tune, its melody as it made itself familiar recalling forgotten and delightful associations. His stroke-play acquired a dream-like smoothness, all angularities and awkwardnesses smoothed away. When it was over he was near collapse, but the song's echoes were of the kind that linger indelibly."

The other book, pilfered from my father's study, never to be returned, was *Kings of Rugby* by T P (later Sir Terry) McLean, the doyen of New Zealand sports journalism and arguably the finest rugby writer yet to grace the game.

Kings of Rugby is his account of the tour of New Zealand by the 1959 British Lions, a richly-talented group who, had they enjoyed better luck with injuries, might well have been as successful as the 1971 vintage.

I saw them play the South Canterbury-Mid Canterbury-North Otago combined team at Fraser Park, Timaru, and remember my father, a proud Welshman, being uncharacteristically bitter on his return from Dunedin, where he'd watched Don Clarke's six penalties trump the Lions' four tries.

McLean, a proud Kiwi, was similarly unimpressed, his stern judgement evoking a time when the All Blacks weren't surrounded by a noxious cloud of advertising agency-generated faux patriotism (the sort Samuel Johnson was referring to when he declared that patriotism was "the last refuge of the scoundrel") and defeats didn't prompt outbreaks of self-lacerating analysis and talkback radio rabble-rousing:

"Shall one ever forget the cry of 'Red! Red!' which burst from 40,000 throats when D B Clarke had placed his sixth and what proved to be the winning penalty of the match? Here was an expression, from a community which had always honoured forward play, of a distaste for forward play supplemented by goal-kicking, which had produced so fortuitous and distasteful a result. Not one person in the crowd, perhaps not one true lover of rugby in New Zealand, would have been in the least distressed or dismayed if the Lions had scored the try the tremendous chants so much encouraged them to attempt."

His artfully-crafted pen portraits reveal a shrewd observer with a deep appreciation of the quirks and foibles of his fellow men.

Of the Welsh prop Ray Prosser, he wrote: "Though comparatively ill-educated, he had a dramatic fluency in both the Queen's and Billingsgate English; his descriptions of the effect upon the human frame, especially the male frame, of various types of excavator and/or bulldozer driving were classical in the bare, terse phrases."

(Prosser later became a celebrated coach of his beloved Pontypool club. His emphasis on hard-nosed forward play did wonders for the Welsh national team, but appalled those who subscribed to the myth of Wales as the spiritual home of dashing back-play. Prosser enjoyed stirring the pot by claiming he had two tactics: "Up and bloody under." Nor did the years dim his command of the vernacular. The night I attended Pontypool training, he told one of his less athletic forwards: "You run like the hairs in your arse are tied together.")

Of the glamorous 23-year-old Irish wing, Tony O'Reilly, McLean wrote: "At a long-range guess one felt reasonably sure that he would in time become president or premier of the Irish Republic."

O'Reilly did indeed go on to great things, but as a businessman whose holdings, including the *New Zealand Herald,* and influence extend far beyond his native land.

I met McLean once, in a Cardiff television studio where I'd gone to meet Carwyn James, the coach of the victorious 1971 Lions. T P politely but firmly deflected my praise and James' invitation to join us for lunch. I put his wariness in the first instance down to his innate modesty and, in the second, to inside knowledge, gleaned from research in the field, that the great coach's idea of lunch was several large gin and tonics.

Stephen Tindall

DANYON LOADER

Stephen Tindall founded The Warehouse in 1982. The chain now has more than 180 outlets and Tindall has become one of New Zealand's most successful businessmen.

Getting up in the dark and heading for very early morning training at the pool, the slog of swimming all those lengths day after day and the single-mindedness needed to excel in that sport.

As someone with a strong interest in swimming all my life, I have some understanding of what those champions in the water have to contend with if they are to make it to the top of their chosen sport.

So I have total admiration for Danyon Loader, who won two Olympic Games gold medals in 1996 in Atlanta, after picking up a silver medal four years earlier in Barcelona.

In passing, though I could never forget Danyon's feats, I would rate Rob Waddell right up there for his extraordinary ability to switch from being a gold medal rower to the America's Cup and then reinventing himself again as an oarsman. He is a marvellous man, too, but on this occasion I have plumped for Danyon.

I guess I had some comprehension of what sacrifices he had to make, what adversity he had to overcome to compete in those games, and a lot of the detail about what was happening, because his father, Peter was working for me as a storeman in our Dunedin Warehouse.

I had no idea Danyon was going to win a medal, let alone twin golds, but I remember putting out a challenge to our staff and eventually we managed to raise enough money so that both Peter and his wife, Daphne, were able to travel to Atlanta to watch their son perform so brilliantly.

There they were decked out in their red Warehouse T-shirts, shouting the house down as Danyon powered through that water to collect his double reward. It was quite something.

Because of Peter's involvement at work, I had quite a lot of inside knowledge about what Danyon was going through, how his training was progressing, what he thought was working and what wasn't in his build-up to those games.

It was just a staggering achievement for him to come away with twin first-place finishes in a sport that New Zealand had never really excelled in, certainly not to the extent that the country has found success in rowing and middle-distance running. It was a remarkable feat by an extraordinarily gifted and dedicated swimmer.

Renowned coach Duncan Laing was a significant part of the package, too, because he was in Dunedin and was able to listen to Danyon. If he had any technical issues, he could talk to him, offer him ideas and push him when required. Duncan was great because he knew all the buttons to push with Danyon.

It wasn't like these days, when all the swimmers train in a group, like the national squad does at the Millennium Centre. There is a lot more help, competition and drive from a concerted, extended group than there was for someone like Danyon, who had to do the bulk of the preparation himself.

Danyon was an incredibly modest, even shy, young man, which was perhaps best captured by the way he came back from the games and put the two gold medals in a shoebox in his bedroom. There was no way he was going to hang the medals on the wall or show them off around his neck, or any of that sort of carry on.

There was nothing about Danyon that said: "Look at me. I'm an Olympic champion."

He has come out of his shell a bit lately, by appearing on such programmes as *Dancing with the Stars,* which is a heck of a leap compared to the television interviews he did after winning his golds. Back then many people considered Danyon to be an unusual character when really he was very shy and uncertain about being in the limelight. He did not really connect with the country then, and I think many people were left feeling disconnected from this sporting phenomenon.

Even though Danyon had won an Olympic medal four years earlier, not much was known about him. He was not much in the public eye – he was considered a bit of a recluse, a little bit alternative, and was left to get on with his area of expertise. He would go to the pool and would play video games while he waited to train, but in terms of dedicated training and the pain that the guy put his body through, he could not be questioned. For a New Zealand swimmer to take on the rest of the world at an Olympics and come away with two golds was staggering.

When he came back from the Olympics, he sent me a really nice poster which he had signed, to thank everybody at the Warehouse, and we had that displayed proudly in our lobby. He is close to his mum and dad, and the fact that we'd been able to raise the money for them to be able to accompany Danyon meant an awful lot to everyone in the community.

Brian Turner

BROTHERS GLENN AND GREG

Brian Turner played hockey for New Zealand, and
has become one of the country's leading poets.

I've always had a few sportspeople I admired, especially when I was young. Their
influence on me was related to what they stood for, as much as for the quality of
their performances. Since then, many have come and gone and left a favourable
impression. But none have affected me quite as much as those I knew, or knew of, in
my formative years.

Nowadays it often seems that some of our most notable sportspeople see themselves
as fully-formed by the time they're in their early 20s and are reluctant to accept that
those who went before have much to offer them. Then again, exceptions breed like
flies, and always have.

In the 1950s Bert Sutcliffe was a hero to me. He was inoffensive, genuinely modest,
a nice mover in the field and composed and elegant at the crease. Then there was
my cousin, the cyclist Alan Larkins. "Larks", as I wrote in my memoir *Somebodies and
Nobodies,* "was, and always will be, a great... the local colossus... As a lean, super-fit
teenager, then as a young man... Larks reigned supreme on both road and track. He
trained hard. He rode with guts and enormous determination. Put them together and
you achieved glory."

By the time I was 20, hockey coaches Tom Eggelton and Cyril Walter, both from
Canterbury, inspired me. They believed there was no substitute for skill, and that you
had a duty to assert your right to display it. At the highest level, sport was an art and it
was necessary to aspire to practise that art.

Then, in my mid-20s, after having stupidly pissed off one or two key, vindictive
individuals in the hockey administration, and realising I would very likely never play
for New Zealand again, no matter where and how well I played, I was appalled to watch

what some in New Zealand cricket were endeavouring to do to my young brother, Glenn. He behaved and played heroically, as I saw it, and he also got offside with some in the media and, crucially, that segment of the New Zealand cricket administration run from Christchurch.

Glenn's was a roller-coaster ride, no doubt about it. As his older brother, I felt a bit protective of him, naturally. My parents and I were often hurt and sometimes incensed by the way he was treated. When he started playing first-class cricket at 17, he was lightly-built and, inevitably, unworldly.

But by the time he was 20 he was a professional, playing for Worcestershire in the UK. It wasn't long before I twigged that, as our only professional cricketer at a time when Walter Hadlee and his faction were utterly opposed to professionalism, he was doomed to be harassed and disparaged, as well as envied, for much of his career.

Of course, Glenn was not always diplomatic, but there were no agents or players' associations in those days, so he was flying solo most of the time. He was paid very little and told that he was lucky to be getting that.

No-one in my lifetime has been so viciously and relentless slandered and impugned by his parent sports body and certain senior players alike.

I admired Glenn's resolve, his thoroughness and attention to detail, his self-reliance. He was always straight, self-effacing, genuinely modest, reliable, and not given to boasting or histrionics. He was reserved and often quite shy in the sense that he never liked or sought to be the centre of attention. He was also a bit stubborn, not to be annoying, but simply because he believed you needed a good argument, one that was based on considerable experience and knowledge, before he'd go another way.

A knee-jerker he was not, nor was he in the slightest bit vain. How frightfully old-fashioned.

He wasn't collegial enough, or sunny enough, for some. And he wasn't always right, no-one is. But for the most part he set professional standards that most couldn't meet, and some disliked him for that. It exposed them. So they turned on him.

Several times I told him to practise the sly art of ingratiation and, basically, do what you're told. Tell people what they wanted to hear, or you'll be savaged, was what I said. I'm not sure I could have, so I'm not surprised that he just gave straight answers to questions and tried to be true to himself and the proper spirit of the game as he saw it.

That Glenn has stuck with New Zealand cricket, given the way he was treated, amazes me. But there's no doubt it's mainly because he absolutely loves and is fascinated by the game; also, because he's always felt he had a lot to offer and still wants to contribute.

More than once, laughing, I told Glenn that if he'd been brought up in Christchurch and had been playing for Canterbury, he'd have been fêted and lauded there. I'm not sure if he agreed, or if he'd have liked it.

I enjoyed listening to him talk about, or commentate on, cricket. Insight, analysis and a dry wit were evident, and he loved to discuss technique and strategy.

Then in my late 30s, I got really interested in my brother Greg's golf career. He was more extroverted and effervescent than Glenn or me. Cheekier, too, and often lippy.

Some might say that is right in the family grain.

Greg was clever, talented, determined, analytical, inventive, innovative and intelligent – his native intellect superior to Glenn's or mine. He didn't have anything like the reserve that Glenn had, and he always appeared to have much more confidence that I did. I envied him for that and still do. Of course, he is 19 years younger than me, and the "climate" in New Zealand had altered a bit by the time he came along.

Nevertheless, some were heard to say that he was "a typical Turner", meaning that in their view he had too much to say for himself. What they really meant, most of the time, was that he wasn't deferential enough. New Zealand is full of officials and others who often respond as if they don't really want to hear what others think. They want to be assured that you know what they think, and that you comply. They were always going to be averse to my brothers and me – we were brought up among adults who argued the toss, enjoyed vigorous debate, and felt that was a right you were entitled to exercise. That way everyone was likely to learn something.

I did quite a lot of caddying for Greg from the late 1980s until about 2002. Despite my presence, as much as because of it, he had a good deal of success during these years, including winning the New Zealand Open at Middlemore in 1997 and the Australian PGA a few years later. There were also a fair few top 10 finishes. I loved working for him; they were some of the highlights of my life in sport.

I saw Greg "under the gun", as is said, on many occasions, and admired his ability to respond to pressure and get the job done.

Both Greg and Glenn admired people with skill, technical and tactical excellence, an ability to make good decisions under pressure, and to accept that while winning is the object, it is not pursued at all costs – the way you play, the spirit you embody, and the importance of worthy tradition is also of the highest importance. Sometimes, in sport as in other facets of life, you succeed by dint of good fortune, as well as effort and skill, including composure. And none of us are bigger than the game.

I've been lucky with my brothers. They've been, often, exemplars to me and others.

So they have been heroes for decades.

Of course, for the likes of me, this country has thrown up very many sportsmen who have struck me as worthy of enormous respect: Steve Gurney, Erin Baker, Hamish Carter, Anton Oliver for his generosity, sincerity and loyalty, Murray Halberg, Danyon Loader... the list goes on. So many...

Glenn Turner

BILLY IBADULLAH

Glenn Turner was one of the world's leading opening batsmen during a first-class career that lasted from 1964-83. He played 41 tests and led New Zealand from 1975-77. He is currently a national selector.

My love for cricket seemed as natural as the matches we played in the backyard or at nearby Logan Park in Dunedin, while my disdain for being dismissed grew from the exceptionally keen games we had among our family and those who boarded with us.

When we shifted to south Dunedin, the intensity of our backyard battles increased, especially if it was a duel with older brother Brian. Outdoing my brother at cricket was a relentless target and three men, in particular, helped me along that route.

Much of the encouragement in my early career started with Lankford Smith, who was my first real coach and taught me the basic skills in the game, then remained my mentor. He was forceful but encouraging and his considered tuition gave me the basis for a strong game. I learned the main strokes I needed and practised them over and over in front of a mirror.

Lankford was an all-rounder who had a successful career with Otago, and his patient encouragement was an invaluable weapon for a youngster who was mad keen on the game.

In my early years at secondary school I was lucky enough to get along to a couple of coaching sessions being run by Bert Sutcliffe. Just attending those practices was massive. Being near one of the New Zealand legends of the game was a massive fillip for someone like me, who was consumed by the summer game. Bert was a very natural player who was also marvellous in encouraging kids to get involved in cricket.

But it was Billy Ibadulla, the Warwickshire professional who had come out to Dunedin as coach for the Otago Cricket Association, who really helped push me to the next level. He was a marvellous instructor, patient enough to meet me at the Logan Park nets at 6.30am, when he would bowl and teach with great sympathy and

255

understanding. While he increased the technical excellence of my cricket, Billy was also able to push me across the psychological boundaries in the sport.

He threw all his experience, knowledge and technical expertise at me. We went through a myriad of scenarios about conditions, theories, techniques and ideas. Having Billy almost to myself was cricketing nirvana. Here was someone who had scored 166 on his debut test, for Pakistan against Australia in Lahore, giving me extensive one-on-one coaching clinics in Dunedin.

Billy gave generously of his time, information and advice and for someone like me, who was so smitten with the game of cricket, his guidance was a pot of gold. He was patient, caring, and supportive when the critics lampooned my slow approach.

He encouraged me to attempt a career in county cricket, running me through a list of what to encounter along with the difficulties of being a professional cricketer. We worked on it together and my success had a great deal to do with Billy Ibadulla's guidance.

It is great to still see Billy round Dunedin these days. He is in his mid-70s and often rugged up in his beanie, scarf and sheepskin jacket in the Edgar Stand, but nothing can keep him away from watching his favourite sport and continuing to make a contribution to the game.

Greg Turner

MY ENVIRONMENT

Greg Turner was a professional golfer for 20 years
from the early 1980s and is now involved in course
design and tournament promotion.

When you have had a career that spans in excess of two decades there is inevitably an
enormous number of contributors to your development. Trying to assign some sort of
scale of importance is difficult, especially in a sport such as golf, where there is such a
technical element to go along with the psychological and physical elements.

And when you come from a sports family such as mine, the influences from within
that family are also rather significant. In many ways I had three fathers, rather than
two brothers, although both of my brothers visibly cringe at the mere suggestion.
From my earliest recollections, both my brothers, Brian and Glenn, were representing
New Zealand in their respective sports, hockey and cricket, and were therefore role
models and idols rather than competitors or playmates.

That said, this did not stop them both, by the time I was showing some promise as
a fledgling golfer, from pushing my comfort zone to its limits. Glenn was especially
adept at trying to antagonise me. In later years, he would justify this constant baiting
as a determined effort to force me outside my comfort zone so as to accelerate my
development and understanding of the debilitating effects on performance of losing
control. I'm sure this was so, although I reckoned his clear delight and enthusiasm at
making me lose my bundle was too great for it to be entirely selfless!

Brian was more restrained in that sense, more likely to probe, question and
rationalise than deliberately bait. Perhaps I'll give him the benefit of doubt and say he
was a reluctant participant in the goading process. Then again – that's not really the
way brothers should think, is it?

There were countless others, too, who contributed significantly to my development as
a golfer. Early mentors and coaches included irrepressible Australian club professional
(then resident pro at Chisolm Park) John Evans, the quirky but always encouraging pro
from my home club, Peter Hamblett, and my final coach, Englishman Denis Pugh.

Pugh and I would go on a journey of immense magnitude in terms of reconstructing the technical side of my game, and I will always be grateful for the time, enthusiasm and insight he invested in me. I have no doubt that my career would have been significantly shorter had it not been for Denis.

But as I tried to assign relative significance to these and others, it became apparent to me that the real foundation of my career was not so much a matter of who, but more of when and where. The New Zealand that I grew up in, that of the late 1960s, '70s and early '80s, was a utopia for a kid like me.

We were very much a working-class family and yet there seemed an enormous opportunity to participate and develop any number of sports-related skills. Money was always very tight, although I have no recollection of wanting for anything or feeling like entry into any sport was out of reach. This circumstance obviously owed much to my parents' attitude and priorities, but it was also directly related to New Zealand's egalitarian nature, and Dunedin seemed at the most balanced end of that spectrum. That's not to say there wasn't significant wealth around, just that in that part of New Zealand (and maybe something to do with the strong Scottish ancestry), it certainly wasn't the done thing to show it ostentatiously.

In those days much of our family life revolved around sport and sports clubs. As a child I was exposed to an enormous range of sports, and played cricket, hockey, soccer, squash, tennis and badminton. People tended to work from Monday to Friday, and therefore the weekends were awash with club-related sports endeavour. I had the opportunity to play with and against the older generation. There always seemed a number of adults to coach and mentor the kids' teams, and then as I grew I was able to make the transition into the lower adult grades.

The impacts were in two main areas.

The first, and sometimes underestimated, factor related to the variety of sports we were exposed to. Far from encompassing the specialising ethic more prevalent today, I can remember being encouraged to try many different sports. I have always believed that the multiple skills learnt and developed by a multi-code approach stood me in good stead for later specialisation. The experience of having to deal with the issues involved in team sports was also an important factor.

The second was the continuing presence of more senior players. Much development was by virtual osmosis. You learned to watch what the older players were doing, how they handled themselves in various circumstances. And when you stepped out of line, you tended to be brought down to earth with a rather large thump. You learned to grow up pretty quickly in that environment. I have little doubt that this was probably the most important area for accelerated development. There is no substitute for coming face to face with more experienced adversaries and team-mates.

As a youngster, you're always prone to putting all your emphasis on hitting the ball well – on admiring the elegance of a great ball flight. But watching the likes of Geoff Clarke, then one of New Zealand's leading amateurs, manoeuvre his way around the course to a low score while seldom ever hitting a beautiful shot was incredibly instructive. You learned to "win ugly" – to concentrate on outcomes rather than inputs – to "play smart rather than pretty".

Sarah Ulmer

DAME SUSAN DEVOY

Sarah Ulmer, New Zealand's most noted cyclist, won the
3000m individual pursuit Olympic gold medal in 2004,
plus the 1998 and 2002 Commonwealth Games gold medals,
and set the world record in the event.

Before I got the sports bug, and especially the hit I got from cycling, I was, like many of
my mates, quite happy when we got time off school in the weekends to be entertained
by *What Now* during Saturday morning television. That was way more fun for us then
than cranking into some activity which was going to send our heart-rates climbing.

Fortunately, though, when I started secondary school and began to be far more
interested in a whole variety of sports, there was this amazing Kiwi sportswoman, Susan
Devoy, whose exploits I could follow in the newspapers and on television. Here was
this extraordinary woman who had gone across to the other side of the world, trained
and competed unbelievably hard and conquered the world squash circuit.

Susan's success was just perfect for me. It showed me that I could follow my dreams
and ambitions on the global stage if I worked hard enough.

Of even more influence was her full-noise approach to squash and the intensity
of her preparation. Her effort, drive and competitiveness were inspirational – well, it
certainly was for me.

At that stage as I was battling to fit the mould at a private girls' school, Susan's
outstanding success just hit the right note for me. Being in the public eye she gave me
someone to try to emulate.

Her approach easily crossed over into my cycling domain. Not only did Susan show how
acceptable it was for chicks to give it everything in their sport, but she also demonstrated
that there were no shortcuts either – giving it death was the only way to go.

Squash is a wicked game, but it was not going to be the sport where I was going to
reach any great heights. However, I could watch Susan and her approach to her work
rather than dwelling too much on the intricacies of her sport.

It was more about evaluating what squash and Susan showed me needed to happen if I was to get anywhere near the top in cycling.

The parallels were not hard to identify. You needed huge levels of fitness, tenacity and competitiveness, all of which Susan had in bucketloads. She was courageous, too, making it to the top of her sport on the other side of the world, so far away from all her friends and family.

Susan had her moments, but she was mentally tough, way too tough for the others trying to pinch her crown, and she showed no let-up until she decided to call it quits.

Her success was a great basis for me to start from and there is no question her achievements played a part in forming my approach and work ethic towards my own sport. Those attitudes, which were created when I was a wee kipper, remained with me throughout my career. They were the pillars in my progress, and I can say Susan's exploits were a really positive influence in my ride to the top.

Valerie Vili

MY MUM LILIKA AND KIRSTEN HELLIER

Valerie Vili has become one of New Zealand's greatest athletes, with world, Olympic and Commonwealth Games shot put gold medals.

There is no question about the initial pillar of my life, my greatest supporter. It was my mum, Lilika, who was the rock of my family, the rock of my heart.

She kept everything moving, no matter how sick she was. She was the Tongan side of my family, a proud full Tongan lady who pulled me right through on everything. My family did not have a lot of money and when she passed away, the person who took over significantly from about 2001 was Kirsten Hellier, who remains my throwing coach and is still my really great buddy.

I was brought up in Rotorua, but left there when I was very young to move to Mangere and the Southern Cross Campus middle school. I was the biggest kid there and like everyone else was made to compete in all the track and field events.

My physical advantages and aptitude helped, and I found I won just about everything there before I graduated to compete for Counties Manukau, then the North Island champs, and it went on from there.

When I was about 13, a Samoan lady named Tina Tugaga, who was my intermediate school PE and social studies teacher, gave me a pair of Nike shoes. I treasured them like nothing else, took them home every day, cleaned them and marvelled how lucky I was to have them. Tina used to help out by taking me to and from training. It might seem like a simple task, but it involved a huge transfer of belief for my mother to agree to deliver me into Tina's care.

I could not have been more fortunate because Tina understood how south Auckland kids worked and thought. She got to know mum well and earned her trust.

About that time I went to the track to do some training and heard about this woman, Kirsten Hellier, who was highly regarded as a coach. I had no idea who she

Valerie Vili and her coach, **KIRSTEN HELLIER,** at a Halberg Awards ceremony.

was, what she had done or anything about her and it must have been a month or so before our paths crossed, in November, 1998, at one of the sessions.

It was clear that this busy woman knew what she was about and was in charge. There was no mucking around. Once I met Kirsten, she started giving me times to go to training and specific help about how to improve.

As the Sydney Olympics rolled around in 2000, I was very involved in athletics, but was also looking after mum, who by then was very sick in a south Auckland hospice and died the day after the September 15 opening ceremony. I remember lying on a lazy-boy watching that ceremony on television while mum was asleep on the bed next to me. It was the first night in an awfully long time that she'd had a good sleep and the following day she died.

It was a terribly difficult time because I was only 15, but I remember watching the Olympics and thinking I wanted to be there one day.

It took me some time to get over that whole experience and I moped around for some time after mum died. My motivation took a hit and it seemed I went to school only to eat my lunch.

My mum was pretty strict, but that influence had a positive impact on me. She was brought up as an only child on the tiny island of Houma. She was a strongly religious person in the Mormon church and served her mission in Tonga. She subsequently only ever travelled to Fiji and New Zealand.

She gave me boundaries and if I crossed those I soon learnt about my mistakes.

My elder sister pushed the envelope far more than me. I felt I couldn't because I did not want to offend or upset my mother because our bond was so strong. I stayed home, I did the work and helped my mother because I loved and respected her so much.

There were no regrets about that at all. When mum was sick, it was natural for me to stay home for about three months to care for her, to tend to her when she went to hospital, to give back what she had given to me.

She was not too keen on the nurses looking after her, anyway. She was a big woman who felt more comfortable if I was there to help her get in and out of bed, wash her, help feed her and take care of her, as she did when we were kids.

It was a sad and hilarious time. I remember she would tell off the staff and warn them not to touch her until I arrived. It was tough and it is still hard when I think back to those times.

I was way too young to lose my mum. She was only 39 when diabetes claimed her, and I am an orphan now because dad died in 2007, just before the start of the world championships.

The lesson I learned from those two episodes is the importance of looking after myself.

Mum was suspicious of people she did not quite understand, like Europeans, or professionals like doctors and nurses, but when Kirsten arrived on the scene that broke down another of those barriers and my mother felt comfortable that someone else of great character could help me through my life.

It was okay for me to go and stay over at her house or for Kirsten to pick me up from training even on Sundays, which was church day.

After mum died, that relationship with Kirsten carried on and developed. She had lived in Samoa and so understood the island way of life. We shared the same birthday. She was an athlete, a good teacher and communicator, and understood what we do.

Kirsten did not want me to make the same mistakes she had in training, technique and tactical approach. Even though her speciality was javelin, when I came along she threw herself into learning all about the shot and we grew together.

I was a bit of a guinea pig as we tried a few ideas in the early stages, but we learned together and discovered what worked for me. We did not follow the Russian technique or the German ideas; we worked out what suited me.

I had fun with the discus and hammer, too, and went well with them, but the shot suited me best when I had to make a choice about specialising in one field event.

You have to be tense and deliver short, fast, violent actions for the shot and that "rip, shit and bust" style suited me. For example, I can't throw the javelin anywhere near the distance Kirsten can – she is still the New Zealand record-holder. She has a long rhythmical delivery, whereas I still try to throw it like the shot, with an explosive burst. I was so bad I knocked myself out once trying to throw the javelin.

Kirsten understood all these things, and we learned the technical side of things together, we got advice from all sorts of international coaches and authorities on the bio-mechanics of the sport, we devoured books on the subject, we worked very hard together.

I have discussed the shot with some other awesome coaches around the world, but Kirsten has never tried to get me to throw like one particular thrower. She would suggest ideas, and we might try them and then either adopt them or give them away. For example, German throwers all throw the same way and have done since the 1980s, whereas I throw the way that suits me.

Kirsten and I have developed my technique and we have not stopped learning. We are always trying to find new ideas and make subtle changes all the time. It is awesome and exciting.

While I glean some ideas from overseas coaches, I could not find anyone better than Kirsten to help me, because she also provides the emotional structure and support for what I do. She understands me all the time – she knows how I will react and feel on a day before a competition.

We have worked out the ingredients together. Some people rest the day before a competition; others might go for a jog. I need to lift, I need to sweat and I get in there and do it. If I don't do anything, I feel lethargic on the day of competition and that's another of the things we have learned together over the years.

Kirsten also knows when to back off. Does she know when I am going to get shitty? Let's say we have developed such a relationship that she will know if something is up, but I have never thrown a hissy fit at her, not one. She has never thrown one at me either, though we have both been close. We have learned it is better to walk out or just not say anything at all, because we value our friendship so much.

We spend a lot of time together on a daily basis, but we are not in each other's pockets. It works. And I would not have it any other way.

Mum started me and guided me on this wonderful life and Kirsten has carried on that wonderful example. I have been very blessed having these two proud, determined, tenacious women mentor me.

I put huge expectations on myself. I am very demanding and put a lot of pressure on myself, but no more than my mum and Kirsten would expect.

That is the way we work. We train hard and we work hard, because if it was a breeze every Tom, Dick and Harry would do it.

I always wanted to do a sport because of my physique. It was all about finding a sport that suited me. Basketball took me from Mangere to Otara, track and field took me to Poland and the world youth championships at the age of 14, and then the world.

Two years later, just after mum died, I won the world youth champs. It was a shame she was not alive, but I knew she was around and Kirsten was there to guide me.

I have had my moments, but I just need to think of all the work those two wonderful women put into me and count my blessings.

Beverley Wakem

RON JARDEN

Beverley Wakem was chief executive of Radio New Zealand from 1984-91 and has been the Chief Ombudsman since 2008.

Ron Jarden was my sports hero, but Tony O'Reilly, the great Irish winger, ran him close for a while.

My father was a big rugby fan, and seldom missed an important game at Athletic Park. He had season tickets in the main stand. Sometimes I got to go with him, which was always a thrill. My love of rugby has continued until this day. I remain a faithful supporter of the Hurricanes, and live in hope for the time when they will be not only brilliant, but consistent!

In Wellington rugby in the 1950s, Ron Jarden was the glamour figure. Playing on the left wing, he ran like the wind and he scored some sensational tries. I once sat on the western bank at Athletic Park watching him play for New Zealand Universities. He scored a length-of-the-field try, beating several defenders with his speed and elusiveness. It was always exciting when he got the ball, because he made things happen.

So he was my special sports hero, but in 1959, Tony O'Reilly achieved almost the same status. He was touring New Zealand with the Lions team and was a sensation. He used to wear the shortest shorts imaginable on the field! What cemented his appeal was that when he was in Wellington he came down to St Mary's College, which I attended, so that Sister Mary Lawrence could do a painting of him. She was a noted artist, but even so it was quite a thing to have one of the Lions players dropping in on the school.

Both Ron Jarden and Tony O'Reilly became very astute businessmen once they were finished with rugby. They were cultured, educated men, fully rounded – renaissance people, really. Ron, of course, set up a stockbroking firm, then in the 1970s became chairman of the BCNZ. Unfortunately, very soon after taking over the job, he died of a heart attack, at the age of just 47. It was such a tragedy because he was so young. I'm sure he would have been a wonderful chairman.

I never met Ron. I did not become chief executive of Radio New Zealand until several years later, and though I had worked for the BCNZ, as it was then called, it was at a lower level than where Ron was operating.

I did meet Tony O'Reilly later in life, though. I was involved in public relations for a time and our company had the Heinz Wattie's account. This was one of Tony's companies. He was just as engaging then as he had been all those years earlier when he'd come along to my school to have his portrait painted.

Sir John Walker

ARCH JELLEY, PETER SNELL AND OTHERS

Sir John Walker won the Olympic 1500m gold medal in
1976, the year after he became the first person to run the
mile in under 3min 50s.

Athletics began in earnest for me at intermediate school, when one of the guys from
the Manurewa Harriers Club encouraged me to join. I had always loved running, just
as I loved tennis and many other sports.

Running was just such a natural part of my life. We shifted to Hunua and as a five-
year-old I caught the bus after school. It dumped us and left us with a two-mile run
home. My parents were working and there was a big goat and dog on the way home
and I wasn't going to be munched by either of those, so I ran home as fast as I could.

Often at the weekends I would be told to take lunch to dad out the back of the
400-acre farm and I guess that all helped with my conditioning, which helped me win
the primary school championships. We moved again when I was about six, this time to
Manurewa, and I would run to the tennis courts to play, then run home again.

When I joined Manurewa Harriers there were two guys, Graham Douglas and Ian
Craig, who both gave me plenty of encouragement. Graham encouraged me and
pointed me in the right directions. He was very positive, always helpful and someone
who believed if you turned down an opportunity that it was a chance which had passed
you by.

Those two men nurtured me and encouraged me through those important years.
When I did not want to get out of bed on a Sunday morning after going to a party,
they would come round to the house and throw stones at my room and mum and dad
would be yelling at me to get out of bed. I would then go and run 20 miles with them
and without that I would not have made it.

Ian Craig would meet me after work and run home with me and it was that sort of
care and attention that helped me along the way. There was always someone there for

me. It is so important because you can't do it by yourself.

So these guys were my heroes, but it was a collective package. Along the way I was inspired by Peter Snell and was grateful for the knowledge of coaching guru Arthur Lydiard. The final piece of the jigsaw was Arch Jelley and the framework was Manurewa Harriers. Arch and the guys at Manurewa Harriers might have been normal people, but they were all heroes who offered their time, their help and advice. Everyone in sport needs those sorts of people, because it always takes a long time until you find your final coach. The initial inspiration is only a small part of the puzzle, but it is so crucial.

When I was about 17, I was introduced to Arch, who became such a huge part of my career.

Much of my inspiration came from Peter Snell.

I did not know him, but his deeds were the beacon for me to follow, to aspire to. As a 13-year-old boy, I remember standing behind the toilet block listening to a transistor radio broadcast of Snell at Tokyo, without really realising who Snell was or what he represented in the world and what he was all about.

He wrote a book with Garth Gilmour called *No Bugles No Drums,* which I must have read 50 times. It was like my Bible. I modelled myself upon it, not because I thought I could be better or anything like that, but because Snell ran the same distances I did. He was a miler, a half-miler and 1500m man, and those were the distances that seemed to suit me.

Snell had also trained in the Waiatarua Ranges in Auckland, and his coach, Arthur Lydiard, also had a huge influence on my mentor, Arch Jelley.

There were all those connections which were important. We all came from similar backgrounds, but I was fortunate to have a bit more ability than others of my age.

I enjoyed reading books about the American miler, Jim Ryun. I read them all as a youngster. I was hugely interested and I think I was destined to be a runner. All these guys, through their books, confirmed and assisted my love of running, because at that stage I had never met any of them.

Then I remember Snell running in the Auckland cross-country championships on the same day as I won the junior cross-country title. I lined up for about half an hour in the pouring rain to get his autograph. He was a legend then and later on he had a significant influence my career. In 1975, the year before the Montreal Olympics, Snell urged me to go to Davis University to be a guinea pig for him.

I stayed with him, but Peter was an enigma. His time was precious, even though he invited me over there. He was studying for a PhD and would shut himself away for long periods in his study. The philosophy he applied to his running, he applied to his studies and he would shut himself away for ages. He never considered himself especially intelligent, but more of a hard worker, although I think he must have been pretty switched on to get his degrees.

I think he undersold himself, as he did throughout his career, but I stayed with him for a week. We played tennis at nights and would go for a bit of a run, and during the day I would read all his diaries, which was pretty amazing. I wanted to know what it was like to run in the Olympics, which were coming up for me. I wanted to learn from the guru about how he attained his three gold medals. I figured that reading about those special times was going to help me mentally and inspirationally.

As a teenager you have little idea how good you are and if you were to say to a kid today: "Give me seven years of your life and I will make you a champion", they would look at you and say, "Stuff that", because at that age it is very rare for anyone to be able to see that.

When I was 17 and won the Auckland 800m champs, I improved my time by a second and that was the only inspiration I needed. The tough years, though, are between 17 and 21 because New Zealanders mature very late, unlike the Europeans, who do a lot of interval work. However, we did the slow Lydiard-inspired work and we were so fortunate we had him as a guru because his principles still apply today to everything. He was the master. His disciple was Arch Jelley, who was my coach and motivated me though my learning years.

Lydiard was an inspiration through speech, whereas Arch was much quieter, more reserved. He would write me screeds of letters saying that he thought I could be the best, that he thought I could be the world record-holder, and those were pretty big statements to a guy who was 17.

He was the one who believed I could be a sub-3min 50s miler, even against my own belief. That was the essence of a good coach.

Tim Whelan

ANTHONY WILDING

Tim Whelan was the founder of the Lone Star restaurant chain in 1988 and is a sports junkie.

There were many Sundays growing up in Christchurch when my father would load up the family car and drive us out to enjoy South Brighton beach. One time on the way out there, he pointed out Wilding Park to us.

We were none the wiser, then, about the man in whose honour they named that sports arena, but it did not take long to discover and appreciate the impact Anthony Frederick Wilding had made on the New Zealand and global sports scene.

Four times Wimbledon singles champion, five times Davis Cup winner, Olympic Games medallist in Stockholm in 1912, gentleman, war hero.

Wilding was an exceptional man in many respects, an outstanding sportsman whose tennis feats remain unsurpassed in this country and whose deeds were among the most glorious in the first part of the 20th century. His successful life ended at just 31 when he was killed by a shell that landed on his trench during the Battle of Ypres on the Western Front in 1915.

He was an uninterested scholar who had been sent to finishing school in London and then studied law at Cambridge. He only scraped through his studies, but his passion for engines helped him in his subsequent motorbike travels across Europe as he became involved on the tennis circuit.

Wilding entertained royalty and many layers of the rich and famous with his sports and social skills. He was great company, a ladies' man and in modern times would have been the ultimate sponsor's dream.

He was also one of the first to champion fitness as a major weapon in sport and often prevailed through that superior conditioning when his tennis matches went beyond three sets. He was a trailblazer in that he did not smoke and prided himself on his physical superiority, which he had developed during rugged training runs through the Cashmere Hills.

Wilding grew up in Opawa on the way to Lyttelton and the old place still stands today. He was taught the tennis arts by his father in the back yard and then he left for England not long after the turn of the century.

There Wilding worked hard on changing his grip and other parts of his game. He began his Wimbledon career in 1904. Though he had success in the doubles, it was not until 1910 that Wilding made his singles breakthrough and began a domination of the tournament that was really only stopped by a German shell.

New Zealand has waited a long time for another tennis hero like Wilding. Onny Parun and Brian Fairlie had some success and Chris Lewis lost a Wimbledon final to John McEnroe. But no-one has matched Wilding's deeds. He was as much a hero in life as in death, a forgotten hero, but an absolute champion, a remarkable athlete and person, and one of New Zealand's finest.

Ruben Wiki

MAL MENINGA

Ruben Wiki played rugby league for the Canberra Raiders and the New Zealand Warriors, a total of more than 300 first-grade games. He played a world record 55 test matches from 1994-2006.

I know most people can tell you who their childhood sports idol was, but I can't. For whatever reason, I didn't have one when I was growing up in Otara in south Auckland. The only idol I had then was mum. She was everything to me then, and still is.

While rugby league became a big part of my life from a young age, it was really all about the Otara Scorpions and just playing the game with the kids from around the neighbourhood on the south side. We were in our own little world then and I didn't really know anything else.

It wasn't until I was in my teens that I began to notice things on a bigger scale, especially once I was able to see a bit of the Winfield Cup on television. By then I was playing my club footy for Otahuhu and, while there were legends who came out of the Leopards – none more so than Mark Graham – there was one team and, above all, one player who grabbed my attention.

I was right into Canberra back then and you just couldn't help noticing the big man in the centres, Mal Meninga. I knew something of him a couple of years earlier, but it was the 1989 grand final between the Raiders and Balmain – the one Canberra won in extra-time – which was the trigger for my special interest in Big Mal.

For a start, he was a centre and that's where I was playing my footy in those days (before the leg speed went just a little and I headed towards the forwards). I loved watching Mal whenever Canberra was playing and to see him in that grand final was awesome.

He always stood out so much because he was such a big and powerful centre, with plenty of speed to match his size. There are lots of huge guys playing in the backs these days – Manu Vatuvei is just one of them – but back then Meninga was called Big Mal for the right reasons. He was a monster in every team he played in, quite often the

273

biggest man in the team (forwards included).

The way he played the game appealed to me to the point where I tried to play just like him in my junior years.

This is how much I wanted to be like him. You know how he had his broken arm, the one he broke a few times? Well, I didn't have a broken arm then, but I bought one of those shin pads and strapped it around my arm so I had an armguard just like Mal used to wear! I wanted to be like him, play like him and look like him, doing the old Meninga bump-off and things like that when I had the ball. He was such a damaging player and he was someone to aspire to.

The crazy thing was that within just a few years I was actually at the Raiders with Mal. It's still hard to believe that I could have been lucky enough to play alongside the man who was my sports idol, but it happened. Best of all, I was blessed to be able to team up with him in the centres in his last first-grade game, when the Raiders beat Canterbury-Bankstown in the Winfield Cup grand final in 1994. How good was that!

That whole season was unbelievable, training and playing with Mal and learning so much from him. Soon after, he also became my coach.

He mightn't have been my childhood sporting idol – I didn't know he existed then – but Mal Meninga certainly helped me make up for lost time. He was, is, and always will be, my sports idol.

Steve Williams

IVAN MAUGER

Steve Williams has been caddying for world-class golfers since 1979, but rose to the top of his profession when he began carrying Tiger Woods' bag in 1999.

Motor-racing has always been a huge passion of mine, an interest fuelled when I was growing up in the Hutt Valley. As a family, we used to regularly go to the Te Marua speedway. It was a big deal. My dad was pretty keen on the whole thing, so it wasn't hard to persuade him to take us whenever the meetings were on.

We would do the whole thing, from eating hot dogs to milling around the pits area after the racing was finished. I can still remember all those smells from bike fuel, oil-encrusted leathers, the food and the people.

When I was about nine or 10, I got to meet my hero, Ivan Mauger. I had seen him race on television and here he was at our local meeting. I couldn't wait to see him up close down at the pits afterwards, and it turned out to be no big deal to be able to talk to him.

Those were the days when we were spoiled as kids and could spill out on to the park at any sports event and get autographs or talk to our heroes. It was such a buzz for a young kid like me to go and see Mauger, let alone have a word to him. He could not have been more normal, more helpful or more accommodating. To someone like me, who was fascinated by the sport, it was just magic.

I loved the way Mauger used to ride. You would look at most of the other riders around him and they would be banging their bikes or hitting bumps or slewing round the track, but Mauger was just so smooth, so classy, so effortless, it looked as though he never hit a bump or a rut in any ride.

At that time New Zealand was right up there on the world stage in speedway. It was incredible – Barry Briggs and Ronnie Moore were up there in the top group with my man Mauger. Speedway was certainly not a mainstream sport down in our part of the world, but on reading how they performed in other parts of the globe, I realised how massive the sport was in Europe.

Since those early days, I've met Mauger several times and he is always the same – a self-effacing man, a real down-to-earth Kiwi who has such a great desire to succeed and has made the most of his talent. He has promoted this country enormously overseas and while the sport has lost some of its popularity in New Zealand, speedway and Mauger are still huge drawcards overseas.

I just loved Mauger's style. It was unique and was what made him such a champion. He would lay the bike down lower than anyone else. It was just remarkable how he could lean it down and keep the throttle wide open to make passing manoeuvres that others were unable to emulate.

Riding motorbikes has been in my blood from those very young days in the Hutt. I still love it and I must say I have been able to pass on that fervour to Tiger and persuade him to follow the sport when he can. He has become a bit of a devotee.

I know Mauger comes back home regularly and this country should be immensely proud of what he has achieved and how he continues to promote New Zealand.

Yvette Williams

JESSE OWENS AND MR AND MRS BELLWOOD

Yvette Williams became New Zealand's first female Olympic gold medallist when she won the long jump at Helsinki in 1952. She also set a long jump world record and won four Empire Games gold medals.

Jesse Owens was my role model, an inspiration during my career. His picture is on the front page of the first scrapbook I kept about my sports career.

He was the perfect stylist and the photograph is taken at the start of the Berlin 100m final, where he won the first of his four gold medals at those 1936 Olympics. While he was a magnificent sprinter, it was Owens' long-jumping ability and the distances he reached that impressed me most.

He did what we call the hitch-kick – running in the air during his long jumps – and I decided to try to emulate him as best I could, starting by jumping off the top of the sandhills between St Clair and St Kilda beaches in Dunedin.

I also have a small newspaper cutting on the front page of my scrapbook, just above the picture of Owens, which reads: "Ideals are like stars. You will never succeed in reaching them with your hands. But like the seafaring man on the valley of waters, you choose them as your guide and, following them, you reach your destination."

I liked that quotation very much, so I clipped it out of the paper, stuck it in my scrapbook, and often referred to it.

From as far back as I can remember, I was always keen on sports. At intermediate school and high school in Dunedin, I played outdoor basketball, which is now called netball, tennis, swam in our schools championships, ran in the Otago primary school athletics championships, attended gymnastics classes and went roller-skating on Saturday mornings.

When I was very young, our family often visited our grandparents in north Dunedin, where I can recall my grandfather telling me off for jumping over his perfectly-kept flower garden and breaking the edges.

I also was very keen on horse-riding, taking lessons during my mid-teens and competing in showjumping. My uncle owned several racehorses. His son was Arthur Didham, one of the South Island's leading trainers back in the 1940s and 1950s.

Our family followed the horses and I often spent a day or two at the Didham stables at Wingatui, where I rode the horses to the track and even in their training gallops.

Surprisingly, I didn't get involved in track and field athletics until I had left Otago Girls' High School. We didn't have organised athletics at our high school, just what we called tabloid sports – tunnel-ball relays, skipping races and so on.

I left high school at the end of my sixth form year when dad said: "I think it's time you got yourself a job."

So I did, working at the health department pricing prescriptions. I continued playing outdoor basketball, for our high school's old girls team, the winter after I left school. Then when the season ended I mentioned to the girl sitting next to me at work that I wanted to keep fit during the summer. I asked her what she thought I should do.

She said: "I'm a member of an athletics club, so why don't you try that? Come out

The incomparable **JESSE OWENS.**

to the Caledonian ground where we compete and see how you like it."

That's how it started.

All the events were handicapped and in the 100 yards I started off the front mark.

I won that and also the high jump. There was a small write-up about this outstanding new girl winning the two events in Monday's *Otago Daily Times*. So that was encouraging.

Then I was extremely lucky when I went to a national athletics training camp in Timaru over the Christmas-New Year holidays and met my future coach, Mr Jim Bellwood, and his wife, Emmy.

Mr Bellwood had been captured in Greece in the early days of World War ll and had spent several years in a prisoner-of-war camp in Germany. When the war ended he was given the opportunity to study at Loughborough College in England, where he learnt all the modern methods of athletics coaching from Geoff Dyson, one of the world's best coaches of his time. And Emmy Bellwood was an international gymnast from Estonia, which was then part of the Soviet Union.

When they started coaching in New Zealand, they were way ahead of their time. For example, we trained very hard during the winter months, something that had rarely, if ever, been done by athletes here in the past.

As a result I improved quite dramatically.

Mr and Mrs Bellwood were huge influences throughout my career. I would have never achieved what I did had it not been for them. I owe everything to them.

By 1952 I was ranked first in the world in the long jump and was the favourite to win the gold medal at the Helsinki Olympics that year. But it did not go quite to plan.

In the morning's qualifying round, I hurt my knee during a practice run-up. There were 35 competitors from 22 countries, including the Russians for the first time. It was the largest field of competitors for any of the track and field events at those games.

I qualified for the afternoon's final. But on my first jump in the final, I was slightly over the front edge of the take-off board and it was ruled a foul (no jump).

I had a 40-minute wait until my second jump, during which time my knee was seizing up. My second attempt was also ruled a foul. So I had just the one jump left to make it into the top six for the medal round. Fortunately I qualified for the final three jumps.

On my fourth attempt I gave it everything, reaching 6.24m, just one centimetre short of the world record, to win the gold medal.

What a relief it was as there was huge pressure on me, especially from the expectations of everyone back home in New Zealand.

Receiving the gold medal from Sir Arthur Porritt, standing on the podium watching the New Zealand flag being raised and hearing our national anthem being played so far from home was the proudest moment of my life.

Immediately after the victory ceremony, a dozen or so Kiwis who had made their way to Helsinki to watch the games defied security, raced on to the track, celebrated with a haka and then carried me shoulder-high from the ground with the New Zealand flag draped across my shoulders.

John Wright

BERT SUTCLIFFE AND FERGIE MCCORMICK

John Wright was a successful test opening batsman from 1978-93. He captained New Zealand from 1988-90. Later he coached the Indian team for five years.

When I was growing up as a cricket-obsessed youngster in Canterbury, Bert Sutcliffe was almost a mythical figure for me. His skill was staggering, his courage and humility so endearing. All those qualities were brought to life with so much flavour by Pat Booth in *Bert Sutcliffe's Book for Boys* with its distinctive green cover, a book that I devoured so intently I'm sure I could still relate whole passages of it now. It had pride of place in my bookshelf and was almost mandatory nightly reading, because we did not have television in those days.

Cricket was my thing and when I read Bert's book and learned about the things he did as a youngster, when his father made him a bat which he had cut down from a full-size model, it was almost like he was standing alongside me telling me how to bat. I can remember those things even now. It was a great book, aimed at kids like me, who were obsessed with cricket. It was topped off when my parents went on holiday to Dunedin one year and returned with a Bert Sutcliffe bat bought from his sports shop.

My whole family was interested in cricket, but there were no organised matches in our rural surroundings. I did not get to play club cricket until I was 12 and rarely saw any first-class matches. My dreams, though, were all about playing for New Zealand, about trying to emulate some of Sutcliffe's style and skill as we played out our dreams in games of pick-up cricket at West Melton.

I missed seeing Bert Sutcliffe bat, but I knew from my parents, relations and friends that he was one of the greatest, perhaps the greatest New Zealand batsman. He was a left-hander and I could relate to that. I met Bert subsequently, when I had played for New Zealand. But never having seen him bat live, and never seeing those flowing crisp strokes except on film is one of my great sports regrets.

I would follow all his deeds on the radio and the great thing was that although I never saw him bat, through those commentaries and that book, I could imagine how Bert was at the crease. Even at a young age I apparently had dreams of playing at Lord's and of being involved in matches on those great grounds. Much of that fantasy grew because I had devoured his book. In a way, he was my pathway. It's pretty interesting really when you look back on it, and it could be said that Bert helped prepare me a little bit for life as a cricketer.

When I met Bert, he turned out to be such a modest, good person, and it was reassuring to have a boyhood hero who kept that status through my adult life. He was a wonderful, unaffected gentleman.

When winter came and the cricket gear was stashed away, my father and I would join the enormous crowds who watched the rugby at Lancaster Park. In those days, in the early 1960s, W F McCormick was the champion Canterbury fullback.

I loved Fergie's attitude. He just looked like a rock, a very fierce one, and every time the opposition mounted a lively attack, I thanked God or someone, that Fergie was on our side. I loved the way he hauled his shorts up over his thighs and exhibited an attitude which said there was no way past him, that he was the last line of an impregnable defence.

There used to be the great national debate about who should be the test fullback. D B Clarke was the main man for a while, but I could not have cared if he had kicked 80-yard penalty goals, because McCormick was my man. It was no race. Mick Williment, the Wellington fullback and another All Black contender, was not even in the picture.

I just loved the way Fergie competed. You could see it in everything he did. He was just so fierce and so proud and I loved him for that.

In 1971, I played the curtain-raiser to what ultimately proved to be Fergie's last test match, against the Lions in Dunedin. I played for Christ's College against Otago Boys. The Lions conned us by saying the All Blacks had a weak link, and then Barry John gave the ultimate tactical kicking display. It made it seem as though Fergie had a bad game, when it was really the masterful skills of John. I don't think the Lions looked back once the All Blacks dropped Fergie after that test.

As a kid, McCormick had shown me that never-say-die attitude, that never-give-up, unrelenting mindset you need if you are involved in the international sporting arena.

I met him later and he was fairly direct. But I loved him for that – that was how he played. Even as a youngster you could see his unrelenting determination, you could see that attitude, feel his emotions and what the jersey meant to him, all those direct ingredients that we talk about in much more flowery terms these days.

Watching W F McCormick, you knew he ran on to the rugby field and never, ever contemplated coming second.

BERT SUTCLIFFE, the prince of New Zealand batsmen.

About the author

WYNNE GRAY started his journalism career on the *Auckland Star*, then worked overseas before being appointed senior rugby writer for the *New Zealand Herald* in 1989.

He has since covered most All Black tests around the globe and written several books, including Buck Shelford's autobiography. He has been a regular guest panellist on Sky Television and won a number of print media awards for his work.

Wynne lives in Auckland with his wife Erin, children Tim, Emma and Sam and, when the weather permits, likes to test his sporting temperament on the golf course.